## About the Author

Oscar Ugarteche is a former Professor of International Finance at the Catholic University of Peru. He was educated at Fordham University in New York and subsequently at the London Business School. His many and varied roles have included economic consultancy for a wide variety of organizations. These include UNCTAD (which he advised on debt questions for over a decade), UNDP, UNICEF, the Pan American Health Organization, Radda Barnen and the Friedrich Ebert Foundation. He has served on the boards of several NGOs in Peru and on the boards of various Latin American journals. In 1993 and again in 1995, he spent time at the University of Bergen's Centre for Development Studies in Norway, where the first draft of this book was prepared. Professor Ugarteche is the author of numerous books on foreign debt and its impact on development issues which have been published in various Latin American countries. His most recent work has caused a considerable stir in Peru. It is entitled *La Arqueologia de la Modernidad: el Peru entre la Globalizacion y la Exclusion* (Desco, Lima, 1998).

## Zed Titles on Globalization

Globalization became the new buzzword in the late 1990s. Despite the very different meanings attached to the term and even more divergent evaluations of its likely impacts, it is clear nevertheless that we are in an accelerated process of transition to a new period in world history. Zed Books' titles on globalization pay special attention to what it means for the South, for women, for workers and for other vulnerable groups.

Nassau Adams, *Worlds Apart: The North–South Divide and the International System*

Samir Amin, *Capitalism in the Age of Globalization: The Management of Contemporary Society*

Asoka Bandarage, *Women, Population and Global Crisis: A Political-Economic Analysis*

Michel Chossudovsky, *The Globalisation of Poverty: Impacts of IMF and World Bank Reforms*

Peter Custers, *Capital Accumulation and Women's Labour in Asian Economies*

Bhagirath Lal Das, *An Introduction to the WTO Agreements*

Bhagirath Lal Das, *The WTO Agreements: Deficiencies, Imbalances and Required Changes*

Bhagirath Lal Das, *The World Trade Organization: A Guide to the New Framework for International Trade*

Diplab Dasgupta, *Structural Adjustment, Global Trade and the New Political Economy of Development*

Graham Dunkley, *The Free Trade Adventure: The WTO, GATT and Globalism: A Critique*

Bjorn Hettne et al., *International Political Economy: Understanding Global Disorder*

Terence Hopkins and Immanuel Wallerstein et al., *The Age of Transition: Trajectory of the World-System, 1945–2025*

K. S. Jomo (ed.), *Tigers in Trouble: Financial Governance, Liberalization and the Economic Crises in East Asia*

Hans-Peter Martin and Harald Schumann, *The Global Trap: Globalization and the Assault on Prosperity and Democracy*

Harry Shutt, *The Trouble with Capitalism: An Enquiry into the Causes of Global Economic Failure*

Kavaljit Singh, *The Globalisation of Finance: A Citizen's Guide*

Henk Thomas (ed.), *Globalization and Third World Trade Unions*

Christa Wichterich, *The Globalized Woman: Reports from a Future of Inequality*

David Woodward, *Foreign Direct and Equity Investment in Developing Countries: The Next Crisis?*

For full details of this list and Zed's other subject and general catalogues, please write to: The Marketing Department, Zed Books, 7 Cynthia Street, London N1 9JF, UK or e-mail: sales@zedbooks.demon.co.uk
Visit our website at: http://www.zedbooks.demon.co.uk

# THE FALSE DILEMMA
## Globalization: opportunity or threat?

**Oscar Ugarteche**

Translated by
Mark Fried

**Inter Pares**
OTTAWA

Zed Books Ltd
LONDON • NEW YORK

*The False Dilemma – Globalization: opportunity or threat?* was first published by Zed Books, 7 Cynthia Street, London N1 9JF, UK and Room 400, 175 Fifth Avenue, New York, NY 10010, USA in 2000 in association with Inter Pares, 58 Arthur Street, Ottawa, Canada K1R 7B9.

Revised and updated from its original publication in Spanish under the title *El falso dilema: America Latina en la economica global,* Fundacion Friedrich Ebert-FES (Peru) and Editorial Nueva Sociedad, Apartado 61.712 Caracas, 1060-A, Venezuela in 1997.

The translation of this book was financed due to the generosity of Inter Pares.

Distributed in the USA exclusively by St Martin's Press, Inc., 175 Fifth Avenue, New York, NY 10010, USA

Cover designed by Andrew Corbett
Set in Monotype Baskerville and Univers by Ewan Smith, London
Printed and bound in Malaysia

A catalogue record for this book is available from the British Library.

ISBN 1 85649 689 9 cased
ISBN 1 85649 690 2 limp

# Contents

# Tables and Figures

## Tables

## Figures

# Prologue

The overall thesis of this book is that a productivity crisis in the G-7 countries lies at the root of the instability in the global economic system. Fortunately for this English-language edition, appearing five years after the Spanish original, events in the interim – the Mexican crisis of 1994 and the so-called Asian crisis in mid-1997 – have shown the validity of the hypothesis put forward in Chapter 2: when financial transactions across the globe add up to 360 times the value of transactions in goods and services, the global economy is walking on eggshells.

In previous books I have argued that taking the dollar off the gold standard in 1971 was the first sign of the crisis. Oil prices soon rose to compensate for the monetary effects of de-linking the dollar from gold. The jump in oil prices rendered oil-based technology, which had shown signs of a marked decline since the 1960s, obsolete and sparked an urgent need for technological change. From that point on, growth rates for the productivity of capital have been unstable and have rarely moved substantially above zero. Negative growth rates are indicative of the fact that the velocity of innovation in knowledge-based technology prevents investments in innovation from being recouped, thus strangling capital. This, in turn, has led to calls for a change in the technological paradigm.

Chapter 5 reviews the economic theory behind the policies implemented over the past decade, and examines the results of the first five years in Latin America; Chapter 7 reviews the evidence of the past five years. It would seem that the theory is insufficient, or at least has failed to achieve the expected results. Some theoretical modification will be required if Latin American development is to reach a safe harbour, even as defined by the goals of those who believe the market functions perfectly. From my vantage point, a person-based approach is required, one that focuses on the internal market, with the external market as a complementary element, and that contemplates a role for the state independent of the private sector.

The systemic crisis has deepened and we have not as yet seen light at the end of the tunnel. In terms of both theory and productive output, and in the end in institutional terms as well, neoliberal policies have shown themselves to be insufficient. The productivity of capital, which is what makes capitalism work in an orderly fashion, must be regained, or instability will continue. In this sense, today's crisis is similar to that of 1930, and even more like the crisis of the end of the nineteenth century.

Disparities between countries have grown larger, financial volatility has been accentuated, the advances achieved by some societies in terms of economic organization have been eroded, and their potential for recovery has become dependent on larger economies which are ever less able to carry the world economy. At the same time we lived through a financial bubble in Japan lasting from 1985 to 1994, and another one in New York that began in 1994 and has yet to end. The global economy is more fragile than in the past. The so-called Asian crisis affected everyone, not because it was virulent, but because the system was, and remains, fragile. Contagion is a symptom of weak defences. Problems with the circulation of capital are symptoms of a problem with the functioning of capital per se.

The market as new philosophical truth was presented, starting in the 1970s, as a revelation that would solve such problems, but in fact it has only deepened them. The problems that plague the system as a whole are present in every sub-system and within each country unit. Gaps widen, instability worsens, with no indication of real development or conversion of the productive plant. The economies of the South are becoming markets for the finished goods the North produces, but the impact is doubtful as can be clearly seen in the rising external deficits of southern economies – deficits that are financed with short-term capital that makes those economies even more vulnerable.

In 1991, due to the changed international context, new questions emerged for the overall shift in economic policy. The Soviet bloc had disappeared, technological change was accelerating, developed countries plagued by persistent economic stagnation had failed repeatedly to meet economic forecasts, China was experiencing dynamic growth, the dollar was weak, Mexico had signed a free trade agreement with the United States and Canada, and the debt crisis had come to its supposed end. The turn of the century appeared to be a change in epoch, characterized by a paradigm shift positing knowledge as the basis of the economy and by a capitalist counter-revolution in Eastern Europe.

Latin America had recently emerged from an economic depression, the second in the century, and the president of the Inter-American Development Bank (IADB), the now-deceased president of the World Bank, and even the executive director of the International Monetary Fund (IMF) were speaking of a Latin American recovery. Global governance had superseded the national framework and international organizations had taken on the role of overseers of economic policy. Meanwhile, the developed capitalist economies faced slow growth or stagnation.

Nineteenth-century debates about mercantilism were dusted off with the broom of modernity and raised their heads again. New liberals brought the state vs market question to the table and, employing a free association of state = socialism, market = capitalism, they radicalized popular beliefs, inverting 1970s common sense regarding the importance and relevance of economic development. There is only one economy, one set of economic rules, one price, they proclaimed, and obeying all this will usher in an era of balanced development and modernity. Apostles of the new doctrine spoke of a new borderless world and the nation-state as an obstacle. In retrospect, what is extraordinary about this new economic theory is that it is based solely on capital, leaving labour entirely out of the picture. In declaring Keynes's thought to be obsolete, the economy's relevance to society was consigned to the realm of oblivion, as was its relevance to workers specifically. This will be the subject of Chapter 1.

From my first publications, I have maintained that there is a relation-ship between the productivity crisis, particularly of capital, in advanced countries, and the export of capital in the form of long-term credit. Empirical studies on the productivity crisis have finally appeared that allow for exploring that notion, which I undertake to do in Chapter 2. Apparently the solution to the existing productivity crisis in mature capitalism is to be sought through the introduction of new technologies derived from a new conceptualization of knowledge. But that fails to tackle the rusty paths of international trade in the twentieth century and ends up re-instituting past trade patterns: Latin America once again as a producer of raw materials. This is also examined in Chapter 2, a chapter that owes much to Anwar Sheik and Andrew Glyn, even though their work is not cited.

Now that we have some long-term evidence and my thinking is clearer, I have come to the conclusion that Latin America went through a depression in the 1980s, euphemistically called 'the lost decade', and that depression was a systemic one. Unlike the 1930s, when the advanced capitalist countries (ACCs) suffered an economic depression and Latin America managed to overcome it quickly, in the 1980s Latin America and Africa sank into the abyss of the international depression while the ACC managed to survive without any economic contraction, despite the pro-ductivity crisis of capital. My hypothesis is that this was due in part to the transfer of resources from the South to the North during that decade, which was what precipitated the depression in the South.

However, the countries of Southeast Asia managed to avoid the depression, which raises a question: Was it the entire concept of industrialization that failed, or the way in which industrialization had been attempted in Latin America? The link between industrialization and progress was indeed broken, but the countries that managed to progress in Southeast Asia did so with new sorts of industries. These complications are discussed in Chapter 3. The related subjects of competitiveness and globalization, two concepts frequently used and poorly understood by those who use them, which have to do with the new forms of production, are discussed in Chapter 4.

Attempts at stabilization in Latin America ran up against structural adjustment programmes designed by the World Bank to fit each country into the new international structure for production, trade and consumption. These programmes were imposed from the top, leaving little room for national leaders to manoeuvre. Ostensibly to address the debt problem, these programmes contained elements aimed at resolving problems linked to the organization of state and society, as well as the economic system. While the structural adjustment template in vogue was one and the same, the results of these policies differed according to the ways they were handled internally. The success of stabilization in controlling and reducing inflation, however, whitewashed structural adjustment, portraying stabilization and adjustment as a single phenomenon, with the result that, in the minds of Latin America's people, what kept inflation under control was the opening of the economy. This is discussed in Chapter 5.

The question is: Why was state policy in Latin America never able to encourage businessmen to become efficient and effectively substitute imports? And why do they now believe the market will be able to accomplish that? Are they expecting new economic actors? Or do they envision some sort of Latin American cultural revolution that will transform businessmen into efficient agents in a market characterized by tight margins? Or is it the law of the Wild West: become efficient or die? Perhaps it has less to do with Latin America's businessmen and more with Latin America as a region that produces raw materials and consumes finished goods, the international division of labour that has been with us since the sixteenth century.

The argument put forward by the renewed ideology of the marketplace is that the overall framework of globalization must be pursued, or the future will be very dark. 'There is no alternative ...' in the words of Margaret Thatcher. The false dilemma of having to choose between exporting or dying, conveniently leaves out why a country exports in the first place: to favour the development of the internal market, which is another way of saying the collective well-being of society, which is, after all, the beginning and the end of economic relations. This is why I pay great attention to the work of Fernando Fajnzylber and others related to equity, a subject that has been abandoned today in favour of the market.

The international arena is relevant and it always has been, even when Latin American discussions of economic development treated world events as an abstraction. But it is relevant only for the opportunities it offers and the challenges it poses. It is not relevant per se. External factors are not going to rain on Latin America and turn the region into what we Latin Americans want unless we take the initiative. There is no reason why the unilateral opening proposed by all governments for reasons noted above – the need for universal rules of the game – should benefit all citizens. It benefits some people and modernizes some things, while excluding the bulk of the population, offering them only the fantasy that owning a cellular telephone will make them part of the new world order. Other factors, cultural factors, continue to hold sway in society, like the memories of my grandparents.

One fascinating topic not taken up here is how, in pursuit of modernity, political discourse on progress has become conservative, turning progress into a nineteenth-century notion. The traditional values of private property and the family have come back on to the political agenda as part and parcel of modernity. The classical liberals were anti-clerical, but the new liberals are awfully timid. As the old joke has it: he may be black, but he's blond, blue-eyed and can't dance. Latin American modernity is covered with rust, the rust of domination and dependence. Paradoxically, just when Latin America is embracing democracy, only one way of thinking prevails. How can there be democracy without two theoretical frameworks at least?

This book is not intended to be comprehensive. It is an attempt to explain international political economy to a well-informed general public. Each chapter would have been a book in and of itself if I had given in to the temptation to spend five more years reflecting and observing. However, I felt it was important to sketch out an overall vision of what is occurring, within a broad conceptual framework and from a long-term vantage point, to help us think about the future. In the ten years since I began this reflection a number of events – Chiapas, the Mexican crisis, the attempts of presidents to engineer their re-elections, the rise in social violence – have taught us that not all people benefit from this global version of modernity. The excess of narrowly focused research and the dearth of broad encompassing studies obliged me to undertake this attempt at synthesis. This book offers a vision and proposes a reading of Latin American development in the new global context from the standpoint of international political economy.

My reading began in the middle of 1991 and concentrated on authors published in *Pensamiento Iberoamericano* and *World Development*. In January 1993 I was invited by the Centre for Development Studies (CDS) of the University of Bergen for a six-month stay, during which I ought to have written up the study. However, my ideas were not yet clear and the more I read the more confused I became. By the end of the six months I had written something which I then presented at the universities of Helsinki, Oslo, Liverpool, Bergen, George Washington, FLACSO-Quito and Centro Bartolomé de las Casas in Cuzco, as well as at various seminars, particularly in Europe. That document became the framework for this book, which I finished writing in July 1995, thanks to another invitation from the Centre for Development Studies, the School of Philosophy and Letters, the Institute of Romance Languages and the International Relations Office at the University of Bergen. I then shared the draft with my students at the Universidad Católica de Lima and, thanks to their critiques, improved it in several respects. I am indebted to two of my students, Augusto Tzukazan Nakaima and Veronica Trelles Thorne, for the summary that appears in the epilogue.

At the time when the Spanish edition was published in May 1997 in Caracas, the global economy began to suffer disturbances. First in Asia, then in Russia, then in Latin America. In my view, these disturbances demonstrated the validity of the argument I make in Chapter 2. Brian Murphy realized this and suggested I write an additional chapter and publish an English-language edition. I immediately set about studying what was happening and reading philosophical works on the concept of modernity. Having been commissioned to write a piece on the crisis in light of the 150th anniversary of *The Communist Manifesto*, I was able to sum up what was happening from both economic and philosophical points of view. Due to its seriousness, the current crisis transcends simple economics and requires a reframing of the *raison d'être* of truth and the economy. The urgency of placing human beings once again at the centre of economic debate and putting aside the truth of the market moved me to write a lengthy, but idea-filled final chapter, passages of which were discussed at the Universidad Católica de Lima and in the seminar for the critique of capitalism at SUR in Lima during the first half of 1998.

The patience of several people has been invaluable: Jon Askeland, Gunnar Sorbo and Leif Manger of the CDS at Bergen, Heidulf Schmidt of Nueva Sociedad Editores in Caracas, Dietmar Dirmoser and Yesco Quiroga of the Fundación Friedrich Ebert in Lima. In the final discussions, if any discussion is ever final, the comments of Javier Iguíñiz, Jurgen Schüldt and Alberto Acosta helped to order the chapters, complete the introduction and round out several ideas. I am responsible for what I have insisted on writing despite their warnings.

This book would have been impossible without the assistance of Tom Johnson, director of the library at the School of Social Sciences at the University of Bergen, who made me feel at home not only in his library but also in Bergen. The detailed discussions I had with Rory Miller and David Hojman at the Institute of Latin American Studies in the northern spring of 1993 were very important. The discussion at the seminar conducted by Cynthia MacClintock in the northern winter of 1995 at George Washington University in Washington, DC, eased my mind. I saw that I was not entirely out of touch. The sporadic conversations I had with Alain Lipietz on his travels through Lima were invaluable. Pleasant evenings with Teivo Teivanen in Bergen, Helsinki and Lima helped me clarify ideas, and my students in Quito, Lima, Havana and Cuzco, along with my colleagues at Bergen, gave me the opportunity to come up with ideas and put them to the test. Finally, discussions in class with my students in international finance and economic cycles at the Universidad Católica de Lima were very helpful for clarifying my ideas. My students gave me courage to carry on. To all of them I am grateful.

Nearly all my colleagues at CDS in Bergen had to put up with my moodiness when writing this book. Percy García is the one who perhaps suffered most from my distraction and the nearly inevitable internal reflections during supper. For the patience of all, I am grateful. Finally, I would like to thank Brian Murphy of Inter Pares for his faith that an English version of the book would be useful, and his embrace of the new vision it contains. To all who insisted that this was too ambitious a project, I thank you for your realism. It is too late now.

*Lima, August 1999*

# 1. Old Debates and New on Globalization and International Trade

In the books of Hermes, it is written that what lies below is the same as that which lies above, and what lies above the same as that which lies below; in the Zohar, that the lower world is a reflection of the upper one. Buffoons founded their doctrine on a perversion of this idea. (Jorge Luis Borges, *The Theologians*)

An essay on spring by André Gide, published in Paris in October 1939, begins with the phrase '... the world is no longer the way it was when I was young.' One feature of progress is that nothing remains the way it was before; improvement is always hoped for. However, contemplating Latin America midway through the final decade of the twentieth century, a number of questions arise. Modernity, in the sense of Habermas's universalization of language, is only half present and therefore is not universal, since globalization – and alongside it, progress – simultaneously presents the younger generation with doors wide open to the world via cable TV, and with doors shut tight to impede illegal migration. The growth of industry, a foundation of progress ever since the industrial revolution, has suddenly been frozen as a result of the concepts of post-industrial societies and the crisis of Fordism. But does this mean that the role of industry in the creation of surplus value and employment has also disappeared? Transnational corporations that thirty years ago were threats to national sovereignty have been cast as responsible economic entities. Basing development on foreign investment is today considered not only positive but indispensable. Thus primary production has once again become the spearhead of economic modernization in economies with small domestic markets, and raw materials are a growing source of foreign exchange in nearly all countries. Since employment is not a concern, supplemented as it is by self-employment, industry has become marginal – or better put, irrelevant – in the new debate. At the same time, small industries emerging in the informal sector have become a vital source of job creation.

Greater access to technology today is limited by a nation's capacity to make use of it, given its rapidly changing nature, thus requiring higher levels of basic technical education. Today more than ever, anything international is considered to be modern, current, yet today as never before anything international comes from the North, as Ohmae has pointed out. Nowadays, Europe and the United States are ever less interested in Latin America, while developments in the countries of the North, and the search for markets there, are of growing importance to us in the South. Has the new order brought an end to the role of Latin America and Africa as 'store-room continents', providers of raw materials? The internal markets of these regions, with a few exceptions, are insufficiently important to place these regions back in the debate.

The exit of Africa and Latin America from the international economic agenda, and the entrance of Eastern Europe, Southeast Asia and China, are indicative of how much conceptions of the world have changed over the past thirty years, and of how roles have shifted among developing economies. Southeast Asia and China have become regions that boast cheap and highly skilled labour, whose products can compete with the manufactured goods of the advanced countries themselves, while Eastern Europe has become a new market and supplier of cheap labour for the economies of Western Europe. In the context of globalization, this turn-around in interests has accentuated the process of unequal development, with some areas of the world pushed progressively backwards and others incorporated into advanced capitalism.

Even though Latin America cannot be spoken of as a single economic unit, it is a region where the same arguments regarding economics are heard and read and where political actors implement the same policies based on that economic discourse. The new economic liberalism holds that economic laws must be adopted universally and that economies must become internationalized if societies are to be modernized. Liberalism has established itself as a politically conservative current in the countries of the region, a departure from the liberals of the eighteenth and nineteenth centuries, especially the English ones who were anti-clerical and irreverent. The liberals of past centuries advocated tolerance, live and let live, and improving the common good by keeping the state from intervening in the economy. The new liberals do not take into account the common good or, better put, the common good does not exist; all that exists is their own good. If progress is conservative, then to be an economic liberal in Latin America is to be a political conservative. Something is backwards. The modern approach is not to belong to political parties, to denigrate them, like Primo de Rivera in 1920s Spain. A blue-blooded Latin American new liberal favours privatization of public services, when it was precisely the liberals who introduced public education in England and the United States.

Suddenly we find ourselves confronted with a discourse by which the inefficient state should be replaced by no state at all, or by much less state. The opposition of good and bad is displaced by the opposition of more and less. That discussion is carried on in isolation from the debate on the fiscal deficit and the urgent need to reduce public spending. From that viewpoint, the political debate is hiding a real economic problem. The state had to be reduced because the existing levels of fiscal deficit were unsustainable, given the lack of external and internal financing, a situation that would have worsened if the economic modernization of the state as a whole was undertaken at the same time.

But the state vs market debate goes even farther: after papering over the fiscal deficit, it launches an unsettling conceptual assault. If the state should intervene only when the market does not work, there is no need to have a large state. In a developing economy, competing economic entities act like jackals and that's the only way capitalism works. The 'market' functions on the basis of the inefficiency of the other and the state must set the rules for competition. It was the state that compensated for the lack of private investment in the 1960s and 1970s, dynamizing effective demand à la Keynes, without crowding out anyone from the private sector.

No one was crowded out because the economic actors were not investing at the same rate as previously, or in fact were divesting. It seems that when Latin American economic actors are prepared to invest, they prefer to do so without a state being present. In the 1990s, they bought bankrupt companies or public companies, which are not the same thing, rather than put up new investments and broaden gross capital formation. This grew out of the discourse on privatization and efficiency. With the exceptions of Colombia and Chile, and possibly Brazil, Latin America's private sectors are not only not efficient, they never had to be in the past. The great critique of import-substitution industrialization policies (ISI) was that they allowed the private sector to remain inefficient. In this sense, privatizing to increase efficiency is theoretically as logical as placing the oven in the sun to heat it up. Perhaps it should be turned on.

Suppose the problem of efficiency really had to do with people, with culture, with education and institutionality, as Morishima proposes, and not a mathematical equation? Suppose the corruption and inefficiency that plagues the public sector also affected the private sector? I believe what Hernando de Soto says about the state in Latin America being a trap is true. But to pose as a solution the elimination of the state, rather than its absolute improvement, has displaced the debate on the modernization of society and efficiency, and constitutes an ideological response in the name of pragmatism. The elimination of the Soviet state has reduced Russian life expectancy from seventy-seven to fifty-six in just five years of liberal revolution. What has emerged is a mafia economy. In the final analysis, doesn't the economy exist in order to achieve the common good?[1]

This book is about the connection between globalization and de-linking, about concepts that emerged from the debate between liberals and mercantilists, and those that arise from the state vs market debate. A reflection on today's reality, it posits that the crisis in capitalism is not over, that Latin America's difficulties are the expression of a systemic crisis, and that internal responses to economic problems generated by the systemic crisis have given rise to new and varied forms of relations among national economies within the global system.

In the following section I shall present a discussion from the past that remains current, because the 1980s was in the end a stage for re-enacting an old debate. What makes the old debate applicable is the change in the techno-economic paradigm that has taken place since the mid-1970s. I am referring to the debate between 'mercantilists' (Hamilton and List) and 'liberals' (Smith, Ricardo, J. S. Mill). This first chapter will set the parameters for the six chapters to follow, by summing up some of the basic ideas that have been debated over the past two centuries regarding trade and protectionism, summarizing the new theory of globalization and its opposite, de-linking, and providing a synthesis of the state vs market debate.

From my point of view, and as the reader will discover, today's debate on globalization, liberalism and the market fails to answer the central question of how to recover the productivity of capital and profitability in the advanced capitalist countries (ACC). Neither is the debate relevant to Latin America's systemic crisis, insofar as our crisis is an offspring of the greater crisis and of the techno-economic transformation, which appeared to be a solution worth trying. All the many changes in the system of world trade and in conceptions of the world have been aimed at trying to resolve the crisis of capital, but all evidence indicates they have not achieved it.

There is no doubt that globalization as currently proposed excludes a large part of the world and bestows on only a few countries significant purchasing power and a high level of productivity. Globalization is really a rich-country phenomenon and, to be more exact, something for the richest sectors within those rich countries. In other words, inside the North there is now a North and a South, just as both exist within the South. Ohmae is quite clear on this when he includes a few Latin American countries in the new 'Inter-Linked Economy' (ILE), made up of only the richest countries (over US$10,000 GNP per capita). Africa is entirely cut out, as is much of Latin America. What is occurring is greater inter-relation among the Norths, and the exclusion of the Souths of this world. The new Inter-Linked Economy forms an island, just like the French acronym, in the middle of a world which for some has no borders and for others has nothing but borders that cannot be crossed. The exception is East Asia where Tigers and Dragons with active states, and China with a highly institutionalized state, have managed to overcome the systemic crisis, achieve technological change and stride forwards. All other countries and regions in the world have been left out and face the huge challenge of finding a way to insert themselves into the global economy again.

If such insertion is predicated on high productivity and the capacity to use new technology, then people with low productivity and little or no technological capacity will be excluded. Given that women and children are currently at a disadvantage in relation to men, and given that the logic of the market tends to accentuate such disadvantages, a free-market economy could become socially and politically unsustainable, particularly if the state does not intervene to help these groups become part of the economic dynamic as a whole; that is to say, if the state does not bring equity into the picture. But improvements for disadvantaged sectors would be hard to sustain if income differentials are so great that policy measures are unable to bring the varied social sectors to a similar starting point. Once again the state has to be the fundamental actor. Technological paths must also be organized and promoted to allow for productive linkages. The same is true of sufficient education to put those technologies to work, understanding technology as a series of processes and not only as equipment.

Today's debates centre on globalization and de-linking, liberalism and mercantilism, and state and market. The debate on capitalism and social-ism has disappeared. State and socialism are not synonyms, and neither are capitalism and the market. Globalization, market and liberalism are not synonyms either, nor are de-linking, state and mercantilism, though at times they have need of each other. Ohmae's theory of globalization is not a real theory in the proper sense of the term; it is an ideological proposal based on the recent evolution of communications and multi-national companies, basically in rich countries. *The Borderless World*, the title of Ohmae's book, may be a reality for western Europeans, North Americans and the Japanese, but 'The Growing Borders' could be the title of a book about the rest of the world.

## De-linking: Samir Amin's proposal

The essential terms for understanding the ideas put forth by Samir Amin (1990a) are 'centre' and 'periphery'.[2] 'Centre' is a product of history.

In some regions of the capitalist system, history has allowed national bourgeoisies and national capitalist states to exercise hegemony. The bourgeoisie and the bourgeois state are indivisible. There is no capitalism abstracted from the state. The bourgeois state is national when it controls the process of accumulation, within external limits that always exist, but become relative in light of the state's capacity to react to them or to participate in their creation.

'Peripheries' are defined in negative terms: they are regions within the capitalist system that do not set themselves up as centres. They are countries and regions where there is no national control over the process of capital accumulation, which is essentially defined by external restrictions. Peripheries are not 'stagnant', although their development is not like that of the ACCs in any of the successive stages of the expansion of capitalism. The bourgeoisie and national capital are not necessarily absent and peripheries are not synonymous with pre-capitalist societies. The state may exist, but its formal existence does not make it a national capitalist state as long as it fails to control the process of accumulation. Control over accumulation is understood to mean control by the local bourgeoisie and the state over five essential conditions in the process of accumulation:

1. Reproduction of the labour force, which presupposes agricultural development policies that provide for sufficient food production at prices compatible with the demand for a return on capital; and later on the production of wage-goods that can simultaneously accompany the expansion of capital and wages.
2. Centralization of the surplus, which presupposes the existence of a national financial system that is autonomous from transnational capital, guaranteeing national capacity to finance direct investment.
3. A market fundamentally reserved for national production, even when tariffs are low and there is no protectionist policy, along with the complementary capacity to be competitive in the world market, at least with selected products.
4. Natural resources. Not only ownership of them, but also national capacity to exploit them or to maintain them as reserves.
5. Control over technology, in the sense that technologies, whether nationally generated or imported, can be reproduced rapidly without long-term dependence on imported essential inputs.

The question for Amin is whether the peripheries are in the process of becoming new centres. The thesis that the contradiction centre vs periphery is innate to the world capitalist system leads to a particular conclusion. If the formation of a national bourgeois state and the construction of a self-centred capitalist economy are impossible on the periphery, then some other model of development is necessary: de-linking and socialism. Self-centred development is defined by national control over accumulation according to the terms indicated above. De-linking is not synonymous with self-centred development. It is a requirement of self-centred development. The concept is to 'de-link' the rational criteria for internal economic selection from those that govern the world system. Real examples have been offered by China and the Soviet Union. Transnationalization (which bypasses nations) is no more than an expression of the subjugation of the diverse segments that constitute really existing capitalism to the existing worldwide law of value (S. Amin 1990b). The relation between national productive systems and the established national bourgeois state has begun to break down, a rupture that operates within the framework of a triple 'revolution': cybernetic, cultural and military. In this framework there are three possible directions for the development of the global system: (1) a continuation of new patterns set by the narrow demands of capital on a world scale; (2) the collapse of the system; and (3) the reconstitution of the system on a new regionalized polycentric basis.

## Globalization: Ohmae's proposal

The most extreme liberal stance, in terms of the functioning of a globalized economy operating with 'new rules of the game', is presented in the work of Ohmae (1990). His would become the dominant theory of globalization. The argument is that large companies have to relearn the art of invention, but this time they ought to do so in industries and businesses that are global, where worldwide economies of scale can be achieved with made-to-measure products for consumers in niche markets. Companies ought to do this because there are more and more informed and demanding customers in developed countries. They hold the power, not the organization selling to them. There are still some who believe that transnationals impose products and select the countries where they will operate, but the new economic order is ruled by ever-more-demanding consumers.

The new role of the state is to protect the environment, to educate the labour force and to build comfortable and secure social infrastructure. Governments do not understand that their role has changed, away from protecting the population and their natural resources from external threats, towards ensuring that citizens have the broadest possible range of choice among the best and cheapest products and services available in the world. States are still mercantilist and for that reason they discourage investment and encourage the impoverishment of their people. There is little awareness that an 'island' is emerging, one larger than a continent, and that the rules of the game have changed. The 'ILE', made up of the Triad

– United States, Europe and Japan – along with aggressive economies like Taiwan, Hong Kong and Singapore, has transformed macroeconomic theory and the functioning of the macroeconomy. A Keynesian economist, hoping to see growth in employment as a result of economic growth, would be disappointed today, since employment could well be created elsewhere. If a government restricts the money supply, international lending will replace domestic lending. If a central bank raises interest rates, cheaper international credit will replace it. In this case, ILE has made the traditional instruments of the central bank obsolete.

Within ILE – with a population of about a billion people and a per capita income of at least $10,000 a year – most of the world's wealth is created, consumed and distributed. And there are no absolute winners or losers. A loser becomes attractive as its currency weakens and unemployment makes its labour desirable. ILE will grow more rapidly and will include most of the countries of Eastern Europe, nearly all of the newly industrialized countries (NICs) of East Asia and a few in Latin America. The interdependence of economies builds security and in ILE that basic fact will supersede the notion of security based on armies.

Ohmae believes the global economy will be led by the richest economies in an inter-related fashion, and other countries will have no alternative but to buy into the rules of free trade or wither away chasing the bit of international trade that remains outside ILE. Inward-looking mercantilists are out of touch with an economic reality by which the dynamic of the world economy is the only dynamic that exists for the bloc of rich countries that leads the march of the world economy.

### A synthesis of the classical debate between liberals and mercantilists

These proposals are the continuation of a debate that has been on the table for two hundred years, ever since the liberal Adam Smith published *An Enquiry into the Nature and Causes of the Wealth of Nations* in 1776 and his ideas were taken up in the United States. In *Report on Manufactures*, presented to the US Congress in 1791, the mercantilist Alexander Hamilton responded to Smith from the optic of a developing country. Later on, the liberal David Ricardo deepened Smith's arguments and introduced the notion of comparative advantage to continue advocating for free trade in his *Principles of Political Economy and Taxation*, published in 1817. Immediately following the unification of Germany in *Zollverein* in 1834, the mercantilist Friedrich List published a new argument favouring trade barriers, *The National System of Political Economy* (1841). J. S. Mill, arguing for free trade, would be the next to follow in this debate.

The theory of international commerce preached by Smith begins with the principle that the wealth of a country does not lie in its reserves of gold and silver. Wealth grows from the general productive capacity of the economy. To achieve growth in national wealth, the state does not need to intervene in the market. Productive profits are best achieved by rational self-interest, by the free pursuit of individual interests. Thus, the rewards of higher productivity achieved by the free market can spread to the rest of the world through free trade.[3] Smith's line of argument against mercantilism is that the wealth of all nations is assured through free trade. Internally efficient production and wealth are based on a division of labour and economic interdependence. These same principles should be reproduced for the world. In the same way that the agents of the state can not administer the multiplicity of economic inter-relations in a national economy, states should not interfere with international trade. When a country finds itself in a deregulated international economy, it will discover a productive niche in which it will enjoy absolute or comparative advantage. The division of labour can and ought to be reproduced globally. Merchants may benefit from protection, but the broader national interest is best pursued through the prosperity that flows from international trade.

Smith does not propose a unilateral opening or unconditional free trade for four reasons. First, because free trade should be limited by the demands of national security. In this sense, he agrees with the Navigation Act that gave British ships a monopoly on the transport of British goods. Second, tariffs should be charged on foreign products to bring them into line with the prices of national products; these could include domestic taxes to prevent a preference for imported products. Third, reprisals may be taken in the form of high tariffs in response to unjust trade barriers erected by a partner country, as a way of forcing the other country to reduce its tariffs. Finally, free trade ought to be achieved in stages, so that domestic industry and the labour force have time to adapt to growing international competition (Crane and Amawi 1991: 58–71).

David Ricardo builds his argument in terms of rents, wages and profits. From his point of view, the economy tends towards an average rate of profit independent of the activities in which investment is made. When profits are greater at the outset of an economic activity, they will soon fall in line with the economy as a whole, no matter if the activity is part of the internal or the external market. On another tack, he notes that the demand for labour will increase the demand for food, which in turn raises the income of landlords and returns in the form of wage increases, undercutting the profits of the bourgeoisie. In this sense Ricardo proposes that the profits of landlords are the losses of the barons of industry. International trade in this framework is beneficial only when it contributes to lowering wages, which will allow for a rise in profits. To earn more from international trade requires concentration in activities that offer a comparative advantage arising from differences in the cost of natural resources and labour. Such differences will lead to economic specialization in certain activities which can be carried out more efficiently in one country than in another, and this differentiation will lead to international trade that is beneficial for all (Crane and Amawi 1991: 72–82). Ricardo starts from the premise that capital and labour are immovable factors, a premise that changed dramatically even in the nineteenth century.

Following the Napoleonic Wars, Britain undertook a slow process of dismantling tariffs with France. The reason why a system of free trade had not been established up to that point was the lack of alternatives to tariffs for public finance. Free trade had to begin with the repeal of the 'Corn Laws' which, by placing tariffs on imported grain, protected British farmers from international competition (Kenwood and Lougheed 1992: 61–2). Previous to this, following the independence of its American colonies, Great Britain demanded that the United States maintain open trade free of restrictions, even though British farmers were still protected by the Corn Laws. It is generally accepted that this provided Hamilton (1791) with the basis for his arguments in favour of promoting manufactures in the United States (reproduced in Crane and Amawi 1991: 37–47).

> The embarrassments which have obstructed the progress of our external trade, have led to serious reflections on the necessity of enlarging the sphere of our domestic commerce. The restrictive regulations, which in foreign markets abridge the vent of the increasing surplus of our agricultural produce, serves to beget an earnest desire that a more extensive demand for that surplus may be created at home. (Hamilton 1791: 178)

The total success of manufacturing industries, Hamilton said, justifies the expectation that obstacles to the growth of those industries will be less formidable than some people thought, and that finding full compensation for foreign disadvantages is not difficult, just as it is not difficult to find access to favourable resources for national independence and national security. This is the first proposal in his *Report on Manufactures* to the US Congress, which sought the introduction of a trade protection law.

US liberals of 1780 believed that agriculture was the most beneficial and productive objective of human activity.

> This position, generally if not universally true, applies to the United States on account of their immense tracts of fertile territory, uninhabited and unproductive ... To endeavor by the extraordinary patronage of govern-

ment, to accelerate the growth of manufactures, is, in fact, to endeavor, by force and art, to transfer the natural current of industry from a more to a less beneficial channel. Whatever has such a tendency must necessarily be unwise; indeed, it can hardly ever be wise in a government to attempt to give a direction to the industry of its citizens. This, under the quick-sighted guidance of private interest, will, if left to itself, infallibly find its own way to the most profitable employment; and it is by such employment that the public prosperity will be most effectively promoted. (Hamilton 1791: 178)

Hamilton argued that it is not evident that agriculture is more productive than other areas of economic activity. Manufacturing enterprises not only bring about improvements in products and income for society, they also contribute to making us greater than we would be without that industry. This occurs through the following circumstances: the division of labour; the extensive use of machinery to substitute foreign products with manufactures made domestically, thus generating domestic employment and increasing employment even in activities that are not directly related to production; the promotion of emigration from other countries to the United States; a broader environment for existing talents; a broader field for business; the creation and broadening of more stable demand for agricultural products.

The domestic market is more trustworthy than the foreign market, Hamilton continued. That is because extensive regulations in trading-partner countries create problems and obstacles that make foreign markets less secure. In its trade with Europe, the United States was assigned the role of an agricultural exporter, which was not in the US interest since it created an unfavourable situation of dependence. One country's superiority early on in the development of a certain branch of industry makes it difficult for those who enter that branch later on to compete. To achieve a level playing field is impossible. Besides, there are incentives and rewards given to exports in some countries, which allow them to sell below cost. In this way, those who enter a new branch of manufacture must begin not only with the disadvantage of being new in that area of production, but also without the incentives that other nations offer for the export of those goods. To compete successfully, obviously one must count on the intervention and assistance of one's own government. The angle from which such an initiative can be objected to is that it could lead to the creation of monopolies, which at first would cause higher prices; but when proper scales have been achieved, prices would fall. 'When a domestic manufacture has attained to perfection, and has engaged in the prosecution of it a certain number of persons, it invariably becomes cheaper' (Hamilton 1791: 223).

Friedrich List (1840) critiqued the notions of Smith, Ricardo and Say, and offered a theoretical alternative. The school of liberal thought, he said, assumes the existence of a world that does not yet exist – a state of global unity and perpetual peace – and from it deduces the benefits of free trade. Economic union grows from political union, not the reverse, and it is via political union that there can be perpetual peace to consolidate the benefits of free trade. There is not a single instance of the reverse being true. Under existing conditions in the world, the result of generalized free trade will not be a global republic, rather its opposite: global subjugation of less advanced nations to the prevailing supremacy of industrial, commercial and naval power. A union of nations is possible only if each nation enjoys the same rights and that is possible only if each has the same degree of industry, civilization, political development and power. List does not question free trade per se,

> rather only in the case of nations that have not yet achieved the necessary internal development to submit themselves to the doctrine of absolute or comparative advantage in international trade. This should be followed, in its concept, only as of the moment when a nation manages to achieve general and generalized development of 'industrial education', which in his epoch would only have applied to England (which benefitted from the ruling doctrine, as the author demonstrated with exemplary subtlety), while all other countries (Germany, France, United States) were still 'underdeveloped' relative to England. *The mission of political economy is to carry out the economic education of the nation and to prepare it to enter the universal society of the future.* (Schuldt 1995: 107–8)[4]

The system of protection is a step toward the economic education of nations and towards their final union to promote true free trade; it is the only means for more backwards nations to achieve parity with the dominant country that enjoys a monopoly on industry, not by natural right but because it happened to advance sooner than others (List 1840, in Crane and Amawi 1991: 48–54).

To achieve a nation's economic independence (Germany versus the dependence it experienced in relation to Great Britain) requires empowering productive forces such as education, the formation of institutions and other social circumstances, the capacity to innovate and adapt technologies, national unity and balanced development among the various sectors. He acknowledged the differences in life and education between farmers and manufacturers. From all this the need to encourage a country's industrialization arises: 'Manufactures and factories are the mothers and children of civil liberty, of enlightenment, of arts and sciences, of domestic and foreign commerce, of navigation and of perfected means of transport, of civilization and of political power. They are the means for freeing agriculture, for elevating it to the level of industry, art, science' (List 1840, in Schuldt 1995: 108–9). List suggests that the classical school attributes a civilizing role to foreign trade because it confuses the intermediary with the cause. The unity of political and economic analysis, for List, is the Nation. The development of the domestic market, through the production of articles to meet basic needs more than merchandise destined for the middle and upper strata, lies at the centre of the author's thinking. In this way, it differs from the proposals that Prebisch would make a hundred years later. Finally, each nation will discover its own path to economic development. Unable to avoid being a man of his time, List the Eurocentrist expresses a vision of the world divided in two: the hot zone and the temperate zone. The temperate zone (Central Europe, United States) has the natural conditions for industrial development; while the hot zone (everything to the south) is best for agricultural development.

## Mercantilism in Latin America

In Latin America in the 1940s, Hamilton's ideas, as distinct from those of List, had a significant spokesperson able to explain events since 1930. Raúl Prebisch,[5] with his theory of import-substitution industrialization (ISI), opened the way for a style of development that had been undertaken with some success by Argentina, Chile and Peru since the 1930s. For Prebisch, the continual deterioration of the terms of trade results, over the long term, in balance of payments problems for economies on the periphery. Therefore, such economies require an industrial base to substitute the importation of intermediate and capital goods for that of finished goods, in order to transfer the benefits of employment, as well as the terms of trade, from the centre to the periphery. The industrialization process ought to have backward linkages and be vertically integrated, so that it achieves full internal economic integration and thus a modification of the external restrictions the region suffers.

Prebisch's first text came out in the 1940s, following the crisis in the balance of payments of the 1930s, and it reflects a process already underway. Building on this, he posited a role for the state as a promoter of the economy to replace or complement the private sector in activities that the private sector would not undertake or would do so only partially. It could be said, in one sense, that Prebisch was a mercantilist in his search for economic autonomy through industry supported by state intervention, but the difference lies in that while Hamilton and List proposed an industry that would produce for the masses, Prebisch favoured a consumer industry based on the market, which in Latin America represented only a small fraction of society. What Prebisch sought was precisely to widen that market, broadening the income base through industrial employment.

To some degree, later problems with foreign debt were the consequence of this intervention. Prebisch's assumption was that industrialists would reinvest their surpluses in the national economy, setting in motion a process of internal capital accumulation that would then broaden the productive base, just as Hamilton and List suggested. His second assumption was that state intervention would compensate for the inefficiencies of a monopolistic industrial sector. This theory held from 1930 until the end of the 1970s, when it was evident that the rate of private investment in Latin America had fallen to alarming levels and that the state had taken over and suffocated the initiative of the private sector. At the beginning of the 1980s, the theoretical crisis of the mercantilist paradigm became evident when the Economic Commission for Latin America and the Caribbean (ECLAC), the institution where Latin American mercantilism was culti-vated and developed throughout the 1950s, 1960s and 1970s, abandoned this theoretical stance. The debate that has replaced it today is presented in Chapter 4.

### The state vs market debate

A discussion regarding the state and the market began at the same time as the debate about globalization (Wolf 1988). The argument for the state was represented by Galbraith, who followed Schumpeter's ingenious approach to view the state from the vantage point of an open economy. And the side of the market was represented by Friedman, who took up Adam Smith's line of argument. The debate between Hamilton and Smith, between mercantilists and liberals, has become a discussion among shades of liberalism, turning on state regulations and the market as regulator, more than on real protectionist barriers. It is a mistake today to speak, as Ohmae and others do, of the debate as being 'state versus market', in the same terms as the early nineteenth-century debate was 'mercantilism versus liberalism'. The arguments put forth by neoliberals today are countered by liberals of different stripes who question the purity of the market in regulating economic affairs and the perfection of the market for allocating resources. The neoliberal critique of the state follows the theory of 'public choice'.[6]

The argument put forth by Wolf, Buchanan and others is that the Third World is filled with a great diversity of countries, but in most of them the economy is directed. The exceptions to state direction are Hong

Kong, Malaysia, Singapore, South Korea, Taiwan and Turkey. In other words, lack of state intervention is what produces the best macroeconomic results in the countries of the so-called Third World. Wolf's work is oriented towards developing 'a theory of non-market failure so that the imperfect performance of governments can be analyzed with a clarity, and anticipated with a degree of accuracy, closer to that already reached in analyzing the imperfect performance of markets' (Wolf 1988: 11). This would fall within the 'theory of public choice' as an anti-statist theoretical current.

TABLE 1.1 Sources of support and opposition: state vs market

|      | Market | State (non-market) |
|------|--------|--------------------|
| Pro  | Theory of competitive markets, supported by country examples and experiences | Theory of planning and welfare economy, supported by country examples and experiences |
| Anti | Theory of 'market failure' supported by country examples and experiences | Theory of 'non-market failure' and 'theory of public choice'* |

*Note*: * My addition, since this is what Wolf says he is doing.
*Source*: Wolf 1988: 5.

Wolf proposes a theoretical division into four sides: pro and anti market, and pro and anti state (non-market), as laid out in Table 1.1. Two criteria ought to be used to judge the success or failure of the market: efficiency and distributive equity. The effects of the market can be called efficient if overall benefits cannot be obtained at a lower cost, or if greater profits cannot be achieved for the same cost. In both cases, overall benefits must be greater than the costs associated with them if the result is to be considered efficient. This is in reference to 'static efficiency'. 'Dynamic efficiency' à la Schumpeter is related to the capacity of free markets, or other institutional arrangements, to promote new technologies that reduce costs, improve product quality or create new products for the market and promote a lower cost than other forms of production (Wolf 1988: ch. 2). Porter (1990) is the great contemporary Schumpeterian theorist, whose book has been widely read and debated.

The second criterion for judging the results of markets, distributive equity (from here on referred to as equity), is more complex to measure and evaluate. Viner (1960) suggests that state intervention in the free market should occur when prevailing income distribution is not satisfactory. Wolf suggests that the meaning of equity varies because it can mean either equality of results or equality of opportunity, horizontal equity or vertical equity, or the Marxist meaning ('to each according to his need, from each according to his ability'), or in the sense that the most disadvantaged should see improvements before improvements are made for the most advantaged.

Wolf identifies four types of restrictions or limitations of the market:

1. *Externalities and public goods*, where pollution, for example, is an externality of private activity which affects a public good, for example water, air. In reverse, public education is a public good which generates externalities for the private sector. In both cases, the participation of the state helps compensate for the tendency of the market, which, if not reinforced, could lead to insufficient results.

2. *Improved performance can make marginal costs fall and lead to monopoly*, when innovators, through the scale of their production, reduce their marginal costs and bankrupt their competitors. This causes inefficiencies because monopolistic prices do not reflect the market, and in terms of dynamic efficiency the producer has no competition to force him to innovate. In this case state intervention is justified a) to regulate the prices of a natural monopoly (such as public services) or b) to create legal protection and thus avoid the creation of a monopoly and promote competition through anti-trust legislation.

3. *Imperfections in the market*, when price, knowledge and factor mobility, characteristics of perfect markets, do not fill the bill in real markets. In such cases, the state and public policy ought to facilitate access to information, and eliminate entry barriers and barriers to capital mobility.

4. *Equity*. Economists generally fail to raise this point, Wolf says, even though they acknowledge that it is an imperfection of the market and that income distribution is a public good. However, they also acknowledge that a market that functions well may not live up to socially accepted standards of equity or to a social preference for reducing the distributive spread. In the welfare economy, the trade-off between efficiency and equity is addressed with distributive measures in favour of the latter to achieve the desired redistribution.

## In sum

The discussion of the transformation the world is undergoing is framed by opposing understandings of globalization, by Samir Amin on one extreme and Kenichi Ohmae on the other. One focuses on the lack of alternatives within transnationalization for countries on the periphery; while the other says that globalization is not for countries on the periphery, rather for a select few who will gain entry to an 'island'. From this point of view, the news is not that transnationalization or globalization will leave few alternatives for countries on the periphery, understood as Amin defines it, rather that globalization does not even take them into account. In other words, there is a universe of countries that are not being considered by the new proposals and rules of the game for the global economy. Some Eastern European countries will be included – Hungary, the Czech Republic, Slovakia and perhaps Poland could be on the list of countries that will join the European Union – but the rest will not, especially those east of the Urals. A few Latin American countries will also be incorporated – basically, Mexico, Chile and Argentina through the North American Free Trade Agreement (NAFTA) – and finally the Asian Tigers or Dragons. There is not much room for the rest of the world in the global economy as we have described it.

In the debate between liberals and mercantilists, the discussion was whether or not protected industrialization was positive in light of the barriers Great Britain erected for its trade with the United States. It was the Americans who established the importance of industrial protection to achieve improvements in national economic development, employment and the broadening of the domestic market. It was they who railed against the English liberals until they finally acknowledged with Ricardo that there could be comparative advantages that would benefit England's trading partners and, therefore, protection was not necessary to improve trading relations. Hamilton believed that the monopolies that protection might create could end up setting prices and, therefore, he did not get caught up in questions of monopolistic behaviour. This discussion, later retaken between liberals and mercantilists, left aside the question of whether protection is required for nascent industries, and avoided entirely the topic of growth or the importance of the internal market. However, no economic development is possible without the development of the internal market, by which improvements are achieved in the overall consumption patterns of the population. Such improvements, in turn, allow for the development of economic activities whose surpluses can be exported competitively, to put it in the terms of the debate on self-centred economies.

Finally, the intervention of the state when the market fails in countries of emerging or intermediate capitalism implies a very large regulatory state because the nature of competition in such countries is much more oligopolistic or monopolistic than in mature capitalism. Despite the crisis of Fordism, because there are so few companies that produce a particular good in an industry, those that participate in the market set prices practically by industry or by product. International competition could block monopolistic pricing only in the case of products whose international distributors are not monopolies or oligopolies, and there do not seem to be many of them (as we shall see in Chapter 4); in fact, the evidence points the other way. At the same time, if the state does not supplant or complement the private sector in the process of development, investment risks are not ameliorated and only highly profitable international investments are undertaken. In the cases of Central America and part of Latin America, this has led to a specialization in primary exports. It could be argued that this is not a problem if the overall level of exports rises. A counter-argument would be that income from exports is only positive to the degree that it allows for a reactivation of the internal market. Otherwise, in Latin America we will have returned to the dual economies that produced the sort of exclusive development that occurred from colonial times up to the first third of this century.

Nowadays, economic debates focus on how to achieve maximum efficiency from larger markets and larger producers, to use Ohmae's terminology. In a new inter-related world, there is an 'island' of countries that trades most of the goods in international trade, receives the lion's share of income, and has the greatest productive capacity. The other countries are not even worth mentioning and are certainly not part of the 'island'. One billion people benefit from this 'island' of inter-related economies, and four billion are left out. This inter-relation is called globalization. From the point of view of market theory, efficiency is the central question and the problem of equity is set aside because no one can agree on what it means. In the theoretical framework for globalization defined by Ohmae, it matters little what happens with equity either among countries or within countries. Ohmae goes back to Smith and affirms that nations do not exist, that universal interests are above nations. There are no borders and peace is built via economic interest.

Viewed from Latin America, where the attempt to create a system for protected industrial development à la List and Hamilton was relatively successful for the thirty years leading up to 1980, Ohmae's proposal seems more like a threat than a promise. Probably some country will say it will come out ahead, but Ohmae is hard even on Brazil, the most successful country of the region in terms of export growth and industrial development. On the other hand, he says: 'We have to accept the fact that, for developing and developed economies alike, for Canada and Australia as well as for Brazil and the OPEC nations, natural resources are no longer the key to wealth' (Ohmae 1990: 193). So much for Ricardo's ideas on comparative advantage.

'[N]ational borders have little to do any longer with the real flows of industrial activity. We have to accept that information and knowledge – a trained and literate population, not military hardware, are the real sources of strength' (Ohmae 1990: 193). The role of government is to educate the people and provide first-class infrastructure for the companies that will employ them.[7] Governments ought to turn their countries into attractive places for companies to set up operations. Truly global companies serve the interests of consumers, not governments. They do not exploit local situations and then repatriate profits, leaving areas poorer than before. They invest, train, pay taxes, build infrastructure and provide well for consumers in all the countries where they do business. Here Ohmae hints that, beyond a new theory of borderless international trade, he is offering us Latin Americans a new theory of the flagless, nationless, civically responsible multinational company. This is not only wildly out of touch, it does not even lead to economic development as it is generally understood theoretically: improvement in the welfare of the population as a whole.

The neoliberal proposal, laid out more extensively in Chapter 4, begins where these discussions end. This instrument of globalization is presented in Latin America as the only alternative to barbarism. The dilemma is posed as either do what neoliberal theory proposes or be left out. Conceptually, however, Latin America and Africa are excluded from globalization anyway. Therefore, this is a false dilemma. Modernization through opening up to outside influence is attractive bait to get us to bite the lure of globalization which global communications dangles in front of us. Globalization is not posed as a given, the way imperialism was at the end of the nineteenth century until the middle of the twentieth century in Latin America. The policies baited on that hook grow from the universalization of economic policy, not the needs of Latin American development.

This book has been written for the lay reader who has no formal economic training. It is framed in terms of international economic policy and interdependence. These subjects will be taken up repeatedly throughout these six chapters from various points of view, in an attempt to summarize a vision of where Latin America stands and where it is going at the beginning of the twenty-first century.

## Notes

1. A reflection on what has been occurring in Peru during the 1990s from the point of view of society as a whole, as an effect of global changes and domestic economic reforms, can be read in Ugarteche 1994b: 207–30. The debate that follows it on pages 231–73 is very important. Jorge Oshiro (1995: 237–48) carries forward this debate with a philosophical presentation of what is modern.

2. This section sums up the main ideas of the debate found in Chapter 1 of Samir Amin (1990a). The original edition came out in 1985 in French and precedes both Ohmae and events in Eastern Europe. After the disappearance of the Soviet

Union and the opening up of China, Amin's examples lost their validity, although the theoretical proposal remains current.

3. Taken from the summary of Chapter 2 on Smith and Ricardo in Crane and Amawi 1991.

4. Chapter 4 offers an in-depth summary of List's thinking.

5. BID 1971 provides a synthesis of Prebisch's thought.

6. Chapter 4 in Wolf (1988) sums up the ideas of Buchanan (1969), Buchanan and Tullock (1962), Niskanen (1971) and Forte and Peacock (1985).

7. An example of the way such thinking has entered the world of Latin American politics can be found in Peruvian President Alberto Fujimori's second inaugural address, in which, according to the BBC (London), he said that the redistribution of the benefits of economic growth will reach the population through improvements in highways and education.

## 2. Systemic Crisis and Technological Change: A View from Latin America

During the 1980s much was said about the debt crisis, and quite a few of us joined in and used that label, which tended to focus the critique on the poor use of resources and on the overextension of credit in the international financial system. Some argued that this excess had to do with the recycling of petrodollars following the rise in oil prices. Others argued that states were irresponsible in their use of international resources; that there was corruption, poor administration, and that, in general, Third World governments were to blame for the problem. Finally, another group of authors attributed responsibility jointly to the excesses of the banks and the irresponsibility of governments.

All of this literature was written in a historical vacuum, as if in the past there had never been debt crises and as if this one was unique. In reality, the first Latin American debt crisis began in 1824 and lasted until the 1840s (Marichal 1989: ch. 2).[1] Interest rates rose and the price of primary resources fell, strangling the balance of payments of the recently founded nations. This was repeated in the 1870s when credit was cut off and governments stopped paying, with a rise in interest rates and a fall in primary resource prices between 1872 and 1876 (Marichal 1989: ch. 4). The culmination of this debt crisis occurred at the end of the 1880s, when for the first time the concepts of swaps and privatization were introduced through the Grace Contract in Peru. Finally, from 1929 to 1931 there was a repetition of the same phenomenon of credit drying up, interest rates rising and raw materials prices falling.[2] The credit drought did not end until the 1950s.

What occurred at the beginning of the 1980s was a repetition of a pattern seen before: rise in interest rates and fall in raw materials prices, which when added to the cutoff of new lending necessarily led to what we called a 'debt crisis'. The way out of the crisis was sought through changes in the technological paradigm (Pérez 1985), which would imply that we were not facing a debt crisis at all, but rather a crisis in the model of accumulation. The crises of 1826, 1876 or 1931 in Latin America were not called debt crises. The global system was the same, but the institutional framework was not, as this changed significantly after the Second World War.

Advanced capitalist countries are suffering a severe productivity crisis, a result of the previously existing techno-economic model. The crisis is evident in the reduction of the rate of growth of factor productivity, which has led to a change in the techno-economic model and a new model of accumulation. The change unhinged international economic relations and undercut Latin America's productive base. This is what this chapter intends to demonstrate. An important debate on the crisis (Sheik 1990)[3] is as yet inconclusive, but recovery of productivity and profitability has been attempted through the spread of a new knowledge-based technological paradigm (Doşi 1982).[4] The hypothesis that this book will seek to prove is that the crisis in developed capitalism grew out of a fall in productivity in the advanced capitalist countries, which in turn caused technological changes and fierce competition on technological frontiers, forcing accelerated innovation in those countries.

During the initial period of decline in productivity there was a surge in the export of credit to more backward regions of the world to dynamize trade and broaden the markets for the industrial production of advanced capitalist countries.[5] Once the crisis became widespread, a reverse process occurred: resources were redirected towards the productive restructuring of advanced countries, and a negative net transfer of resources from developing countries emerged, deepening the economic crisis that had been introduced by the change in the model of international trade and by the crisis in profitability which had kicked off the lending binge in the first place. In this way, the financing of accelerated technological change in advanced capitalist countries 'dried up' the credit resources available for the Third World. What we call the 'debt crisis' in Latin America and Africa was but a reflection of a systemic crisis that affected advanced capitalist countries first and later on everyone else. The big question is: Why did it not affect Southeast Asia?

## The productivity crisis in advanced capitalist countries

Numerous studies in recent years have sought to determine how much productivity has fallen and why. Baumol (Baumol et al. 1991) and Caves (1992) did comparative international and inter-industry studies to measure how US industry was faring in comparison to other economies. Baumol says what was most satisfying about his study was that he found the US economy to be in better shape than he expected. Although the growth of US productivity has fallen off over the last fifty years, the trend has been stable, with only a slight downturn attributable to the maturity of the economy and the high level of productivity achieved. Caves (1992) shows Japanese industry to be more efficient than American, although he finds no major correlation between efficiency and international trade.

However, studies by the Organization for Economic Cooperation and Development (OECD), published between 1991 and 1994, show that this is not the case for the economy as a whole. A wide-ranging study by Angus Maddison (1991) of the principal OECD countries demonstrates that there has indeed been a long-term decline in productivity, as indicated in Table 2.1. The variety of approaches in these studies all conclude that productivity has declined in every member of the Group of Seven (G7), but particularly in the wealthiest countries: the USA, Japan and Germany. It is noteworthy that, despite the deterioration in the productivity of capital, there has been a recovery in the productivity of labour, leading to an improvement in aggregate productivity, particularly over the past few years in certain countries.

Englander and Gurney (1994a: 111–28), using growth in factor productivity as an indicator, show that the use of new technologies is spreading rapidly in several countries. A close examination of Table 2.1 reveals a fall in factor productivity between 1960 and 1979. In no country were there improvements and all of them saw deterioration in the growth of factor productivity. The deterioration of the productivity of capital, in particular, as well as that of labour, explains the technological revolution that took place in the middle of the 1970s. It also explains the rise in the export of capital throughout the period of decline in factor productivity, in light of capital's need to recover that productivity. The inverse relations noted arise from simultaneously needing to sell in new markets, while undergoing technological change at home to recover first domestic and then international competitiveness. The need to recover factor productivity, particularly that of capital, must have led to the massive spread of technological change in advanced countries. Thus, the beginning of the 1980s would have seen growing absorption of capital in developed countries, feeding in turn the further spread of technological change.

The evidence from 1980 on is moderately encouraging. Apparently the introduction of technological change in advanced capitalist countries produced a moderate recuperation of factor productivity and kicked off a phase of accelerated technological competition. Perhaps technological change has turned out most beneficial for the United States, as an examination of the data from 1986–90 against 1986–93 shows a renewed deterioration for all except the United States, which doubled its rate of improvement in factor productivity from 0.3 to 0.6 per cent annually (see Table 2.1).

The implication is that a process of accelerated technological change is under way and will tend to spread farther afield. Technology is the 'what' and the 'how' of production. Thus, while technological progress, in terms of knowledge and inventions, is relatively autonomous, the application and spread of specific techniques in the productive sphere are governed by social conditions and economic decisions regarding profitability (Pérez, 1985: 442). To the degree that profitability, understood as the productivity of capital, does not improve, the need to dynamize technological change becomes more urgent.

According to Pérez, the techno-economic paradigm that ended its cycle in the 1970s was based on the intensive use of raw materials for energy, above all petrochemicals, which presupposed the low price of oil. Companies were organized in line, they were corporations and operated in oligopolistic markets. The introduction of micro-electronics, which brought a fall in the cost of processing information, is the basis of the new techno-economic paradigm. The characteristics of this new paradigm based on micro-electronics are:

1. intensity of information versus intensity of raw materials and energy
2. economies of scope or of specialization based on flexibility versus economies of scale based on homogeneity
3. new concepts of organizational efficiency

The paradigm change, Pérez says metaphorically, is more like crossing an ocean than following a railroad line. The future is built on the past, but in a paradigmatic change the future is innovation on the past and cannot be extrapolated from the past. In this sense, Latin America's crisis

TABLE 2.1 Productivity of all factors in G7 countries, 1960–93 (annual percentage change)

|  | 1960–73 | 1974–79 | 1980–85 | 1986–90 | 1986–93 |
|---|---|---|---|---|---|
| USA | 1.5 | -0.4 | 0.1 | 0.3 | 0.6 |
| Japan | 4.6 | 0.9 | 1.4 | 1.8 | 0.8 |
| Germany | 2.5 | 1.7 | 0.4 | 1.6 | 1.0 |
| France | 3.8 | 1.6 | 10. | 2.0 | 1.4 |
| Italy | 4.11 | 1.9 | 0.6 | 2.0 | 1.3 |
| UK | 2.51 | 0.5 | 1.5 | 1.6 | 1.5 |
| Canada | 2.0 | 0.8 | 0.3 | -0.1 | -0.2 |

*Source*: Englander and Gurney 1994b, table 2, 116–17.

stems from the fact that the paradigm change requires the destruction of the existing productive plant and a change in social behaviours and institutional structures to allow the new paradigm to function well (Pérez 1985). The crisis of capital as a whole, however – since productivity did not recover with the introduction of new technology – is due to the fact that the lower cost of processing information (the technological revolution) brings with it greater technological obsolescence and a quicker depreciation of capital than in the period before 1975.

The effects on the global economy were felt first in variations in investment patterns caused by the paradigm change; then in direct impacts on patterns of trade in goods and especially now in services, as well as on the patterns of international trade. It is worth warning that a process of generalized technological change can end up strangling capital itself, since the investment required to carry it out cannot be recouped before the next phase of renewal must begin. This is the difficulty posed by the shortening of the technological cycle, fruit of competition on the technological frontier and so short at this point that one cannot even speak of a product cycle (Cantwell 1995).

Other evidence (Pianta 1995) suggests that when productivity levels and incomes are high, and economies approach the technological frontier, a new group of inter-relations between technological factors and the evolution of the economy emerges. The virtuous cycle between technology and growth – reflected in the high correlation between growth in the per capita gross domestic product (GDP) and spending on research and development per employee, and the levels of investment per employee – can no longer be sustained by concentrating on a particular aspect. There emerges a new inter-relation between knowledge, learning processes, human capital, research quality, non-material investment, organizational innovation and favourable institutional conditions (Pianta 1995). In addition, there are higher levels of competition on the technological frontier itself (Pianta 1995), which suffocate the relation between technological change and growth, while opening new non-material spheres of technology in relation to growth.

It could be that competition on the technological frontier is leading to very low capital productivity (see Table 2.2). The pace of innovation and the difficulty of recouping investments could lead to extremely low rates of capital productivity, despite showing high rates of return in the short term. It could be that the problem of profitability – an integral part of the world system for over two decades, particularly in advanced capitalist countries – is related to competition on the technological frontier (Scherer 1992).

This phenomenon could also be related to a process known as 'catch up'. The need for competition among firms in advanced capitalist countries gave rise in the 1970s to a 'catch-up' process in the technological realm (Hansson and Henrekson 1994). The idea came from Gerschenkron (1952) and basically means that there can be advantages to being a bit behind the most advanced capitalist countries. The hypothesis is that when productivity levels are much lower in a sub-group of countries than in others that are more advanced, the former will marshal all their technological resources to catch up to the latter. This could have been happening in Europe in the period 1960–90, accentuated during the decade from 1970 to 1980. This seems to have occurred with the countries of East Asia, especially the Tigers. Usually this concept is applied to advanced countries relative to less advanced countries, but if we use it in the broad sense of countries with high labour productivity relative to those with lower labour productivity, it could help explain changes between dissimilar advanced countries or, in this case, also between advanced and backward countries. The question is why Latin America did not enter this catching-up process in the 1970s. Perhaps inertia made innovation difficult, since the development model based on the depleted techno-economic paradigm of the 1930–75 period had positive results in terms of growth, especially between 1950 and 1970. It is probable that something similar occurred in the socialist countries of Eastern Europe (Pérez 1985: 446). The countries of Southeast Asia did not experience such inertia because they began industrializing twenty years after Latin America and the Soviet Union.

The evidence (Englander and Gurney 1994a, 1994b; Maddison 1992) shows that production by worker/hour has tended to come into line with US levels, which are taken as reference points. This was made possible by high levels of investment in countries that are 'catching up' and by a decrease in the productivity of capital. As the levels of international competition around the same products and the need for innovation both

TABLE 2.2 Productivity of capital in G7 countries, 1960–93 (percentage variations)

|         | 1960–73 | 1974–79 | 1980–86 | 1986–90 | 1986–93 |
|---------|---------|---------|---------|---------|---------|
| USA     | 0.1     | -1.3    | -1.2    | 0.0     | -0.1    |
| Japan   | -3.0    | -3.5    | -1.7    | -1.1    | -2.1    |
| Germany | +1.4    | -1.0    | -1.6    | 0.8     | -0.1    |
| France  | 0.9     | -1.0    | -1.1    | 0.8     | -0.3    |
| Italy   | 0.4     | 0.3     | -0.7    | 0.6     | -0.2    |
| UK      | -0.3    | -1.6    | -0.5    | 1.4     | 0.5     |
| Canada  | 0.6     | -0.5    | -2.0    | -1.5    | -2.1    |

*Source*: Englander and Gurney 1994b, table 2, 116–17.

increased, the capacity of capital to recoup its investment was choked off and profit margins narrowed. The pace of innovation knocks products out of the running before investment can be recouped, which explains how production by worker/hour came to be uniform across the world and will continue to be so. Competition on the technological frontier is a competition based on innovations that are more and more costly per finished product. Thus, not only more backward countries are in a race to catch up, so are advanced capitalist countries. Paradoxically, Japan seems to be the farthest behind in this catching-up process, yet it has achieved the most stable improvements in labour productivity. This could mean that Japan is immersed in a process of ongoing innovation, rather than a staged process like other advanced capitalist countries.

Technological competition and constant innovation explain why trade in technology increased among advanced countries over the past thirty years. Innovation, however, does not only refer to equipment (Porter 1990), it also means new methods of production, new designs, new forms of organization and new methods of management. Innovation continually colours all aspects of the life of a company and is primarily a macro-economic phenomenon. Some argue that Gerschenkron's analysis is not applicable because he refers essentially to machinery and physical technology, while the new concept is broader (Amsden 1992–93). However, the concept of technology in its broadest sense covers everything and makes no important distinction between machinery and processes. The substantive issue is that those who are behind in labour productivity imitate those who are more advanced, or purchase their way of doing things. This is the principle of technological competition until the technological frontier advances.

TABLE 2.3 Levels of labour productivity in G7 countries, 1966–90 (production by worker/hour; USA = 100)

|  | 1966 | 1975 | 1990 |
| --- | --- | --- | --- |
| USA | 79.4 | 88.5 | 100.0 |
| Japan | 16.9 | 32.3 | 49.4 |
| Germany | 37.2 | 54.7 | 80.2 |
| France | 38.4 | 57.4 | 93.8 |
| Italy | 34.4 | 56.8 | 80.9 |
| UK | 36.6 | 51.7 | 76.9 |
| Canada | 54.1 | 67.4 | 88.6 |

*Source*: Englander and Gurney, 1994a, according to Maddison's (1991) methodology.

Everywhere except Japan, technological change is tending towards uniform levels of labour productivity matching those of the United States, but degrees of productivity improvement have necessarily been dissimilar. During the process of technological obsolescence, up to the middle of the 1970s, growth in labour productivity in the United States slowed and became stagnant. At the same time, the introduction of technological change in Japan and its need to catch up gave it the highest rate of labour productivity growth for the entire period from 1975 on. It never reached the 8 per cent growth in productivity it had enjoyed before 1973, but given the growth it had already achieved that would have been very difficult. Despite such a high rate of growth in labour productivity, as we have seen, in absolute numbers Japanese productivity is only half that of the United States (see Table 2.3). Countries where innovation has come later have had slower responses regarding labour productivity (France, Italy and Germany). In the United Kingdom and Canada, technological change apparently began at the beginning of the 1980s, but did not continue with the same impetus for the rest of the decade.

The conclusion we can draw regarding the issue of productivity is that although the group of advanced countries faces the problem of falling productivity and profitability, there are countries where both are continuing to grow slowly. All seem to have been affected by the problem at the beginning of the 1990s, except for the United States since its enormous productive base had already experienced technological change and had maintained innovation as a dynamic process, managing in this way to emerge from the long crisis it had suffered. Despite everything, US productivity is higher than that of the rest of the world and, despite the efforts of the rest of the advanced countries to catch up, they have a long way to go. If they maintain the current pace, in another decade Europe could surpass US levels, but not Japan, which is still far behind on this count.

TABLE 2.4 Labour productivity in G7 countries, 1960–93 (rates of growth)

|         | 1960–1973 | 1974–79 | 1980–85 | 1986–90 | 1986–93 |
|---------|-----------|---------|---------|---------|---------|
| USA     | 2.1       | 0.0     | 0.7     | 0.5     | 0.9     |
| Japan   | 8.0       | 2.9     | 2.8     | 3.1     | 2.2     |
| Germany | 4.4       | 3.0     | 1.3     | 2.1     | 1.6     |
| France  | 5.3       | 2.9     | 2.2     | 2.7     | 2.2     |
| Italy   | 6.1       | 2.8     | 1.3     | 2.7     | 2.1     |
| UK      | 3.6       | 1.5     | 2.4     | 1.7     | 1.9     |
| Canada  | 2.8       | 1.5     | 1.6     | 0.7     | 0.9     |

*Source*: Englander and Gurney 1994b, table 2, 116–17.

Technological change is introduced when growth in factor productivity slows to zero. In addition, if productivity must be enhanced to try to achieve parity with an economy that enjoys greater labour productivity, and thus gain a competitive edge, this would be another incentive for introducing accelerated technological change (Romer 1989). In the case of advanced countries, the combination of both factors led to a strong dynamic of ongoing technological change that has been maintained through the acceleration of the product cycle. Despite this, there is still no sign of recovery of the productivity of capital, even though an improvement in factor and labour productivity growth is expected in most advanced capitalist countries. This suggests that the efficiency with which capital is employed is as important as the quantity of capital invested.[6]

## The recession in OECD countries

The 1980s saw a deceleration in the growth rates of advanced capitalist economies, a process which continued into the 1990s. Due to problems with productivity and to the techno-economic change they had been undergoing for over two decades, the advanced capitalist economies entered a period of recession which reduced the demand for raw materials and, at the same time, forced them to export more. The effect was a deceleration in the demand for Latin America's exports in the OECD countries – from 12.7 per cent growth in 1986–89 it fell to 3.8 per cent in 1989–92 – and an acceleration in exports from OECD countries to Latin America, which went from 12.2 to 14.9 per cent in the same period (see Table 2.5). This was possible only because of the widespread application of economic liberalization policies in Latin America after 1990.

At the same time, the United States lost its leading role in world

TABLE 2.5 Trade of OECD countries with regions or groups of countries, 1986–92 (rates of growth)

| | 1986–89 | 1989–92 | 1986–89 | 1989–92 |
|---|---|---|---|---|
| Latin America | 12.2 | 14.9 | 12.7 | 3.8 |
| Asian Tigers[1] | 24.1 | 10.7 | 17.6 | 2.4 |
| Central/Eastern Europe | 11.2 | 11.2 | 8.9 | 11.4 |
| Africa | 7.2 | 5.5 | 8.4 | 0.7 |
| Asia and Pacific[2] | 11.2 | 9.8 | 22.1 | 15.1 |

*Notes*: 1. South Korea, Hong Kong and Taiwan. 2. China and the Dragons: Malaysia, Thailand, Indonesia and the Philippines.

*Sources*: 1986–89: OECD 1991: tables 89–93; 1989–92: OECD 1993: tables 95–99.

economic growth. Even though it is still the largest economy, growth in the USA no longer carries the rest of the world's developed economies with it (the locomotor effect). Growth regions have been China and the countries of Southeast and East Asia, which managed to maintain their levels of export growth in the midst of a systemic recession (see Table 2.6). They may become the new engines of the system when the global economy comes out of the worldwide recession.

The big question is whether the Asian countries, including China, have greater labour and capital productivity, or if it was external factors that allowed those countries to achieve greater profitability through production in scale. Dynamism of exports to the OECD after 1989 can been seen in Table 2.5. The other question is how these countries achieved dynamic export growth when the same external factors affecting Latin America were affecting them. No doubt the answer to that question lies in domestic policies, which will be examined later, and in cultural factors that will also be taken up in another chapter. One factor that ought to be noted is that in the midst of the recession in productivity and the change in techno-economic paradigm, a group of countries previously excluded from the global economy were brought in: Eastern Europe, China and the Asian Dragons (Malaysia, Thailand, Indonesia and the Philippines) – signs of a new order in the global system. The evidence shows a turnaround in the supply of goods from these three to OECD countries and a dynamic growth in that trade, at the same time that trade with Latin America, the Asian Tigers (South Korea, Hong Kong and Taiwan) and Africa decelerated. In other words, the slowdown in OECD growth occurred in a context of a changeover in the actors in the world system, which precipitated modifications in the previous model of international economic relations.

## The characteristics of technological change and its impact on Latin America

Latin America's insertion in the global economy has suffered a shake-up and the effect has been a crisis in the export sector, due to the change in techno-economic paradigm and the slow pace of adaptation to the new demands of the world economy. The reasons are the following:

1. the nature of technological change
2. the de-materialization of production
3. the substitution factor
4. the use of information
5. the accelerating pace of innovation

TABLE 2.6 Growth of the world economy, 1960–93 (annual GDP growth rate)

| | 1960–68[1] | 1968–73 | 1973–79 | 1979–85[2] | 1985–90 | 1990[3] | 1991 | 1992 | 1993 |
|---|---|---|---|---|---|---|---|---|---|
| United States | 4.5 | 3.2 | 2.4 | 2.4 | 3.1 | 1.2 | -0.6 | 2.3 | 3.1 |
| Japan | 10.2 | 8.6 | 3.6 | 4.0 | 4.6 | 4.8 | 4.3 | 1.1 | 0.1 |
| European Community | 4.7 | 4.9 | 2.51 | 1.7 | 3.0 | 3.0 | 1.7 | 1.1 | -0.3 |
| Economies in transition[4] | n/a | n/a | n/a | n/a | 3.1 | -6.3 | -9.0 | -16.3 | n/a |
| Latin America[5] | | 6.8* | 5.3* | 1.8* | 2.01 | 0.3 | 3.5 | 3.0 | 3.2 |
| South and East Asia[4] | 4.7 | 2.9* | 4.3* | 5.4* | 5.9 | 6.4 | 5.3 | 4.9 | n/a |
| China | n/a | 2.9* | 4.7* | 8.7* | 9.9 | 5.2 | 7.7 | 12.8 | n/a |

*Sources*: 1. OECD 1992: table 3.1. 2. OECD 1992: (averages for 1979–85 and 1985–90 are by the author; UN statistics differ). 3. OECD 1994: A4, Annex Table 1 (UN statistics differ; but this series was chosen because it covers 34 years; recent tendencies hold). 4. ECLAC 1994a: 242, table I (the average corresponds to 1981–88). 5. ECLAC 1994c: 37, table A1 (the average refers to 1986–90; these data were chosen because they are more current). * United Nations 1986 and 1989 (the data correspond to 1970–75, 1975–80, 1980–86).

6. the spread of new technologies
7. the changes in the organizational paradigm for production to improve productivity and achieve greater competitiveness

**The nature of technological change**  What has been occurring since the middle of the 1970s is not a continuation of the techno-economic paradigm that existed up to that point, but rather a rupture in the techno-economic paradigm.

> Following a period of crisis, the paradigm is replaced by another, which redefines accumulated knowledge and situates relevant science in a new and fruitful trajectory. A techno-economic paradigm represents the guiding model for commercial technological progress during several decades. It is a model of accepted wisdom for identifying and developing products and economically profitable productive processes, based on the range of what is technologically viable. (Pérez 1992: 26, 3, fn)

The central points of new technology are the displacement of labour and savings in raw materials and energy. Displacement of labour has been achieved through the introduction of computer equipment that substitutes for labour, and therefore raises labour productivity. This has a positive impact on labour productivity and an adverse one on direct employment.

This last point will affect Latin American economies in two ways: the sources of direct productive employment are reduced, and unemployment in advanced capitalist countries affects their migration policies negatively. Second, the primary economy will slow the demand for raw materials and have an adverse impact on international trade in them (see Table 2.7).

The feasibility of putting these new technologies to work opens up some opportunities and closes off others at the same time. It can become

TABLE 2.7 Evolution of world consumption of major metals, 1960–90 (average per cent annual growth)

|                   | 1960s | 1970s | 1980s |
|-------------------|-------|-------|-------|
| Refined aluminium | 9.0   | 4.4   | 1.5   |
| Refined copper    | 4.3   | 2.6   | 1.4   |
| Refined tin       | 1.0   | 1.0   | 1.0   |
| Iron ore          | 4.0   | 2.0   | 0.5   |
| Nickel            | 6.0   | 2.0   | 2.0   |
| Refined lead      | 4.0   | 3.0   | 1.0   |

*Source*: ECLAC 1994d: 36.

a new independent source of jobs, but also can make the established industrial base in Latin America obsolete if companies are not able to incorporate innovations to increase productivity and become competitive. This technological change in Latin America may generate improved levels of production and income, but it is not likely to increase employment, as has occurred in advanced capitalist countries. Industrial obsolescence in Latin America and the requirements for innovation will likely lead to a process of industrial modernization, causing some companies to close and others to open, if investment conditions are given. Otherwise, it could lead to de-industrialization. Pérez maintains that the institutional transformations required by a change in the techno-economic paradigm take thirty years to become consolidated. Under Fordism, to develop mass production based on intensive energy use required state intervention, institutionalized rules for promoting trade and international investment, the creation of the General Agreement on Tariffs and Trade (GATT), the Bretton Woods system, the United Nations, and the recognition of unions and the forty-hour week. Today, in light of the changes, all of this is thrown into question and will require a different institutional framework (Pérez 1992).

There is another angle from which to analyse this same point. The new lines of computerized production are flexible, they can provide delivery on demand, do not require stocking raw materials or finished goods and they do not waste. This implies a drop in the consumption of raw materials per unit of finished goods, with direct effects on world trade in raw materials and particularly on the structure of Latin America's exports. It should be emphasized, however, considering the availability of highly concentrated mineral veins, that investments in the primary sector may continue and even broaden in light of environmental restrictions on mining in advanced capitalist countries.

Nevertheless, it is argued that countries that are technologically behind can catch up and take advantage of the paradigm shift thanks to the discontinuity in technological progress and the prolonged period of adaptation in the leading countries of the previous wave (Pérez 1992). So the adverse effect, in terms of trade in raw materials and its de-linking from the world economy, is also an advantage for those entering fresh on the phase of growth and expansion. This implies that new international insertion will not occur via raw materials, but rather in a manner that is complementary to them.

**The de-materialization of production** Currently, forward and backward vertical linkages on all goods have been reduced, as far as the scope and use of raw materials throughout the process is concerned.

Miniaturization saves on raw materials, reducing still further the demand for them, already weakened by the previous factor as discussed above.

**The substitution factor** Technology – defined as the means for labour-saving improvements in productivity, consumption of raw materials and energy – has led to a massive investment in the development of alternatives to existing raw materials, what could be called the 'saltpeter syndrome'.[7] Biotechnology and research on substitutes for metals have allowed industrial, agricultural and mineral raw materials to be replaced. Two examples are the substitution of cane sugar (produced in Latin America) by beet sugar (produced in Europe) and corn syrup (produced in United States) for sweeteners; and the invention of optic fibres to replace copper. These are two examples of a process of substitution that disrupts international trade in raw materials. Other examples are the utilization of plastics in place of tin for canning, and of hard plastic in place of steel in musical instruments, wristwatches and computers.

Technological changes seeking to bring improvements in productivity and profitability in advanced capitalist economies have had the effect of reducing global trade in industrial raw materials (metallic and non-metallic minerals) and increasing trade in manufactured goods. This led to a reduced presence for Latin America in world trade between 1970 and 1992, from 5.5 to 3.7 per cent, and for Africa from 4.1 to 1.8 per cent (see Table 2.8). The displacement of raw materials affected mono-producing countries more than others, as in the case of Bolivian tin exports which fell by 45 per cent between 1980 and 1987. This phenomenon has been

TABLE 2.8 Structure of world commerce, 1960–92 (percentages)

|                              | 1960 | 1970 | 1980 | 1990 | 1992 |
|------------------------------|------|------|------|------|------|
| USA                          | 15.8 | 14.0 | 11.0 | 11.5 | 12.0 |
| European Community           | 32.2 | 35.5 | 32.5 | 36.8 | 35.7 |
| Japan                        | 3.1  | 6.1  | 6.5  | 8.4  | 9.1  |
| All developed countries      | 65.9 | 70.9 | 62.3 | 71.4 | 71.5 |
| Latin America and Caribbean  | 7.7  | 5.5  | 5.5  | 3.9  | 3.7  |
| Asia including China         | 9.5  | 8.1  | 17.8 | 17.0 | 18.2 |
| Africa                       | 4.2  | 4.1  | 4.7  | 2.0  | 1.8  |
| All developing countries     | 21.9 | 18.4 | 28.7 | 21.6 | 23.9 |

*Note*: The difference in the totals is due to the socialist countries and those, such as South Africa or Israel, that under UNCTAD classification are considered under the heading of other countries.

*Source*: ECLAC 1994a: 35, table I.4.

felt in every economy of Latin America. At the same time, trade in manufactured goods, be they intermediate or finished goods, increased, leading the countries of Asia to increase their presence in world trade from 8.1 to 18.2 per cent between 1970 and 1992. Initially, the United States could not compete in the export of manufactured goods, and lost ground between 1970 and 1980 when the US share fell from 14 to 11 per cent. But the spread of new technologies internally kicked off a recovery, increasing the share from 11 to 12 per cent between 1980 and 1992. Something similar occurred with the economies of the European Economic Community (EEC), now the European Union (EU). Japan, like other countries in Asia, steadily broadened its presence in the world market due to its stable process of innovation and as a result of the quality of its finished goods.

**The use of information** Since information has become available in real time, and both fax machines and electronic mail are widely used, having goods on hand by maintaining an inventory is less important than knowing where to find them when needed. With improved transportation and communications systems, the function of inventories has been modified. This also has an adverse effect on basic trade in raw materials. New technologies, however, touch not only on the availability of information, but also on ways of using it. In other words, they establish a new way of doing things that ranges from telecommunications satellites to running a corner store (Pérez 1992: 36). The globalization of information thus allows for the opening up of capital markets and improved systems of trade in finished goods (since desirable markets are more easily accessed for capital investment or for seeking out markets or suppliers), revolutionizing even supermarkets and university teaching methodologies. The process of liberalization under way would not have been possible without such technological change.

**The accelerating pace of innovation** The past two decades have seen an acceleration of technological change. Ever since the microchip was introduced in 1975, the concept of accumulation of knowledge has been transformed to the point where such knowledge doubles every four or five years (Dahlman 1994). Pérez (1985) identifies the invention of the microchip and biotechnology as the starting points of the new technological revolution. Microchip technology, by allowing information to be processed quickly, accelerates the pace of new knowledge. This is a new dynamic which has shortened the technological cycle from fifty years to five years and then to one year, making the entire concept of the life of a technological process obsolescent. In this process of permanent innovation, the shelf-life of electronic products went from two years to only a few months. For Drucker, knowledge before the industrial revolution was for being, with the industrial revolution it became knowledge for doing, but following the Second World War it became knowledge applied to knowledge itself. Knowledge today is *the* factor in production (Drucker 1993).[8] Applied knowledge is systematic innovation.

**The spread of new technologies**   Having shortened the life-cycle of innovations, innovators are now obliged to obtain benefits on a much shorter term, and they seem more interested in selling technology patents than in exporting manufactured goods or setting up branch operations overseas (Soete 1985, in Antonelli 1990). The spread of technology basically happens through three channels: the export of capital goods, the sale of licences and patents, and within multinational corporations. Generally speaking, the innovators are large companies with high wage costs and low research and development costs. The first innovators are risk-takers. The spread of a technology takes off once a critical mass of those willing to adopt it is achieved. A necessary condition for innovations generated overseas to be adopted in domestic markets is the rapid creation of a critical mass capable of producing the externalities the knowledge requires (Antonelli 1990).

Information technology is becoming so common that it can be used for small-scale production, as well as for small-scale commerce and finance. The real cost of filing, processing and transmitting information has been falling at a rate of 20 per cent per year for the past forty years. In contrast, the real cost of energy that gave rise to the industrial revolution fell by 50 per cent over thirty years (Drucker 1993). This means that new information technologies are being used ever more broadly, with many spin-offs in organizational terms and in terms of new frontiers of efficiency. The use of information has several requirements and establishes new principles of efficiency, creates a new universal language and promotes the interconnection of activities that were previously related but separate (Kaplinsky 1984, in Pérez 1992).

1. *Decentralized integration*: the emerging organizing model rejects organizational pyramids centred on one point, at the top, and favours decentralized organizations, in which the manner of using information is custom-made for the user. This concept revolves around flexible information systems.

2. *Continual improvement, constant learning*: the concept that management knows best has become obsolete and human capital ('humanware') has become essential for achieving a process of permanent innovation, made possible by new forms of information and flexible production.

3. *Flexibility and adaptability*: thanks to the new forms of organization and production, a flexible multi-product plant can adjust to variations in market demand, in volume or product profile, achieving levels of productivity equivalent to mass production.

4. *Inter-company networks for structural competitiveness*: the need for total quality and just-in-time delivery to reduce inventory costs, made possible by information systems, encourages the establishment of networks among users and producers which tend to be more stable. They replace the concept of price with those of quality and opportunity, forging linkages that benefit all parties.

**Changes in the organizational paradigm for production to improve productivity and achieve greater competitiveness** The crisis of Fordism brought with it a crisis in the international division of labour (Lipietz 1985). The engine of the intensive Fordist style of accumulation is the dynamic of mass production based on the intensification of labour, the detailed division of tasks and mechanization to increase productivity, accompanied by monopolistic regulation of capital. The basic international division of labour that grew out of Fordism had advanced capitalist countries producing manufactures and the countries of the Third World supplying raw materials. This form of production and accumulation, as well as the international division of labour derived from it, became obsolescent at the beginning of the 1970s.[9]

New technology made mass production a redundant concept, while also making it possible to subcontract specialized production over several factories. The imposition of new production technologies and concepts, with the radical alteration of the international division of labour it wrought, caused an accelerated growth in the tertiary sector of economies, accentuating the gap between 'global' cities and old 'industrial' cities (Esser and Hirsch 1994). Forms of production and accumulation of capital have changed, allowing for a new sort of international trade in components, as well as in finished goods, based on new concepts of competitiveness. In addition, the social profiles of countries which industrialized more or less recently also changed, as did those of Latin America.

In Latin America the incorporation and adaptation of new technologies are a feature of non-continuous production processes, as distinct from continuous-process industries such as pharmaceuticals and steel (Herbert-Copley 1990). In this sense, innovations in machinery and individual pieces of equipment and products do occur in non-continuous production plants. Nevertheless, previously there had been technological changes in continuous-process industries, affecting parts of the same processes (Rath, 1990: 1434). The paradigm shift made it difficult to achieve autonomous processes of innovation, in some cases, but it also widened the potential for innovation, particularly in non-continuous group production versus continuous mass production.

The manner of organizing production has been modified by the introduction of cost-reduction measures based on the concepts of just-in-time (which refers to delivery of goods precisely on time), zero defect and total quality. These new concepts introduced by the Japanese have become generalized, and are new forms for determining competitiveness. Under this new model, subcontractors deliver components manufactured in different places, geographically close to one another to allow for rapid low-cost transport. This differs from the US model of subcontracting, which requires high levels of inventory due to distances between suppliers, and in this way can affect the producers of components in developing countries (Dahlman 1994).[10]

The management revolution that this required has consisted of training managers to be responsible for applying new knowledge and administering systematic innovation (Drucker 1993). The application of this concept in Latin America will vary, according to the degree of maturity of the management systems in some countries (versus the non-existence or limited existence of management systems in others), the diffuse culture of time, inexperience with subcontracting and the learning curve for producers using new technology. In other words, there is a management revolution, but there is also a revolution in the mode of production that requires changes in the way producers are trained, be they employees or independent workers.

## The systemic crisis, technological change and its impact on Latin America: A hypothesis and a proposal

Given the context portrayed above, the problem of the debt and the crisis in Latin America occurred because, at the time the technological shift began, long-term capital in the advanced capitalist countries regrouped, putting pressure on credit, raising real interest rates significantly and maintaining them consistently high. Prices of raw materials were depressed in constant dollars, generating a balance of payments crisis. In the 1930s, the balance of payments crisis caused by the systemic crisis led to a suspension of debt payments and an about-face in macroeconomic policy, from a reliance on primary exports to import substitution (ISI). But in the crisis of the 1980s the answer was just the opposite: import-substitution policies were dropped in favour of export-growth policies, in an attempt to transform the productive base in response to changes in the techno-economic paradigm.

The changeover did not begin in the 1970s due to inertia resulting from the success ISI had achieved regarding economic growth under the previous techno-economic paradigm. Thus, states and businesses resisted the move towards crossing an ocean rather than following railway lines, to paraphrase Pérez. Latin America's external problems at the beginning of the 1980s were inevitable, given the global context. The dislocation of trade in raw materials and the introduction of trade in manufactured goods to substitute for raw materials limited the region's options. However, the influence of the foreign debt on the use of foreign exchange and on public spending – a symptom of crisis – made the changeover even more difficult to implement, generating political and social conflicts that lasted the entire decade. Structural adjustment was implemented at the end of the 1980s in most countries in the hope that it would achieve the required transformation. The underlying thinking was that neoliberal policies and the notion of public choice *vis-à-vis* the state are appropriate for the new techno-economic paradigm.

Certainly the policy proposals put forward by the World Bank and ECLAC, the only ones that exist to date, are both systemic in nature. They propose to change all the rules of the game for national economies, regarding both their international relations and their ways of functioning internally. The question is whether structural adjustment reforms respond to the demands of the systemic crisis in a way that will lead to future growth for the region's countries (or if they simply introduce new distortions), and whether these in some way reflect the economic achievements of East Asia. From Gerschenkron's point of view, if countries are expected to make a great leap forward to the productivity levels of advanced capitalist economies, then there are gaps in such models for recovery, fundamentally regarding the technological aspects.

The implicit question is: Why did Latin America not make the great leap forward to close the productivity gap in previous decades? ECLAC boils it down to three answers: (1) mistakes in economic policy, essentially import-substitution policy, and the preponderant role of the state in the economy undercut the competitiveness of Latin American industry; (2) mistakes at the company level, 'the lack of an innovative business class would have been the factor that induced so many governments to intervene more and more in the economy to compensate for the lack of drive from business'; and (3) mistakes in key markets, externalities, public assets and problems of industrial organization (ECLAC 1994d). In other words, policies to improve the factor markets were lacking and product-marketing policies were overemphasized.

If the problem was inertia from the previous model, as this chapter seems to imply, then the state should have intervened to shake off the inertia of economic actors and encourage them to innovate. Otherwise, productive innovation would have been left to economic actors acknowledged to have been inefficient and not risk-takers under the previous model. Equally, the need to mobilize resources for investment should have forced the state to act in this realm. Lastly, there was a need for regulation during restructuring, to avoid a monopolistic manipulation of prices in economies with few producers and few large international marketers. The orthodox policies the region has been applying focus solely on the first concern – mistakes in macroeconomic policy – emphasizing privatization, opening the economy and reducing the size of the state in order to improve productivity and launch a process of competitive export-led industrialization.

The crisis of the system has not ended, and the need for Latin America to reinsert itself into the global system is still urgent. Latin America has not yet crossed the ocean, though it has got off the rails of the previous industrialization model. Because of the nature of techno-economic change and the crisis of capital, the way out of the systemic crisis is unclear. More uncertain in this framework is how Latin American countries will manage to cross the ocean. Two options are evident: self-determination and export growth. Either would be difficult. In no case could self-determination be achieved without changes in the export sector and the productive base, given the new techno-economic paradigm and its effects. Problems with the export model, due to the characteristics of technological change and the crisis of capital, could lead to modifications in open-market policies that, while not a turnabout, may make them more apt for facing the challenges presented by the crisis.

## Notes

1. Carlos Marichal (1989) offers an entertaining narrative of the relation between the 1825 London financial crisis and the financial problems of indebted nations in Chapter 2 where he refers to these problems as Latin America's first debt crisis. The institutional differences between the period before 1980 and the decade of the 1980s in terms of the existence of the IMF, the World Bank, bilateral credits and creditors' organizations are laid out in Eichengreen and Lindert (1989). Especially useful is Chapter 3 by Jorgensen and Sachs, 'Default and Renegotiation of Latin American Foreign Bonds in the Interwar Years' (pp. 46–85).

2. One explanation of the mechanics of the rise in interest rates and the fall in resource prices is offered by Charles P. Kindleberger (1985: 366–8). The phenomenon occurred in the same way in the crises of 1825 and 1873, but also in 1985 and perhaps it could be summed up as the effect of investment substitution explained by Tobin in his portfolio theory.

3. Anwar Sheik (1990: ch. 6) offers a theoretical critique of the debate.

4. G. Dosi (1982) uses 'technological paradigm' to refer to the model that guides the trajectory of incremental improvements in each technology.

5. Kenwood and Lougheed (1992) make the same argument, citing A. I. Bloomfield who, in his 'Patterns of Fluctuations in International Investment before 1914' (1968), tried unsuccessfully to prove the theory. There are two essential problems for demonstrating the validity of the theory: there are no data for measuring factor productivity and credit statistics are incomplete. L. H. Jenks (1963), lays out the cyclical history of credits to Latin American countries, where the only exception is Brazil; since Brazil became a republic at the end of the nineteenth century, it was out of synch with the rest of the region's countries. I made this argument to D. C. M. Platt at a conference in Oxford in 1986 and from his point of view the work of Jenks was incomplete and did not reflect real credit flows, which were substantively smaller than what had to then been acknowledged. However, Paul Kennedy (1987) later went over Platt's figures and demonstrated that previous versions were closer to reality. I would like to thank David Platt as much for the discussion as for what he taught me about checking sources.

6. A summary of current discussions on the determinants of long-term productivity can be found in Englander and Gurney 1994a.

7. At the beginning of the twentieth century the spectre of war caused fears of a shortage of nitrogen, which was used both to make explosives and as fertilizer. Nitrogen was a fundamental input into a country's development. With war on the horizon, alternatives had to be found for this raw material found in Chile, on lands which Chile took from Peru on behalf of British interests in 1879. Chile was unlikely to supply the German side in the war if war were to break out. This was the framework for the invention of synthetic saltpeter, using the Birkeland-Eyde method, patented in Oslo in 1904 (Hodne 1975: 294–6). Eyde was a businessman who had the hydroelectric industry in mind. Birkeland, a physics professor at the University of Oslo, undertook experiments on nitrogen-fixing using an arc of light or a flame-thrower. The patent-holders linked up with the Wallenbergs, owners of Sweden's Enskilda Bank, and began producing saltpeter in 1905. The company set up for this was called Norsk Hydro and today it is Norway's largest industrial enterprise. In 1920 they changed the production system to that patented by the Germans Haber-Bosch, which used a quarter of the amount of energy, and at that point the production of natural saltpeter disappeared, Europe was safe from the transport problems a war might cause, profits were made selling synthetic saltpeter for weapons during the First World War, and the north of Chile (previously the south of Peru) was left as it had always been, a desert. The boom and bust had lasted fifty years in all. Ghost towns left from the saltpeter mines can still be visited southeast of Iquique.

8. Chapters 1 and 10. The third part is a reflection on knowledge and its effects on productivity.

9. The specific ideas that Ash Amin (1994) lays out correspond to those of Alain Lipietz (1985).

10. Cited by Dahlman (1994).

# 3. Trends in Industrialization and Foreign Trade

May you live in interesting times. (Chinese curse)

This chapter reviews the issues of industrialization and foreign trade in Latin America in comparison with the countries of Southeast Asia, in an attempt to draw out pertinent lessons. Does international competitiveness exist? What are its abstract and real characteristics in Latin America? Is the export-led development model emerging in Latin America capable of meeting the challenges of the twenty-first century?

## The industrialization crisis

In an article written in 1992, A. O. Hirschman wondered how two contrary explanations for the same problem could have the same solution. He was intrigued by the explanations given for industrialization processes in Eastern Europe and in Latin America. In the former, he wrote, analysts maintain the problem was that heavy industry was incapable of moving on to consumer-goods production. In contrast, in Latin America the problem was that import substitution got stuck manufacturing consumer goods, and linked up to international industry to obtain capital and intermediate goods on a large scale. In both cases, the explanation given was that an excessive state presence and over-regulation impeded the development of successive (or previous) stages.

It is easier to be unhappy with what you have than with what you lack, Hirschman suggested, following the line of Gerschenkron's classic critique of subindustrialization from forty years ago. In brief: How can we distinguish one type of unhappiness from the other? The question was left unresolved. Is there an Asian model of industrialization? Analysts who undertake comparative studies conclude that there are no uniform models of industrialization in Asia, and that none of them has any relation to Latin American models (Wade 1990; van Dijck 1990). On the other hand,

TABLE 3.1 Per capita GNP, GDP growth and export growth for selected countries of Latin America and Asia, 1965–92

| Per capita GNP Latin America | 1972[1] | 1992[1] | Per capita GNP Asia | 1972 | 1992 |
|---|---|---|---|---|---|
| Argentina | 1,430 | 6,050 | South Korea | 330 | 6,790 |
| Brazil | 570 | 2,770 | Taiwan | – | – |
| Mexico | 880 | 3,470 | Hong Kong | 1,230 | 15,360 |
| Chile | 1,080 | 2,730 | Singapore | 1,410 | 15,730 |
| Colombia | 390 | 1,330 | Indonesia | 91 | 670 |
| Peru | 20 | 950 | Malaysia | 450 | 2,790 |
| Costa Rica | 60 | 1,960 | Philippines | 200 | 770 |
| Guatemala | 390 | 980 | Thailand | 290* | 1,840 |

| Average annual GDP growth Latin America | 1965–80[3] | 1980–92[2] | Average annual GDP growth Asia | 1965–80 | 1980–92 |
|---|---|---|---|---|---|
| Argentina | 3.3 | 0.4 | South Korea | 9.5 | 9.4 |
| Brazil | 9.0 | 2.2 | Taiwan | – | – |
| Mexico | 6.5 | 1.5 | Hong Kong | 8.5 | 6.7 |
| Chile | 1.9 | 4.8 | Singapore | 10.2 | 6.7 |
| Colombia | 5.6 | 3.7 | Indonesia | 7.9 | 5.7 |
| Peru | 3.9 | -0 | Malaysia | 7.3 | 5.9 |
| Costa Rica | 6.3 | 3.3 | Philippines | 5.9 | 1.2 |
| Guatemala | 5.9 | 1.4 | Thailand | 7.4 | 8.2 |

| Average annual export growth Latin America | 1965–80 | 1980–92[2] | Average annual export growth Asia | 1965–80 | 1980–92 |
|---|---|---|---|---|---|
| Argentina | 4.7 | 2.2 | South Korea | 27.3 | 11.9 |
| Brazil | 9.4 | 5.0 | Taiwan | – | – |
| Mexico | 7.7 | 1.6 | Hong Kong | 9.5 | 5.0 |
| Chile | 7.9 | 5.5 | Singapore | 4.8 | 9.9 |
| Colombia | 1.5 | 12.9 | Indonesia | 9.7 | 5.6 |
| Peru | 2.3 | 2.5 | Malaysia | 4.4 | 11.3 |
| Costa Rica | 7.1 | 5.2 | Philippines | 4.7 | 3.7 |
| Guatemala | 4.9 | 0.0 | Thailand | 8.5 | 14.7 |

*Note*: GNP per capita data are in current dollars unless otherwise indicated.

*Sources*: 1. World Bank 1994c: table 2 and country tables. 2. World Bank 1992: World Development Indicators, tables 2 and 13. 3. World Bank 1987: World Development Indicators, tables 2 and 10. * The figure corresponds to 1975.

Eastern Europe's industrialization models were clearly the opposite of Latin America's, since they began by setting up an industry to produce capital goods rather than consumer goods, with central planning versus indicative planning.

## Asian industrialization vs Latin American industrialization

The process of industrialization and the development of international trade derived from it are today linked to policies adopted in response to external impacts and balance of payments problems, or as the result of the drying up of traditional opportunities for growth, rather than a concerted long-term strategic plan (Wade 1990: 346–70). Countries without natural resources in East Asia faced the challenge of development following wars in which their economic systems were destroyed and had to be rebuilt. In Latin America, countries had ample natural resources and did not face the destruction of their economic systems. Moreover, Latin America began its processes of import substitution in the 1930s, twenty years before the countries of East Asia.

The evidence indicates that for the sample of Latin American countries in Table 3.1, average per capita GDP increased by a factor of 3.2 over twenty years (1972–92). Brazil led the pack, increasing 4.8 times over the period; and Peru, Chile and Guatemala brought up the rear with between 1.5 and 2.5 times. Growth, however, took place in two periods: previous to 1980 and after 1980. The second section of Table 3.1 shows how growth slowed in all economies except for the Chilean, which rebounded (4.8 per cent average annual growth) in comparison to the period 1965–80, and the Colombian, which although slowing somewhat maintained an acceptable pace of growth of 3.7 per cent over the 'lost decade' of the 1980s.

In Asia, GDP growth per capita in selected countries increased 10.3 times on average, more than double that of Latin America, with South Korea in the lead (20.5 times) and the Philippines at the back (3.8 times). The East Asian country with the least GDP per capita growth still grew more than the average for the eight selected Latin American countries, as well as more than half of them. What stands out is that although growth was slightly higher in Asia in the period 1965–80, countries like Brazil, Mexico, Costa Rica and Colombia had growth rates comparable to those of Asia. However, in the period 1980–92, although GDP growth slowed everywhere except the Philippines, every East Asian country experienced sustained high growth rates of around 6 per cent per year, while this was not the case in Latin America, except Chile.

Latin America's exports during the period 1965–80 grew at rates comparable to those of East Asia, with the exceptions of Peru and Colombia (which grew 2.3 and 1.5 per cent per year on average, far below other countries) and South Korea (which grew 27.3 per cent per year on average, far above the rest). Average annual growth rates were in the range of 5 to 10 per cent in both regions. Yet in the period 1980–92, only one country in Latin America experienced export growth comparable to East Asia (Colombia with 12.9 per cent), and only one in Asia comparable to Latin America (Philippines with 3.7 per cent), even though Hong Kong and Indonesia did slow to rates similar to those of Brazil and Chile, Latin America's best exporters after Colombia.

Another variable that ought to be emphasized in order to understand Asia's success is the ratio of investment to GDP: 50 per cent higher in Asian countries than in those of Latin America. The same is true of the

TABLE 3.2 Gross domestic investment/GDP for selected countries of Latin America and Asia, 1965–1992 (%)

|  | 1965–73[1] | 1973–80[1] | 1980–85[1] | 1992[2] |
|---|---|---|---|---|
| Latin America |  |  |  |  |
| Argentina | 19.8 | 21.8 | 16.3 | 17.0 |
| Brazil | 26.1 | 26.2 | 20.4 | 17.0 |
| Chile | 14.4 | 17.4 | 17.5 | 24.0 |
| Colombia | 18.9 | 18.8 | 20.0 | 18.0 |
| Mexico | 21.4 | 25.2 | 25.4 | 24.0 |
| Peru | 27.7 | 28.9 | 28.0 | 16.0 |
| Costa Rica | 21.8 | 25.5 | 28.0 | 28.0 |
| Guatemala | 13.3 | 18.7 | 13.5 | 18.0 |
| Asia |  |  |  |  |
| Indonesia | 15.8 | 24.5 | 29.4 | 35.0 |
| Malaysia | 22.3 | 28.7 | 35.1 | 34.0 |
| Philippines | 20.6 | 29.1 | 25.8 | 23.0 |
| Thailand | 23.8 | 26.6 | 24.4 | 40.0 |
| South Korea | 25.1 | 31.8 | 30.7 | n/a |
| Hong Kong[3] | 36.0[3] | 24.0 | 21.0 | 29.0 |
| Singapore[3] | 22.0[3] | 40.0 | 43.0 | 41.0 |
| Taiwan[3] | 26.0[3] | 31.0 | 18.0 | n/a |
| China[4] | 25.0 | n/a | 38.0 | n/a |

*Sources*: 1. World Bank 1987: 177. 2. World Bank 1994b: World Statistical Indicators, table 9. 3. Figures for Hong Kong, Singapore and Taiwan correspond to 1965, 1975 and 1985 (World Bank 1987: 210); 1975 data are World Bank statistics taken from Wade 1990: 48. 4. Figures for China correspond to 1965 and 1985 (World Bank 1987: 210)

ratio of savings to GDP. The data in Table 3.2 show that Asian countries, almost without exception, experienced investment rates of over 20 per cent of GDP between 1965 and 1973, over 24 per cent between 1980 and 1985, jumping in 1992 to over 30 per cent for most of them.

Half of the eight selected Latin American countries had investment/ GDP ratios of between 13 and 20 per cent from 1965 to 1973, and more than half between 14 and 20 per cent during the 1980s, with a slight increase to between 17 and 20 per cent for most of them. Overall, then, the investment/GDP ratio was 50 per cent greater for Asian countries than for most of Latin America over the past thirty years, which should explain Asia's high growth rates.

In the same way, the savings/GDP ratio is much higher in Asia than in Latin America; why this is the case will be tackled below. The evidence shows that in Latin America the ratio was below 18 per cent in most countries, but in East Asia it was over 18 per cent in all countries (see Appendix 3.1). Thus, for a given level of investment, the requirements for external savings were lower for Asia, and therefore ups and downs in international interest rates affected Asia's domestic economies much less than Latin America's. That said, the level of investment in Asia was higher than in Latin America, which explains the low rates of foreign indebtedness and the low debt service of Asian countries shown by Wade as one of the features that differentiate the two regions.

The high rate of internal savings per GDP in Asia can be explained as the result of high growth rates (Carroll et al. 1993; World Bank 1993: 204), since households improved their levels of income before raising their levels of consumption. In models developed by World Bank studies, savings does not necessarily lead to economic growth, but economic growth has always led to increases in savings in East Asia (World Bank 1993: 204). Several variables point to why this occurred.

1. Low inflation in those countries due to balanced macroeconomic management, creating a favourable environment for savings (Neal 1990; World Bank 1993: 205).

2. Low growth in nominal wages in Taiwan and South Korea due to low inflation rates, while in Argentina and Chile, for example, inflation was relatively high, causing high growth in nominal wages which in turn fed inflation (Lin 1988a: 161).

3. Stable and slightly positive interest rates in Asia versus Latin America, where they have been highly volatile and have been either very negative or very positive. This was possible because of Asia's low inflation. Price stability in Taiwan and South Korea encouraged financial savings, facilitating financial intervention in the savings/investment process (Lin, 1988a: 164). The lack of a framework of low inflation in Argentina and Chile, for

example, forced people to spend their savings and thus forced the economy as a whole to make more use of foreign savings (p. 165).

4. Public savings. To the degree that there are public savings, the level of consumption is held in check and the general level of savings increases. Public savings does not crowd out private savings. The World Bank points out that 'the method of raising public savings matters: on average, increasing public savings via reduced expenditures is more effective than raising taxation' (World Bank 1993: 207). The evidence shows that Indonesia, Japan, South Korea, Singapore and Thailand had a level of public consumption below 15 per cent of GDP.

Other elements at play were exchange-rate policies that kept currencies undervalued as a way of encouraging the export of manufactures and of keeping the impetus to import in check; reduction of effective protection; and a system of explicit incentives for the export of manufactures (Lin 1988a).

Agricultural yield and the participation of women in the labour force in East Asia ought also to be considered. The moderation of wage demands in Taiwan and South Korea were achieved by an elastic labour supply, the result of increases in productivity in the countryside and the incorporation of women into the labour force. Meanwhile, in Chile and Argentina, agricultural productivity did not improve, says Lin, primarily due to the existence of adverse exchange rates and rural/urban terms of trade unfavourable to the countryside. In Taiwan and South Korea these elements were compensated for by state investment in rural irrigation, research and development and support services in the countryside. In addition, in Taiwan and South Korea agrarian reforms carried out immediately following the war offered incentives to producer-owners. Meanwhile, in countries with substantial agricultural resources such as Chile and Argentina, the state did not offer such services or incentives, nor did it carry out an agrarian reform (Lin 1988b).

Besides the moderation of wage demands, salary costs were controlled in Taiwan and South Korea by increasing labour productivity in manufacturing, which occurred alongside the rapid growth of capital stock and a substantial improvement in its operating efficiency, something that did not occur in either Chile or Argentina, for example (Lin 1988b). The evidence shows that the results of the policy mix in Southeast Asia were very positive, while in Latin America they were not. The neoclassical explanation cited above is that macroeconomic conditions made this possible: high rates of internal savings and high rates of investment, derived from correct pricing. Considering the changes in the structure of international trade and the reduction of trade in raw materials due to the technological shift under way, as discussed in the previous chapter, this neoclassical explanation suddenly provides no answer to the question of why in Southeast Asia there was a change in the export structure and in Latin America there was none.

A second approach to the regulated market suggests that Asia's superiority is due to: high levels of productive investment, which allowed for the transfer and rapid employment of new technologies; greater investment in certain industries than there would have been had the state not intervened; and the exposure of industry to international competition, both in the domestic market and in the international market (Wade 1990). The industrialization of foreign trade is not synonymous with free markets or with export-led growth. Rather, it is a requirement for new exports if a sustained and dynamic external sector is to bring foreign exchange into a developing economy. Other elements were: high educational levels with a focus on areas of production being developed; state planning in concert with companies and workers; the setting of export goals with rewards and penalties; and a public policy of conflict mediation (Fajnzylber 1990; Amsden 1989; Wade 1990; Van Dijck 1990; Gereffi 1990).

The evidence in Table 3.3 indicates that between 1970 and 1992 Asian countries industrialized their exports and that these moved towards the heavy end of the product scale, i.e. exports were broadened to include machinery and transportation equipment. For South Korea, Malaysia, Singapore and Hong Kong, exports in this category represented between 24 and 52 per cent of total exports in 1992, while in 1970 it ranged from 2 to 12 per cent for those same countries. The proportion represented by manufacturing exports of total goods export in 1992 was between 78 and 95 per cent for the Tigers and between 48 and 73 per cent for the Dragons. The only Asian country for whom exports of raw materials continued to be important, while still declining in relative terms, was Indonesia, where manufactures exports reduced the proportion of raw materials (oil) from 98 per cent in 1970 to 53 per cent in 1992.

In Latin America the situation was the opposite. Countries considered to have pursued export-led industrialization (Argentina, Brazil and Mexico) taken together had manufactures exports of no more than 27 per cent (Argentina) and 58 per cent (Brazil) of total exports. However, the total proportion of manufacturing exports did grow for all countries, although Brazil, Colombia and Guatemala had a greater share of light industry (other manufactures). This growth in the proportion represented by manufactures is related in part to the loss of income from primary exports, although that cannot explain the entire turnaround. Except for Brazil and Mexico, heavy industry does not represent a growing proportion of exports.

Brazil's exports became industrialized (Ominami 1991) because the

TABLE 3.3 Export structure by product category for selected countries of Latin America and Asia, 1970–92 (percentages)

| | Oil, gas, minerals and metals | | Other primary products | | Machinery and transportation equipment | | Other manufactures | | Textiles and apparel* | |
|---|---|---|---|---|---|---|---|---|---|---|
| | 1970 | 1992 | 1970 | 1992 | 1970 | 1992 | 1970 | 1992 | 1970 | 1992 |
| **Latin America** | | | | | | | | | | |
| Argentina | 1.0 | 10.0 | 85.0 | 64.0 | 4.0 | 8.0 | 10.0 | 19.0 | 1.0 | 1.0 |
| Brazil | 11.0 | 13.0 | 75.0 | 29.0 | 4.0 | 21.0 | 11.0 | 37.0 | 1.0 | 4.0 |
| Mexico | 19.0 | 34.0 | 49.0 | 13.0 | 11.0 | 31.0 | 22.0 | 21.0 | 3.0 | 2.0 |
| Chile | 88.0 | 47.0 | 7.0 | 38.0 | 1.0 | 2.0 | 4.0 | 13.0 | 0.0 | 1.0 |
| Colombia | 11.0 | 29.0 | 81.0 | 39.0 | 1.0 | 2.0 | 7.0 | 29.0 | 2.0 | 9.0 |
| Peru | 49.0 | 49.0 | 49.0 | 31.0 | 0.0 | 2.0 | 1.0 | 19.0 | 0.0 | 10.0 |
| Costa Rica | 0.0 | 1.0 | 80.0 | 72.0 | 3.0 | 4.0 | 17.0 | 23.0 | 4.0 | 5.0 |
| Guatemala | 0.0 | 2.0 | 72.0 | 68.0 | 2.0 | 1.0 | 26.0 | 28.0 | 8.0 | 5.0 |
| **Asia** | | | | | | | | | | |
| S. Korea | 7.0 | 3.0 | 17.0 | 4.0 | 7.0 | 40.0 | 69.0 | 53.0 | 36.0 | 20.0 |
| Taiwan | – | – | – | – | – | – | – | – | – | – |
| Hong Kong | 1.0 | 2.0 | 3.0 | 3.0 | 12.0 | 12.0 | 84.0 | 71.0 | 44.0 | 40.0 |
| Singapore2 | 5.0 | 15.0 | 45.0 | 7.0 | 11.0 | 11.0 | 20.0 | 26.0 | 5.0 | 5.0 |
| Indonesia | 44.0 | 38.0 | 54.0 | 15.0 | 0.0 | 0.0 | 1.0 | 44.0 | 0.0 | 18.0 |
| Malaysia | 30.0 | 17.0 | 63.0 | 22.0 | 2.0 | 2.0 | 6.0 | 23.0 | 1.0 | 6.0 |
| Philippines | 23.0 | 8.0 | 70.0 | 19.0 | 0.0 | 0.0 | 8.0 | 56.0 | 1.0 | 6.0 |
| Thailand | 15.0 | 2.0 | 77.0 | 32.0 | 0.0 | 0.0 | 8.0 | 45.0 | 1.0 | 17.0 |

*Note.* * 'Textiles and apparel' is a sub-group of 'other manufactures'.

*Source:* World Bank 1994b: World Development Indicators, table 15.

Brazilian government persevered in its desire to industrialize in the 1970s, strengthening its policy of import substitution in intermediate and capital goods, offering direct incentives to industry to modernize via export promotion. The instruments utilized were public enterprises and the National Bank for Economic Development, which provided the long-term financing required for the ambitious investment programmes of both the state and the private sector. This explains the export of capital goods (the aeronautics industry, for example) as well as light manufactures, which include electronics exports.

In sum, Latin America continues to be a region of primary exports. Even though there are indications (Buitelaar and Mertens 1993) that some change is under way, this is occurring much more slowly than in East Asia (Van Dijck 1990). The changes observed took place in a context marked by a shrinking industrial base: industry fell from 26 per cent of GDP at the beginning of the 1980s to 24 per cent at the beginning of the 1990s, while industrial employment fell 5 per cent over the same period (Buitelaar and Mertens 1993). Gross domestic investment has been recovering very slowly since 1991, while companies undergo improvements in their organizational systems and are immersed in efforts to improve factor productivity, of which there is already some evidence in a number of Latin American countries (ECLAC 1994e). This should lead to a change, albeit still incipient, from traditional raw materials exports towards manufacturing exports (see Table 3.3) (Buitelaar and Mertens 1993: 57), even though the trend away from industrial exports is said to have been caused by the de-industrialization of the economy, a result of neoliberal policies (Ominami 1991: 92).

Gereffi groups the different ways of interpreting Southeast Asia's industrialization into six currents.[1] He suggests that several currents of interpretation of the new industrialization are mistaken or contain errors, and he proposes other ideas for understanding the phenomenon. The first current is represented by the interpretations put forth by Fröbel et al. (1981) (which Gereffi believes should be toned down) about the new international division of labour growing out of a world manufacturing system 'based on labour-intensive export platforms, set up by multinational companies in low-wage zones. The objective of the new international division of labour is to exploit labour reserves on a global scale by means of advanced communications and transportation technologies which allow for the spacial subdivision of the production process' (Gereffi 1990: 207).

A second current, the neoclassical school, takes the results achieved by Southeast Asian countries and offers them as unequivocal policy recipes for the development strategies of Third World countries.[2] Balassa (1981), Balassa et al. (1986) and the World Bank (1987: ch. 5) insist that 'the export development strategies of Southeast Asia lead to better results regarding exports, economic growth and employment than the inward-facing development strategies of Latin America. The Southeast Asian NICs ought to be the model for all other developing countries' (Gereffi 1990: 208). From the neoclassical point of view, the functions of the state are:

- to maintain macroeconomic stability
- to provide physical infrastructure, particularly those with high fixed costs in relation to variable costs (ports, railways, irrigation canals and drainage systems, etc.)
- to provide 'public goods', including national defence and security, education, basic research, marketing information, a judicial system and environmental protection
- to contribute to the development of institutions that will improve labour market conditions, capital, technology, etc.
- to correct or eliminate price distortions that arise in cases of market failure
- to redistribute income to the poorest so that they can cover their basic necessities

Wade offers a harsh critique of this current, and says that not even the defenders of the neoclassical school believe it because there is no long-term empirical evidence to back it up.[3]

The third current is represented by Wallerstein (1974) and Arrighi and Drangel (1986) who use world systems theory to propose the concept of 'semi-peripheral countries to identify an intermediate band between central and peripheral countries. The countries in this area can resist becoming peripheral but they can not avoid ascending to the highest band' (Gereffi 1990: 208).

The fourth current is the dependence school, as expressed by Evans (1979), Cardoso and Faletto (1979), Gold (1981) and Lim (1985). Related to the previous current, it maintains that 'the structural dependence of developing countries in relation to foreign capital and external markets constricts and distorts, but is not incompatible with capitalist economic development' (Gereffi 1990: 208).

The fifth current, from political science, is argued by O'Donnell (1973), Collier (1979), Johnson (1987) and Wade (1990), and proposes that

one of the fundamental institutional characteristics of the success of countries that experienced late industrialization is the appearance of a 'developmentalist state,' set up to make selective but substantial interventions in the economy in order to encourage a rapid accumulation of capital and industrial progress. This literature poses the question whether the 'developmentalist state' is a prerequisite for capitalist industrialization on the periphery. (Gereffi 1990: 208)

If the argument can be made that government steerage of the market has been an important factor in East Asia, then the general recipes for developing countries would need rethinking. For it could not then be argued that more economic liberalization is always better; the desirability of integration into the international economy becomes a matter of degree and circumstance, to be weighted against the desirability of improving existing arrangements for planning and controlling, and of relying more on growth in domestic demand than on export demand. (Wade 1990: 5–6)

According to Gereffi, there are some fallacies in the arguments presented above, for the following reasons.

1. The debates on the new international division of labour are based on the reality of the 1960s, which was the initial phase of attempts at exporting. 'More recent export industries are not export enclaves, rather they encourage high levels of integration with a well developed local base.'

2. They correctly emphasize the appearance of a decentralized system of world manufacture, in which production capacity is spread out to an unprecedented degree over a number of developing and industrialized countries. However, this is not done directly by transnational companies; rather, the main exporters are local private subcontracting companies in Third World countries.

3. Recently industrialized countries have not been industrializing recently, nor have they developed as a response to the same sort of global dynamic.

4. The contrast between outward-oriented and inward-oriented development strategies is exaggerated. Each country in these regions has followed a combination of both.

5. Dependence is by nature different in the development of Southeast Asia and Latin America. In Asia, it is on foreign aid and foreign trade, while in Latin America it is on banks and transnational companies. The consequences of these different types of dependence for development relate to the capacity of the state to convert such linkages into national advantages.

6. The objectives, social basis and policy instruments of a developmentalist state are different in each country, a fact which has implications for the relative autonomy of the state.

One element that Gereffi does not discuss is the function of the state. The role of the state, as posed theoretically by the neoclassical school, does not seem to exist in the countries of East Asia. The state in East Asian countries has an active role and is a developmentalist state (Wade

1990; Amsden 1989). The problem posed for the state in neoclassical theory is when to acknowledge market failure and what to do about it. Wolf's definition (1988)[4] in this sense is clear: the state intervenes only when the market does not work. The state in Asian countries, however, does more than re-establish optimum market conditions: it promotes, controls, prohibits, invests, rewards or penalizes economic activities.

Amsden suggests that a strong state emerged in South Korea not as a response to policy decisions, but through social change, that it fulfils a need and that its policy decisions are made within real restrictions and a specific history. In other words, the state is present and acts to encourage the development of the possible within a world of existing restrictions in alliance with sectors of 'winners' within the economic system (Amsden 1989: 63–78 and ch. 4). Certainly, then, the arguments presented by Wolf (1988) and the World Bank (1987) are not self-evident as far as the role of the state is concerned. Westphal (1991) argues that this occurred only in South Korea, but Wade shows a similar degree of intervention in Taiwan.

To compare Asia's success with Latin America's failure, first of all we must note the presence of the state as the regulator and the entity that links different social sectors. This was the central element that determined degrees of success of Southeast Asia's export economies, and not so much the efficiency of production costs in and of themselves. The most important factors in Southeast Asia's success are related to the role of the state. Van Dijck notes three aspects:

> 1) A strong government commitment to economic development and to consistent and flexible policies. 2) A close relationship between the government and the private sector, a situation which led to consistent and flexible policies. 3) Governmental assumption of an important part of the responsibility for the success of its economic strategy through direct participation, which reduced the risks of an open strategy for national companies and business groups. Elements that made these successful policies useful for young industries to achieve international competitiveness early on included the system of export objectives and government verification of their achievement by individual companies, the free-exchange regime for exporters, the restricted use of tariff and non-tariff barriers and a system of incentives that did not favour import-substitution over export-promotion. (Van Dijck 1990: 198)

Amsden adds that export development in South Korea and Taiwan went hand in had with internal development, and neither one nor the other took the lead. State regulation may have sought this to avoid the imbalances that would have resulted from export-led industrialization based on competitiveness or from protected development for the internal market. Protection and regulation were oriented towards helping domestic industries export, rather than protecting them from international competition. The role of the state should not be defined as either 'strong' or 'weak', but rather as 'catalysing' by clearly defining the rules for a set period of time (Bradford 1992–93).

## A note on the process of import substitution

The countries of Asia and Latin America have gone through several phases of import substitution – which in the end is what is being proposed from different perspectives for both regions – and this fact could help explain the situation in several countries. Some suggest that this lies at the centre of Latin America's crisis, but others (Rojas 1991: 61) point out that, ever since the English industrial revolution, industrialization has always gone through periods of import substitution. It is not a feature that differentiates Latin America from other places. The unique features of Latin America's import substitution were: relative abundance of non-manufactured exportable goods, strong protection and dependence of industry on the political system, and an industry oriented almost exclusively towards the internal market. Regarding the stages of import substitution, I will expand on several definitions taken from Gereffi (1990):

1. *Primary products exports phase.* This refers to unprocessed material derived from nature.
2. *Primary ISI phase.* During this phase local manufacture of basic consumer goods develops, i.e. textiles, apparel, shoes and processed food.
3. *Secondary ISI phase.* Capital-intensive and technology-intensive manufacturing is substituted, i.e. durable goods, intermediate products and capital goods.
4. *Primary EOI phase.* This phase refers to the export orientation of labour-intensive industry, i.e. textiles, shoes, apparel.
5. *Secondary EOI phase.* This refers to the export orientation of industry with high technology and capital content.

Some evidence emerges from Table 3.1. First that Mexico, Brazil, Taiwan and South Korea went through primary export phases at the same time as the rest of Latin America, between the end of the nineteenth century and the 1930s. However, Latin America began the primary phase of industrialization during that period, while the Asian countries named only began it after the Second World War. Nevertheless, Taiwan and South Korea moved on to secondary import substitution in the 1960s, while Mexico and Brazil were already well engaged in that phase in the middle of the 1950s. In Peru secondary substitution also began in the 1960s, as in nearly all of Latin America. The break came in the 1970s when Taiwan and South Korea went on to the export phase, while Brazil and Mexico continued with secondary substitution, Argentina got stuck there, Chile went back to primary exports, Peru cut off its state-led secondary substitution, and Venezuela moved forward into secondary ISI following in the footsteps of Brazil with a state-led process. Colombia, at that time, began a diversification of its exports with the introduction of primary EOI (shoes), as well as flowers and other primary products for new markets.

The result is that while Mexico and Brazil struggled to develop an export-oriented industrial sector, followed by Colombia, the rest gave up on that route to industrialization and either went back to primary exports or never left them (Bolivia, Paraguay, Central America except for Costa Rica and Guatemala). In this sense, industrialization is more recent in Southeast Asia, beginning after the Second World War, while Latin America first started in the 1930s, even though neither of the two regions is really recently industrialized. A general conclusion to be drawn is that the Latin American crisis of the 1980s was due to failed industrial policies in the region, and that the indiscriminate opening in Mexico, Bolivia or Peru led to a reorientation of the economy towards exports. No studies show that secondary export industrialization policies did not pan out in practice; there is some evidence that such policies were closed off or not applied. That path was simply cancelled.

What Buitelaar and Mertens seem to be studying is how export industries managed to survive the opening up of the economy by being more productive. In order to survive, exporting is fundamental due to the contraction of internal markets and growing competition within them. If an export industry manages to survive and grow, it is not due to export-promotion policies, rather to the stubbornness of the economic agents who refuse to die: a microeconomic phenomenon rather than a macro-economic one. The state in Latin America has not, since the early 1980s, played the role of promoter of economic development which it still plays even today in Asia, although there are similarities. In most Latin American countries the reorientation towards exports seems to be towards primary exports, which carries with it problems due to history as much as the international context, above all considering that new actors are entering the industrial export sector defensively.[5]

## The conditions for industrialization

The success of industrialization in East Asia and peripheral European economies is due to the fact that they were more equitable than Latin American economies as far as income distribution is concerned. Those countries used the same instruments of industrial protection and governmental intervention as the Latin Americans, but they achieved innovative successes in production (Rojas 1991 on Fajnzylber 1986). Fajnzylber proposed four variables as fundamental for achieving development, and he drew them as four quadrants divided by vertical and horizontal axes. The upper half of the vertical axis represents income distribution (the ratio of the income of the poorest 40 per cent to that of the richest 10 per cent); the lower half represents international competitiveness (represented by the ratio of exports of metal-mechanical equipment and machinery to imports of the same). He used these variables to measure the development style of several countries.

From this analysis (see Figures 3.1 and 3.2), he concluded that Korea and Taiwan's development style was closer to Japan's and Latin America's was closer to that of the United States. The Japanese style was austere, with a high level of equity (understood as a fair income distribution) and a process of permanent innovation. The US style followed by Latin America was characterized by little austerity, poor income distribution, low growth and poor international competitiveness. He suggests that in Latin America the lack of internal savings resulting from poor income distribution constituted an obstacle to development. This, plus the lack of technological progress, would be the central elements for understanding the difference between the two regions analysed.

In other words, in Latin America we have adopted US-style conspicuous consumption without having achieved Asia's levels of income and dynamism. That was feasible thanks to the high concentration of income and the availability of external savings in the 1960s, 1970s and 1980s. The lack of internal savings resulting from this sort of consumption in the high-income sector causes problems with the factors conditioning international competitiveness, in so far as not enough is invested to give investment the desired dynamism. In this context, the structural reforms introduced in recent years, which seek to get the state to pull back from its role as an investor and to eliminate mechanisms that regulated consumption, set off an even more marked surge in conspicuous consumption. This meant, in the end, the consumption of imports financed with external savings by means of short-term inter-bank credits, which cause the exchange rate to become undervalued by increasing the supply of foreign exchange. This in turn led to stagnant exports in sectors linked to manufacture, which aggravated current accounts deficits because most exports are concentrated in one or a few raw materials for which the demand is not elastic.[6]

In a later comparison, Fajnzylber indicates that among the GEICs (Growth with Equity Industrializing Countries)[7] and the countries of Latin

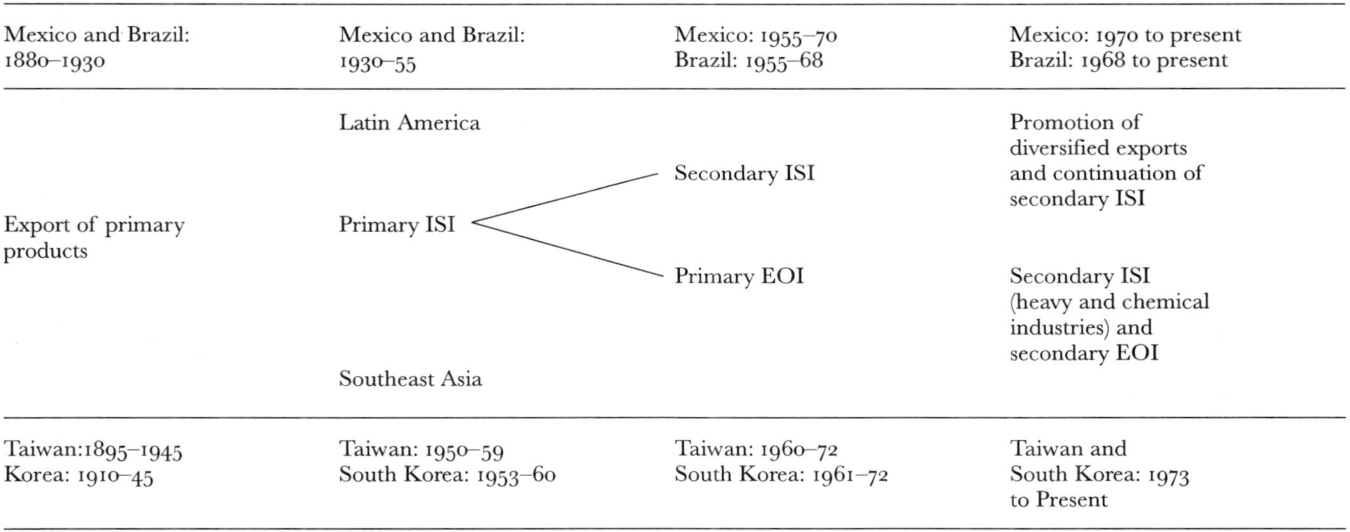

| Mexico and Brazil: 1880–1930 | Mexico and Brazil: 1930–55 | Mexico: 1955–70 Brazil: 1955–68 | Mexico: 1970 to present Brazil: 1968 to present |
|---|---|---|---|
| Export of primary products | Latin America<br>Primary ISI | Secondary ISI | Promotion of diversified exports and continuation of secondary ISI |
| | | Primary EOI | Secondary ISI (heavy and chemical industries) and secondary EOI |
| | Southeast Asia | | |
| Taiwan:1895–1945 Korea: 1910–45 | Taiwan: 1950–59 South Korea: 1953–60 | Taiwan: 1960–72 South Korea: 1961–72 | Taiwan and South Korea: 1973 to Present |

*Notes:* ISI: Import-substitution industrialization; EOI: Export-oriented industrializatioin

FIGURE 3.1 Industrialization paths in Latin America and Southeast Asia (points in common, divergences and convergences)

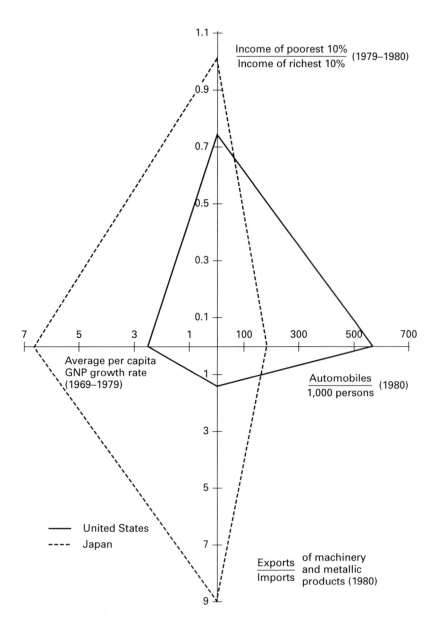

FIGURE 3.2 Profiles of Japan and United States (*Source*: Fajnzylber 1986)

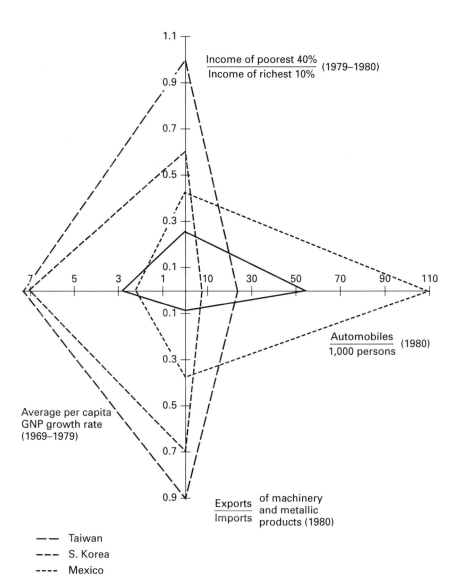

FIGURE 3.3 Profiles of Taiwan, South Korea, Mexico and Argentina
(*Source*: Fajnzylber 1986; *Statistical Year Book*, CGBAS 1981; Report on
the Survey of Personal Income Distribution)

America, the most substantive differences are the lack of internal savings, the excess of foreign debt and foreign investment to compensate for it; excessive population growth; a small industrial manufacturing sector; the scarce presence of technologically innovative sectors in industry, with a subsequent fall in industrial production in years of rapid technological innovation (1980 to 1986); and weak international competitiveness (see Table 3.4) (Fajnzylber 1990).

In general, Fajnzylber says, GEICs exhibited greater equity, austerity, dynamism and competitiveness than Latin American countries taken together (Fajnzylber 1990: 89). 'The capacity of countries to insert themselves solidly in international markets is strongly conditioned by their capacity and potential to keep up with international technological trends. In this sense, the difference pointed out between Latin America and the GEICs is revealing'. (Fajnzylber 1990: 92)

In this framework, the conditions of industrialization in East Asia were:

1. State intervention in order to achieve international competitiveness in the medium term.
2. The formulation of development plans with the participation of the private sector, with precise goals, rewards and penalties.
3. Controlled exchange rates, always offset to make exports profitable and imports costly.
4. Differential management of tariffs and trade barriers.

TABLE 3.4 Some indicators of differences between GEICs and Latin America, average statistics, 1965–86 (%)

| Indicators | Latin America | GEICs |
| --- | --- | --- |
| Gross internal savings/GDP | 16.0 | 28.0 |
| Foreign debt/GDP | 79.0 | 38.0 |
| Direct foreign investment/GDP | 10.9 | 3.0 |
| Population growth rate | 2.5 | 1.4 |
| Industrial manufacturing sector/GDP | 19.4 | 33.1 |
| Gross value of industrial production (GVP) chemical and metal-mechanic industries/GVP industrial sector | 16.9 | 31.4 |
| GVP 1986 (1980=100) | 98.6 | 127.0 |
| Manufacturing exports/all exports | 10.0 | 18.0 |
| Exports/manufacturing imports | 0.3 | 0.8 |

*Source*: Fajnzylber 1990: 88.

5. High indices of professionals in technical fields in proportion to the total population.
6. Production accords between workers, business and the state.
7. A culture that encourages work and savings.[8]

Possibly, in Latin America, some of these elements could be susceptible to replication; however, the function of the state and the perception of that function by a society fed up with inefficiencies that have gone on for decades generate animosity to any notion of regulation and state intervention. On the other hand, Latin American attitudes towards work, drawn from Spanish Catholic culture, have undergone changes since the crisis of the 1980s, when it became necessary for workers at all levels to hold more than one job, each of them paying hunger wages. But attitudes towards work are still not oriented towards effort and savings, rather towards consumption and spending, which indicates a cultural barrier to economic development and the thriving business approach so well developed in Asia.

## Some conclusions

Recent years have given testimony to a number of changes on the international scene which have modified the environment within which economic development is conceived in Latin America. Faced with a crisis, generated in part by such changes introduced since the beginning of the 1980s, the response in Latin America, as in Eastern Europe, has been to point the finger at the industrialization model and, in both cases, proceed to undertake a de-industrializing opening. The hope is that in the end the aggregate value of the new industries will be greater than the aggregate loss of those that have closed, and will thus add to the region's economic development. It has been suggested that the perceived loss in Latin America's market share of international trade indicates a change in the theoretical understanding of development. The response of some countries is to form trading blocs, like the North American Free Trade Agreement (NAFTA) for example, to broaden the internal market. With all the difficulties the concept has always had, the meaning of development aid was also transformed during the 1980s, going from having some link to development to being primarily humanitarian aid, which benefited Africa during the 1990s due to its lack of economic viability. That implied modifications in long-term capital flows from the public sector.

The economic problems facing Eastern Europe were not the same as those in Latin America, but the recipes applied were the same, bringing as a consequence certain difficulties in the management of development in both regions. The results in Latin America were growing current accounts deficits and a balance of payments maintained by short-term deposits at high interest rates, which in the end constituted an obstacle to real new investment. It is not possible today to bring an economy to the state-of-the-art technological frontier without having gone through previous stages and fulfilling all the requirements of industrializing in the current context. Theories critical of subindustrialization that once held true have been rendered obsolete. The state is important for achieving economic development; Southeast Asia's experience demonstrates this. In Latin America there is resistance to the very concept of the state, due to evidence of inefficiency and corruption from past decades. It is impossible to go beyond a certain level of industrial exports without fulfilling a series of requirements, including accords between the state and business on export goals, and establishing the state's function as regulator – not in order to achieve correct pricing nearer to the level set by international prices, rather to keep internal costs competitive with international ones. *Protection and regulation ought to be oriented towards helping domestic industries export, rather than protecting them from international competition.*

Latin America started off down the road to industrialization before Southeast Asia. Yet in the 1970s Southeast Asia went from the secondary ISI stage to the secondary EOI stage, while most of Latin America, with a few exceptions, regressed to the primary export model. There is some evidence of change, but even so it is not sufficient to claim that the region is undergoing export industrialization. The conditions for achieving competitiveness, for Wade, Amsden and most analysts of Southeast Asia, are: proper management of internal pricing (which is not the same as correct pricing); dynamism (high ratio of capital goods exports to total exports); good income distribution; and high levels of internal savings.

Latin America is not following the path set by Southeast Asia because of problems with the activity and function of the state, the indiscriminate opening, a culture not oriented towards work, low levels of internal savings, the volatility of new external savings and the low profitability of a portion of available external savings, as well as the high concentration of income. Finally, the debt crisis has not been overcome and the high level of indebtedness in Latin America's economies continues to be an obstacle to encouraging investment, since it continues to absorb a substantial portion of national income. Meanwhile, given the indiscriminate opening, slow export growth feeds growing current accounts deficits whose limit is a crisis à la Mexico. The return of Latin America at the beginning of the twenty-first century to a development model similar to the one that existed at the end of the nineteenth century seems hardly viable or consistent with the region's social demands and the need for real improvement in the living conditions of the population as a whole.

Gerschenkron invites us to reflect on the originality of industrialization models and not to repeat steps simply because they were taken by the first countries to industrialize. What's more, the spirit and ideology of industrialization in countries that already have an established industrial base are necessarily different from those which are beginning their industrialization process. In this sense, it must be emphasized that Latin America is not beginning its industrialization process; rather, that one stage has come to an end and the region is now *ad portas* in another. Depending on the point of departure, it could be said that Argentina kicked off Latin American industrialization at the end of the nineteenth century, and in the 1930s, under pressure from balance of payments problems, Argentina's industrialization policies were adopted throughout the region. The growth of the state in the economy is a generalization from the 1950s onward, although in banking it was intimately linked to the visits of Kemmerer and others in the 1920s, who recommended setting up public development banks, since Latin American and foreign bankers refused to take risks with their investment capital. That is why Latin America had public development banks from the 1930s until the end of the 1980s.

A prior example of what is currently occurring in Latin America can be found in the tariff-reduction policies and the elimination of import prohibitions applied during the Second Empire in France, which tore down the protected refuge within which French industry had developed (Kenwood and Lougheed 1992: ch. 4). The Cobden-Chevalier trade treaty signed in 1860 opened French industry to British competition and eliminated monopolistic profits in the coal and iron sectors, while at the same time dropping the cost of imported industrial inputs, leading to a phase of accelerated industrialization. However, the development of investment banking (Credit Mobilier) allowed for the required financial resources to be mobilized to sustain the industrialization process and the construction of railways.

This concept does not exist as part of the current model being applied in most Latin American countries, where commercial banking is short term. Once the public development banks were dismantled, the channel for transforming savings into risk capital was broken. British industrialization was achieved without long-term capital and with a short-term commercial banking system. That required a very rapid recouping of investments and very high rates of profitability, as well as low investment costs. At this stage of industrial development, it is difficult to imagine central banks could finance a process of industrialization in Latin America due to the cost of technology and the generalized reduction in profit margins resulting from the pace of innovation and the massive spread of international competition. Because of the terms offered and the prevailing interest rates in Latin American financial markets, national productive investors are obliged to turn to international creditors or to form partnerships with international capital. Undoubtedly, this leads to an outward-facing model of industrialization as far as capital sources are concerned.

In Southeast Asia what stands out is the presence of the state in the economy, as well as the existence of a financial system with state participation in investment capital and specific systems for trade protection. In other words, they did not follow either nineteenth-century European models for industrial development or Latin American ones to achieve the 'great leap forward' in the 1980s, precisely when Latin America got stuck. The policies adopted in Latin America in the 1990s are not like nineteenth-century European policies or Southeast Asian policies of the second half of the twentieth century. They are much more like the ones Latin America, with the exception of Argentina, followed up until 1930. Latin America, caught up in the systemic crisis, is trying to get out of it by applying free-market policies that link private enterprise, the free market and the absence of the state, within the current of 'public choice' (Wolf 1988).

The existence of authoritarian democracies in Latin America for implementing such policies paradoxically parallels the return to democracy in the majority of countries, as well as popular support for the politicians responsible for implementing open-market policies. We are witnessing the definitive dismantling of the import-substitution industrialization model. Some suggest for that very reason that free and open market economic policies may be here to stay (Hojman 1994), while others suggest that policies must be locked in by negotiating international trade pacts (Mexico through the Free Trade Agreement, others through the WTO) to prevent a return to ISI (Oman 1994).

The evidence shows that it is still too early to speak of the end of the Third World (Harris 1986); to use aggregate data for manufacturing exports from developing countries as proof of a new industrialization of the Third World simply masks reality. Several Latin American countries could be going through a phase of industrialization of exports, like Brazil or Mexico, but there is a general tendency towards de-industrialization, against which action must be taken to prevent the destruction of jobs and the return to primary exports, for the effects on Latin America's economic relations with a world that requires ever less in the way of raw materials are bound to be negative. The Asian example sheds light but can not be replicated, for reasons of history, culture and politics, and because Latin America's economies are at a different stage as they seek to redefine their relationship to the global economy.

# Appendices

APPENDIX 3.1 Internal savings/GDP for selected countries of Latin America and Asia, 1965-92 (%)

|  | 1965-73[1] | 1973-80[1] | 1980-85[1] | 1992[2] |
|---|---|---|---|---|
| **Latin America** | | | | |
| Argentina | 19.7 | 21.2 | 11.3 | 15.0 |
| Brazil | 24.3 | 21.7 | 16.9 | 21.0 |
| Chile | 12.9 | 12.2 | 6.9 | 26.0 |
| Colombia | 17.2 | 19.2 | 15.0 | 21.0 |
| Mexico | 19.9 | 21.3 | 23.5 | 17.0 |
| Peru | 27.2 | 24.9 | 23.7 | 13.0 |
| Costa Rica | 16.8 | 13.8 | 16.1 | 23.0 |
| Guatemala | 12.9 | 16.4 | 9.9 | 8.0 |
| | | | | |
| **Asia** | | | | |
| Indonesia | 13.7 | 24.6 | 26.6 | 37.0 |
| Malaysia | 21.6 | 29.3 | 27.5 | 35.0 |
| Philippines | 20.6 | 24.3 | 20.0 | 18.0 |
| Thailand | 22.6 | 21.5 | 18.5 | 35.0 |
| South Korea[3] | | | | |
| Hong Kong[3] | 7.0 | 26.4 | 31.0 | n/a |
| Singapore[3] | 29.0 | – | 27.0 | 30.0 |
| Taiwan[3] | 10.0 | – | 42.0 | 47.0 |
| China[4] | 25.0 | n/a | 34.0 | n/a |

*Sources*: 1. World Bank 1987: 177. 2. World Bank 1994b: World Statistical Indicators, table 9. 3. Figures for Hong Kong, Singapore and Taiwan correspond to 1965, 1975 and 1985 (World Bank 1987: 210); 1975 data are World Bank statistics taken from Wade 1990: 48. 4. Figures for China correspond to 1965 and 1985 (World Bank 1987: 210).

APPENDIX 3.2 Savings/investment gap in relation to GNP for selected countries of Latin America and Asia, 1965–85 (%)

| | 1965–73[2] | 1973–80[2] | 1980–85[2] | 1992[2] |
|---|---|---|---|---|
| **Latin America** | | | | |
| Argentina | 0.0 | 0.6 | -5.0 | -2.0 |
| Brazil | -1.7 | -4.5 | -3.5 | 4.0 |
| Chile | -1.4 | -5.2 | -10.6 | 2.0 |
| Colombia | -1.8 | 0.4 | -5.0 | 3.0 |
| Mexico | -1.5 | -3.9 | -1.9 | -7.0 |
| Peru | -0.5 | -4.1 | -4.3 | -3.0 |
| Costa Rica | -5.0 | -11.7 | -11.8 | -5.0 |
| Guatemala | -0.4 | -2.3 | -3.6 | -10.0 |
| **Asia** | | | | |
| Indonesia | -2.2 | 0.1 | -2.8 | 2.0 |
| Malaysia | -0.7 | 0.6 | -7.6 | 1.0 |
| Philippines | 0.0 | -4.8 | -5.9 | -5.0 |
| Thailand | -1.1 | -5.1 | -5.9 | -5.0 |
| South Korea[3] | | | | |
| Hong Kong[3] | -8.0 | -5.3 | 1.0 | – |
| Singapore[3] | -7.0 | – | 6.0 | 1.0 |
| Taiwan[3] | -12.0 | – | -1.0 | 6.0 |

*Note*: Developed Asian countries are calculated by differences.

*Sources*: 1. World Bank 1987: 77. 2. World Bank 1994b: World Statistical Indicators, table 9. 3. Figures for Hong Kong, Singapore and Taiwan correspond to 1965, 1975 and 1985 (World Bank 1987: 210); 1975 data are World Bank statistics taken from Wade 1990: 48.

## Notes

1. Another classification of interpretations of industrialization in Latin America, is that of Mauricio Rojas (1991: 59–78). In summary, there are two readings of Latin American industrialization: developmentalism as proposed by Prebisch, and dependency theory, according to which greater integration into the global economy brings greater underdevelopment. In both cases the solution is industry for the internal market.

2. Ching-yuan Lin (1998b) of the IMF undertakes a comparative study of Latin America and Southeast Asia. He makes his argument using the examples of Taiwan, South Korea, Chile and Argentina from the 1950s to the beginning of the 1980s. The central thesis of the book is that keeping inflation low will allow for the economic system, financial regulation and wage controls to function better, leading to greater economic growth with all its positive effects. This will be, in essence, Latin America's difficulty versus East Asia. The article 'East Asia and Latin America as Contrasting Models', (Lin 1988a) sums up the central arguments of the book and was used for the neoclassical standpoints on the development differences between the two regions.

3. Chapter 1 of Wade (1990) offers a theoretical debate, but pp. 14–22 seek to refute theoretical positions by means of partial research results. The rest of the book is also an empirical refutation of the principles on which Southeast Asia achieved success, taking as the central example Taiwan.

4. See Chapter 1 on the state–market debate.

5. We shall return to this theme in Chapter 4.

6. Van Dijck (1990) makes a cluster analysis of the orientation of trade and the foreign debt (p. 181) and finds that most Latin-American countries, in spite of everything, are in the primary phase of exports, exporting one or a few products.

7. The GEICs considered by Fajnzylber are Spain, Portugal, Yugoslavia, Hungary, South Korea, China and Thailand. He notes that Indonesia has been excluded from the list because of its low level of industrialization, under 20 per cent of GDP; also Hong Kong, due to its lack of an agricultural sector. He doesn't say so, but it is understood that Singapore was excluded for the same reason. Taiwan was not included because it lacks a data base comparable to those of the other countries.

8. Michio Morishima's (1985) account of Japan's success focuses on the role of Confucianism in Japanese work culture and respect for group initiative. The introduction presents the central features of Confucianism in terms of how they affect work and the use of technology. The book emphasizes the differences between Confucianism in China and in Japan and it is not unlike Weber's work on the spirit of capitalism in the Protestant ethic. To be brief, the spirit of Confucius, the values he considered essential were: benevolence, justice, ceremony, knowledge and faith as fundamental virtues. In principle man is naturally good and social morals are built on the family. It is not a divine being who establishes moral order in the world, rather it is the family. When natural human affection goes beyond the limits of the family to persons outside it or to strangers, then one is said to have acquired love for humanity and these are men of benevolence or virtuous men. Filial piety and the exercise of family duties as a younger brother are virtues of Confucianism. Filial piety is understood as respecting one's parents, caring for them and obeying their desires. And the role of the younger brother is to follow the desires of older brothers and to obey them. Besides harmony, which means that people are in agreement and maintain that agreement in society, loyalty and faith are the two virtues of sincerity. Loyalty is one's sincerity with one's conscience, an absence of pretensions or selfishness of the soul. And faith is defined as always telling the truth.

Morishima quotes from Chapter 16 of *The Analects of Confucius*:

> For the perfect gentleman there are nine considerations. These are a desire to see clearly when he looks at something; a desire to hear every detail when listening to something; a desire to present a tranquil countenance; a desire to preserve an attitude of respect; a desire to be sincere in his words; a desire to be careful in his work; a willingness to enquire further into anything about which he has doubts; a willingness to bear in mind the difficulties consequent on anger; a willingness to consider moral values when presented with the possibility of profit.

> Confucius' moral was: 'Guide by morality, control by ceremony.'

# 4. Globalization, Competitiveness and New Trade Patterns

The further off from England the nearer is to France —
Then turn not pale, beloved snail, but come and join the dance.

(Lewis Carroll, *Alice's Adventures in Wonderland*)

This chapter will review the discussions under way regarding the conditions and results of the new forms of international competitiveness which either allow developing economies to insert themselves into the global economy or prevent them from doing so. In addition, it will examine globalization and the emerging patterns of trade to which it has given rise. The question we will seek to answer is: What do the real conditions of globalization have to do with the notion of competitiveness put forth, and what do both of these have to do with crossing the ocean, to paraphrase Pérez? Finally, globalization is a word that contains many concepts. While these essays take Ohmae's approach to globalization, several conceptualizations ought to be reviewed to clarify the environment in which the crossing or not of the ocean and/or the derailing of the previous model of industrialization occur.

## Forms of competitiveness: A new way of saying productivity

The first theorist to introduce the notion of competitiveness was David Ricardo when he defined the comparative advantages for producing a good that an economy might enjoy over another economy producing the same good. This concept might be summed up as the adequateness of human resources, available raw materials and means of production for manufacturing at the lowest possible cost an exportable good which no one else can manufacture at that cost. Schumpeter introduced the notion of long-range industrial revolutions, ones which remake the existing industrial structure by introducing new methods of production and produce an avalanche of new consumer products and improvements in living standards, but which at the same time open a gap between various income sectors (Schumpeter 1943: part II). In other words, he introduced the concept that comparative advantages are not static and that they do not favour everyone. What Schumpeter explained is that technological revolutions transform comparative advantages, which are dynamic and in permanent flux.

Porter (1990) begins where Schumpeter left off and asks why nations with continual budget deficits such as Japan, Italy and South Korea have been successful at improving their international competitiveness, if, as some maintain, low exchange rates, low interest rates and small deficits are the preconditions for enhanced productivity. He also asks how countries with high exchange rates such as Germany and Switzerland have succeeded, and how Italy and South Korea, with their high interest rates, have as well. He goes over the argument about cheap and abundant labour as a source of competitiveness and observes that Germany and Switzerland have high labour costs, but have still been successful. In the same way, he examines the cases of countries that are poor in natural resources (Germany, Japan, Switzerland, Italy and South Korea), but have been successful regarding competitiveness. In light of the crisis in the productivity of capital in advanced countries and the low growth rates of labour productivity there compared with the emerging new industrial countries, competition today is based on differences in productivity. International trade and investment can improve national productivity, but they can also constitute a threat, since international competition sets an absolute standard for national/ international productivity. In this sense, subsidies are a distortion that, rather than help raise the general productivity level, can suffocate it.

Why does a country come out ahead at the international level in a particular industry? He suggests:

1. *Factor situation*: such as specialized labour or infrastructure necessary to compete.
2. *Conditions of demand*: that is, the type of internal demand that exists for a given product.
3. *Corollary or mutually supportive industries*: the presence or absence of efficient and internationally competitive suppliers.
4. *Company strategy, structure and competence.* A company achieves competitive advantages when the head office allows and supports the quickest accumulation of technologies and assets, when it provides good information and insight regarding what a product or process requires, and when it supports sustained investment so that the national environment is dynamic.

The new technological change has introduced several notions of competitiveness that have to do with productivity and which fall within the concept of dynamic advantages (Dahlman 1994: 72–3; Porter 1990):

1. *Permanent innovation and change*: includes new ways or means of doing common things, changes in design, in production processes and in market focus or organization.
2. *Quality*. The trade-off between quality and cost has disappeared in the new forms of production. Greater quality control reduces costs by reducing waste and the need to rework products or change defective products. To be competitive in the new industrial paradigm, products must be manufactured with the highest possible quality at the lowest possible cost.
3. *Response to client demand and quick delivery*. Computerized and automated technologies have shortened the time between the design of new products and their appearance on the production line. The flexibility of new technologies allows for adapting products to fit the specific demands of clients. At the same time, the time on the production line has been reduced substantially since it does not go through so many 'hands'. The result is greater diversification of products and more competition in design, distribution and services, as well as in production itself.
4. *Aggressive marketing and efficient distribution networks*. To sell products whose life-cycle is short requires aggressive marketing and large and efficient distribution networks to recoup investments in research and development. This is facilitated by information systems introduced by the new technologies, which allow companies to reach the point of sale to track how products are selling. In turn, this allows retailers to carry smaller inventories on high-sales products and to renew inventories quickly, which reduces the financial cost to retailers and accelerates product sales for lower total costs. One factor is that this requires efficient and timely transportation systems to get products from the factory to the point of sale 'just in time'.
5. *International strategies*. A company ought to move towards a global strategy as soon as its resources and competitive position (productivity) allow, in the cases of industries with international projection. An international strategy ought not to be marginal, but rather an integral part of a company's development, seeking efficient distribution networks and deploying an aggressive marketing system.

Dahlman and Porter propose that, given the generalized crisis in productivity, and given that conditions of productivity ought to tend to become equal if economies are perfectly open, it is differentiated productivity that will make some products more competitive if they are manufactured in one place rather than in another. It will be the conditions of competition by productivity that will dynamize industries still swamped by the productivity crisis of capital and/or labour. The conditions for competition, in a situation of technological change, are given by the facilities that the new technology provides in terms of on-time delivery, innovation and high quality. But they also require aggressive marketing strategies and global policies as part of the integral development of the company. Companies will have to develop efficiently in domestic markets and be capable of entering the international market. The conditions to achieve this are not set, although the implicit assumption is that it can be accomplished by means of an open economy.

One debate in this regard is laid out by Krugman (1994a, 1994b),[1] who poses three questions: What will happen when a country has lower productivity than its trading partners? What will happen when a country is behind in productivity improvements in relation to its competitors? And which is more important, growth in productivity in those sectors that must compete with foreign rivals, or improvements in productivity in those sectors that produce for protected internal markets? In this way he provocatively challenges the common wisdom expressed above and affirms that being less productive than trading partners is not a problem. Even if that country has a lower standard of living than its trading partners, trading with countries that have higher productivity will mitigate its problems of low productivity, since wage differentials will compensate for them. Export success will not depend on absolute productivity differentials, rather on comparative ones within the same industry. In the end, unproductivities will be covered by differentials in the terms of trade (Krugman, 1994a: 274).

Regarding the second question, if one country is behind another in productivity growth, this differential will be reflected in the exchange rate. The country that makes productivity improvements will see an improvement in its exchange rate in relation to the one that does not, favouring the exports of the one with the cheaper currency. In sum, what matters regarding improvements in productivity rates is internal productivity. External factors are compensated by the exchange rate.

On the third question, regarding the disjuncture between selling on the internal market and selling on the external one, it is erroneous to emphasize the manufacturing sector (in reference to Thurow) where the internal market is a residual of the external one. What matters are productivity improvements in those sectors that make up the lion's share of GDP and not in industries that constitute a smaller portion of it. US industrial GDP is only 20 per cent of total GDP. Improvements in manufacturing productivity are less than the average productivity of the economy as a whole, due to the small size of the manufacturing sector. Improvements in manufacturing productivity will strengthen the exchange rate to the point that products are no longer competitive due to wage differentials. He concludes by saying that the generalized belief that productivity improvements are essential for international competitiveness is a mistake. Productivity is important, but competitiveness has nothing to do with it. The argument Krugman makes in *Foreign Affairs* is essentially the same, adding that it is not countries which compete, rather industries in specific sectors. But Krugman concludes by saying:

> If productivity is important, why object if some people try to raise the urgency level by claiming the reason that it is important is because we are in some kind of international race? ... There are, I think, two answers. The first is that a misplaced belief that the United States needs higher productivity to face international competition can lead to errors in policy. For example, there has been some talk of trying to focus government-sponsored research on improving productivity in U.S. manufacturing – as opposed to services, which are deemed less important because they do not face foreign competition. Since an extra percentage point of service productivity is worth 3.5 times as much as an extra point of manufacturing productivity, this would be a serious mistake. More important is that the prevalence of fashionable misconceptions about the relationship between productivity and competitiveness provides a kind of test of the reliability of supposed experts ... He might as well be wearing a flashing neon sign that reads: I DON'T KNOW WHAT I'M TALKING ABOUT. (Krugman 1994a: 280)

He acknowledges that it takes courage to affirm that common wisdom in international policy is mistaken. But he insists that competitiveness is a meaningless word when it is applied to national economies. The obsession with competitiveness is wrong and dangerous (Krugman 1994b).

The responses to this solitary stance against productivity improvements to bring about improvements in competitiveness, revolve around the following:

1.   Prestowitz states that if in competition between companies the profits of one are the losses of others, the same is true between countries. He offers as example the $6 billion Saudi Arabian purchase order for aeroplanes which the United States won and Europe lost. In the second place, those who propose competitiveness as an important issue do not ignore the internal economy. International commerce is a secondary issue. The lack of export dynamism is more a symptom than a cause of a lack of competitiveness. Krugman ignores the imports of the United States which add up to 11 per cent of GDP or half of industrial GDP (20 per cent). Global US trade is 21 per cent of GDP, equal to the manufacturing

sector, and it has an impact on half of the country's economy. The price and quality of imports help define internal prices, wages and income in the country. He offers the automobile industry as an example.

2. Thurow declares himself innocent of Krugman's accusations, of giving more importance to international issues than they really deserve. He affirms that improvements in the living standards of the population respond to improvements in productivity and in any economy the growth rate of productivity is determined essentially by domestic investments in machinery and equipment, research and development, infrastructure and public services, and the quality of private management and public administration: 'Ninety-three percent of economic success or failure is determined at home with only seven percent depending on competitive and cooperative arrangements with the rest of the world ... [What is central is] domestic invention and innovation' (Thurow in Prestowitz et al. 1994). From there Thurow argues in favour of protectionism to avoid a deterioration in domestic wages, but he counter-argues when he says that foreign competition at the same time forces an accelerated rate of domestic economic change and produces new opportunities to learn new technologies and new management practices that can be used to improve domestic productivity.

In the world of new technologies, it doesn't matter where they are manufactured, rather who manufactures them. The quasi-rents that come from getting into the market earlier and staying longer have been replaced by the creation of new products and processes that generate higher-than-world-average wages and rates of return on capital. A private producer, if he is not the best in the world, is going to adopt the best practices he finds elsewhere, and will not necessarily try to invent the same product again with his own technology.

Cohen asks why Krugman does not get to the bottom of the issue. The deterioration in the rate of productivity improvement in the United States is a fact stated, but not explained. No one says that the productivity of a company and of a country are the same thing, and he cites *The Report of the President's Commission on Competitiveness* written for the Reagan administration in 1984:

> Competitiveness has different meanings for the firm and for the national economy ... A nation's competitiveness is the degree to which it can, under free and fair market conditions, produce goods and services that meet the test of international markets while simultaneously expanding the real incomes of its citizens. Competitiveness at the national level is based on superior productivity performance. (Cohen in Prestowitz et al. 1994: 195)

Cohen speaks of the recognition that the United States is no longer the leader and that this awareness is good for inducing improvements and comparative measures. Krugman oversimplifies a greater problem for which the economy has no explanation: the determinants of productivity and their relation to competitiveness.

In sum, the debate on productivity and competitiveness is far from over, but it should be understood that competitiveness at the national level refers to differentials in national productivity, and company competitiveness refers to differentials in productivity within the same industry. It could be, in effect, lack of productivity at the company level which compensates for the macroeconomic side, as a way of levelling differences. However, where all are in agreement is that improvements in levels of domestic productivity are essential for improving the living standards of the population and that international pressures can stimulate this. For most of those reviewed above, the international side is relevant, but not for Krugman. From the Latin American point of view, this same argument has derivations regarding the lack of exchange-rate compensation for low productivity and the dependence on one exchange rate, the US dollar, *vis-à-vis* the other currencies of the developed world. Productivity differentials among ACCs can be compensated by exchange rates, possibly, but that does not occur in the same way with Latin America where exchange rates are tied to the dollar.

In addition, low wages due to an oversupply of labour can help at the company level, through improvements in productivity levels, but for the economy as a whole productivity improvements are reflected in reductions in the demand for labour, placing downward pressure on wages as a whole. Lastly, the technological base from which productivity levels and absolute differentials in productivity between ACCs and Latin American countries are measured is immensely different, such that small investments in this part of the world can augment productivity enormously, while that is not the case in the ACCs. However, this would result in an S-curve during the period of productivity improvement, whether or not it is induced from the exterior. But the absolute distance would not necessarily be reduced.[2]

Finally, when added foreign trade (X+M) represents 50 per cent of GDP, but industrial GDP is 25 per cent, international factors are much more important than in the US case taken as an example above. Agricultural improvements are ignored in Krugman's text and these are easily obtainable in Latin America. What is certain is that productivity improvements may or may not lead to improvements in international competitiveness; for example, if the exchange rate is unfavourable, or the cost of capital greater than internationally, or the cost of energy greater than internationally, or the cost of transportation to markets greater than those for similar goods coming from the ACCs. In the final analysis, improvements in productivity levels will be reflected in rising standards of living of the national population. One thing is not a symmetrical reflection of the other. As Thurow points out, the determinants of improvements in productivity will be internal and linked to real investment, rates of innovation, infrastructure and management quality. International factors are derived from that.

## Globalization

Globalization can be defined as growth in economic activity that transcends national and regional boundaries. It is expressed in the growing movement of goods and services through trade and investment – and of human beings – across those borders, as well as in the exchange of information in real time. It is driven by individual economic actors in search of greater profits under pressure from competition. The essence of the discussion on globalization has to do with the integration of the markets for goods, services, capital and labour. For Ohmae, market integration is undertaken among 'island' economies which have per capita incomes of over US$10,000 and which can integrate because they maintain free-market policies and an openness to foreign capital. Globalization is undertaken by global companies and all forms of restriction on them are a hindrance to globalization. The question is what will happen to lower-productivity economies that have no way of entering the market of countries with per capita incomes of over US$10,000. They remain in the hinterland, and the growing income gap between them and the rich countries leaves them without a future.

New rules of productivity, described by Porter and Dahlman as the new international competition, would be one way for such countries to become inserted into the globalized economy. Drucker foresees a potential for countries that are developing today to become developed countries tomorrow, if they follow the example of Mexico, pursuing openness and integration to world markets. However, he says, those countries which choose not to and which continue with 'suicide policies', like Brazil in the 1970s, can turn into problems for advanced countries, because they will send forth a flood of migrants, given that two-thirds of world population will live in those countries by the second decade of the next century.[3] At the moment this essay is being written, following the crisis in Mexico and Brazil's growth spurt in 1995, it is not clear that this reflection is valid, even in terms of the success of the policies proposed or the failure of those not favoured. There is no doubt about the exclusion of the majority of the population of the world from the globalized world. And that is the framework within which new concerns arise regarding the utility of policies that promote integration among economies that are unequal.

The concept of globalization has two distinct meanings. One has to do with companies and their technological capacity to compete; the other, with multilateralism. The world trading system and government trade policy are the pillars of the process. From the beginning of the Uruguay Round of the GATT talks, and the emergence of regional initiatives such as NAFTA, the European Union, the Southern Cone Common Market (MERCOSUR), there has been a debate about whether the world is moving towards a system of trading blocs or universal rules of the game (WTO), and if such blocs are impediments to, or part of, the building of universal rules for the free market (Oman 1994).

Oman offers a summary of the debate between multilateralism and regionalism, and warns of the dangers that each holds for developing countries. The debate revolves around the specific weight that the size of markets holds in a multilateralized system. From this point of view, the larger the market, the more clout it has in defining the multilateral rules of the game. Inversely, countries that view themselves as weak will tend to join together in regional groupings to wield more specific weight as integrated markets within the global scheme. The danger is that these could become inward-oriented integration schemes rather than outward-oriented ones, to compensate for difficulties in competing with other trading blocs. There is evidence that intra-bloc trade has tripled in value since the 1980s, while inter-bloc trade doubled in the same period. However, intra-bloc trade currently represents only 40 per cent of inter-bloc trade (Oman 1994: 6 fn).

Globalization is not synonymous with multilateralism, Oman suggests, for three reasons.

1. There have been three moments of globalization since the end of the nineteenth century, the first of which occurred when multilateralism did not exist. The first came at the end of the nineteenth century and beginning of the twentieth, and was marked by strong movements of capital, labour and markets for goods. The second, after the Second World War, was launched by multinational companies and accompanied by reductions in tariffs on international trade resulting from the GATT rounds. And the third, the current one, which began in the 1980s. The specificity of today's globalization is linked to information and technological knowledge, while those of previous periods were linked to the search for raw materials or new markets in developing countries.

2. The market unification of a few countries, due to their geographic proximity, opens the way to regional schemes for broadened markets. In

the same way, regional integration efforts help guarantee policy continuity, as has been highlighted in the NAFTA accords for Mexico. Such agreements are possible only among countries that share an understanding of the problems each faces, as well as a common long-term vision.

3. To make an equation between globalization and multilateralism obscures the interaction between globalization and regionalization. Mittelman (1995) proposes that what is new in the concept of globalization is the manner and degree of penetration of global phenomena in national economic policies. Regional divisions of labour are emerging, oriented in some way towards global structures, each one entwined in unequal dealings with the world centres of production and finance, and offering a number of possibilities for development (Mittelman 1995: 279).

The initial evidence on both multilateralism and globalization is not very positive. The formation of the World Trade Organization (WTO), for example, does not mean that trade protection has been reduced, rather that the forms of protection in the 'grey area', about which the WTO can do little, are on the rise, and efforts are made to resolve conflict through bilateral negotiations.[4] Meanwhile, in the name of free trade, the countries of Latin America and Africa have unilaterally opened their borders, with effects that are already evident in the current accounts deficit. The agreement of the Uruguay Round will signify an increase in world GNP growth of 0.11 per cent yearly over the next decade, an amount that is insignificant for this issue (Thurow 1994: 7). The director of ECLAC warns of the danger of neo-protectionism and the potential application of unilateral trade measures in a situation of persistent recession and worsening unemployment in developed economies (Rosenthal 1994: 43). The perception that the crisis in the ACCs will not allow protection to be reduced, but rather will tend to increase pressure for greater protection in the 'grey area' is a concern for the economies of East Asia (Pangestu 1995). This viewpoint diverges from the common wisdom expressed by the media and policy-makers in Latin America who think the Uruguay Round will guarantee free trade.

The Uruguay Round contains the following basic agreements (Rosenthal 1994): mutual tariff concessions, which it is hoped will reach a level of 40 per cent reduction in tariffs; an agricultural agreement with commitments to gradually diminish export subsidies; more strict regulation of anti-dumping measures and compensatory duties, in order to limit their use in unilateral and arbitrary ways; strengthening of the legislation on safeguards to eliminate 'grey area' measures; provisions to continue negotiations on the financial, telecommunications and transportation sectors; and a commitment to create the World Trade Organization, which in effect was set up in January 1995. If indeed this summary is not in any

TABLE 4.1 Latin America (certain countries): summary of trade liberalization process

| Country | Start date | Maximum tariff | | Number of brackets | | Average tariff | | Non-tariff barriers | Variation in real exchange rate[a] |
|---|---|---|---|---|---|---|---|---|---|
| | | Start | End of 1993 | Start | End of 1993 | Start | End of 1993 | | |
| Argentina[b] | 1989 | 65 | 30 | — | 3 | 39[c] | 15[c] | In 1988 the value of industrial production subject to restrictions was reduced from 2 per cent to 18 per cent. In 1989–1991 non-tariff barriers were eliminated, as were additional transitory duties and specific duties. | -49 |
| Bolivia | 1986 | 150 | 10 | — | 2 | 12[d] | 7[d] | With few exceptions, all prohibitions and import licensing requirements were abolished. | 92 |
| Brazil | 1988 | 105 | 35 | 29 | 7 | 51[e] | 14[e] | In 1990 the list of imports that were prohibited or required previous licensing was eliminated. However, requirements on national content were maintained for intermediate and capital goods. | 14 |
| Colombia[b] | 1990 | 100 | 20 | 14 | 4 | 44[d] | 12[d] | Nearly all restrictions on previous licensing requirements were eliminated at the end of 1990. | -4 |
| Costa Rica | 1986 | 100 | 20 | — | 4 | 27/e | 14/e | Gradual elimination of import permits and other quantitative import restrictions. | 10 |
| Chile[f] | 1973 | 220 | 10 | 57 | 1 | 94[e] | 10[e] | During the 1970s quantitative import restrictions were repealed. | -10 |
| | 1985 | 35 | 11 | 1 | 1 | 35[e] | 11[e] | Price bands were reintroduced and an anti-dumping system was set up. | 32 |

| | | | | | | | | Notes | |
|---|---|---|---|---|---|---|---|---|---|
| Mexico | 1985 | 100 | 20 | 10 | 3 | 24[c] | 12[c] | Products requiring import permits were cut back from 92% of all production in June 1985 to 18% in December 1990, and official prices for imports were eliminated. | -15 |
| Peru[b] | 1990 | 108 | 25 | 56 | 2 | 6[e] | 18[e] | In September 1990 import licences, controls and authorizations were eliminated, as were quotas and prohibitions. | -28 |
| Venezuela | 1989 | 135 | 20 | 41 | 4 | 35[d] | 10[d] | The number of categories subject to restrictions was reduced from 2,200 in 1988 to 200 currently. Specific duties, which in some cases reached a maximum of 940% before the liberalization pro- gramme was introduced, were repealed. | 15 |

*Notes*: a. From the year previous to the beginning of the liberalization programme up to 1993 the exchange rate for exports was used.
b. Tariffs include surcharges.   c. Weighted according to domestic production.   d. Weighted according to imports.   e. Simple average of tariff categories.   f. Chile's first trade liberalization was completed in 1979. A uniform tariff of 10% was in place until 1982. Therefore, the first line refers to information for that period (1973–82). The second line has information about the reduction in import tariffs from a high of 35% in 1984 to 20% in 1985, 15% in 1988 and 11% in 1991.

*Source*: ECLAC 1994a: 106, Table V.1, on the basis of national figures.

way exhaustive, it does offer a general idea of the issues taken up and the way in which they were addressed (see Table 4.1).

First of all, the 40 per cent reduction in tariffs is being sought over the next decade for all nations, but is directed particularly at the largest ones. Latin American countries already implemented a unilateral tariff reduction of between 10 and 35 per cent and dismantled their 'grey area' mechanisms, as part of their trade adjustment policy. From this angle, what was agreed to in the GATT is insufficient for Latin America.

In the second place, the commitment to reduce agricultural subsidies will continue to be a thorny issue, considering that the farmers of both Europe and the United States receive subsidies equivalent to between 50 and 75 per cent of the value of their production. This depresses Latin American agriculture and does not contribute to improved spacial distribution of income in the region; on the contrary it constitutes an obstacle to change in the distributive structure.

In the third place, strengthening the legislation to help dismantle 'grey area' protection is highly controversial, since the lobbies of the various producer associations or certain transnationals are much more powerful than the clout of a developing country. Such processes work only when relations among the parties are symmetrical and this is clearly not the case. Recently there was even a case of a unilateral application of tariffs on Japanese automobiles by the United States, due to Japan's resistance to opening its market to US cars, a dispute that is still unresolved. The case of arsenic in Chilean grapes proves the argument that I am trying to demonstrate. Legislation can be passed, but its efficacy is highly questionable due to the clout of the specific actors within their national polities.

Finally, the deregulation of national markets in the realms of finance, transportation and telecommunications will naturally favour the larger companies in each industry, while opening some space for a few smaller ones. Fundamentally, this is something for the big companies and banks.

From this point of view it would seem that the GATT agreement at the Uruguay Round, despite what many say (see Leiva 1994), has less to offer Latin America and much more to offer the trading systems among advanced capitalist countries. That is why a process of bilateral, unilateral and plurilateral accords is occurring in nearly every region of the world. There are three plurilateral negotiations under way in Latin America: the G3, MERCOSUR and the Andean Community.[5] A fourth regional initiative is NAFTA, which includes Mexico. Similarly, dozens of bilateral accords were signed in Latin America between 1992 and 1995. Finally, unilateral trade reform measures have been adopted as part of World Bank structural adjustment programmes. In other words, multilateral negotiations are fourth on the list of priorities and in any case do not seem to correspond to the environment in Latin America created by the dynamics of developed countries or even to the implementation of trade reform policies in Latin America, where barriers were removed unilaterally.

The protectionism that exists in the ACCs could mean that multilateral negotiations are held not so much to eliminate trade barriers as to prevent them from growing. UNCTAD (1993: 36–8) tracked the use of non-tariff measures in eight developed countries and the EEC over the period 1981–91, and found that despite the growth of trade during the 1980s and despite the Uruguay Round negotiations, the use of non-tariff measures had not only not declined, it had increased slightly, affecting 18.3 per cent of the imports of all developed countries in 1991 as compared to 16.2 per cent in 1981. The frequency of the use of non-tariff measures has declined since 1987, suggesting that the Punta del Este Declaration did contribute to stemming the expansion of this sort of protectionist measure (see Table 4.2).

Evidently, developed countries place more protectionist barriers on imports originating in developing countries (DCs) than those originating in other developed countries. Barriers affect 20.9 per cent of the former versus 17.7 per cent of imports from the entire world. This means that protectionist barriers affect somewhere in the neighbourhood of 14 per cent of imports originating in developed countries. Barriers are high on textiles and apparel, and shoes – light industries towards which the DCs are orienting themselves as part of the primary export industrialization strategy – followed by steel, fishing and other sea products, another DC

TABLE 4.2 Imports protected by non-tariff barriers in ACCs as a proportion of total imports, by product type (rates of coverage in percentage of imports)

| Definition of product group | Sourced in entire world | Sourced in developing countries |
| --- | --- | --- |
| All products including fuels | 17.7 | 20.9 |
| Fuels | 17.8 | 13.1 |
| Agricultural products | 26.2 | 20.8 |
| Textiles and apparel | 52.2 | 70.7 |
| Fishing and sea products | 51.4 | 54.8 |
| Iron and steel | 50.5 | 40.4 |
| Shoes | 35.0 | 42.5 |
| Vehicles | 41.7 | 0.6 |
| Electronic consumer appliances | 16.1 | 10.3 |

*Source*: UNCTAD 1993: 39, table 19.

area of focus and another area of conflict. For this reason, if DC exports move from the light industries noted towards industries with a higher technological content, more of this sort of protectionism can be expected. Protectionism arises due to the quantity of competitors and the effect they have on reducing the market share of producers in developed countries (light industries) and not due to the technological content of the products (consumer electronic appliances).

Such protectionism, unrelieved by the negotiations of the Uruguay Round of the GATT, sparked regional initiatives. The question is whether these regional initiatives will be stumbling blocks or building blocks for globalization, i.e. will they promote inward-oriented development of the regional spaces or outward-oriented development? This will depend entirely on whether countries perceive the potential for getting ahead under the new GATT rules, or on the contrary fear they will continue losing ground in the global economy, as was seen in Chapter 2 (see Table 2.8).

What is clear is that the regional blocs being set up have differentiated rules for their member countries, with very low tariffs and trade preferences, while raising up common external barriers. This is happening at the same time that the GATT, now the WTO, is imposing universal trade rules. At the Miami Summit, the United States recently proposed a free-trade area for the Americas for the year 2005, with the intention of taking in the regional blocs of South America. This entire panorama gives you the feeling that the future rules of world trade have yet to be defined. GATT does not seem to have much credibility, though the countries of Latin America have joined or are in the process of doing so. On the other hand, GATT does not seem to be enough for the United States, which would like to create an inter-American free-trade area, but that is being attempted over and above initiatives such as MERCOSUR and G3.

There is an apparent contradiction between the multilateralism proposed in GATT, the bilateralism proposed in the US–Canada, US–Mexico accords and the twenty-six bilateral accords signed in South America between 1993 and 1994, and the plurilateralism expressed in the European Union, MERCOSUR, G3 and the Andean Pact. The uncertainties expressed in these plurilateral accords place in doubt the future of free trade in the neoclassical sense of the term, and turn the WTO, in its infancy, into a fragile organization without much clout or credibility. The strength and credibility of the multilateral trade institution will be tested in its capacity to be the arbitrator of trade conflicts among the ACCs. The combination of policies in the European Union is oriented towards internal integration and external protectionism with some openings, while in Latin America it is towards internal integration and external opening, with the exceptions of Colombia and Brazil which, like the EU, combine protectionism and opening with integration. The Association of South East Asian Nations (ASEAN) similarly combines protectionism, opening and integration. The World Trade Organization will be called on to play the arbitrator between these regions and a world free-trade system that does not exist more than in embryonic form. And the question remains as to whether regional blocs will be building blocks or stumbling blocks.

### New patterns of world trade

The minimal relevance of multilateral trading agreements arises from the combination of plurilateral, bilateral and unilateral accords, except in the case where multilateralism occurs among blocs of countries. Trading problems among ACC blocs (NAFTA, EU) are in part responsible for the changes in trading patterns, which show an unmistakable growth in trade among the DCs (UNCTAD 1993: 12). This could be due largely to trade in manufactured goods originating in Southeast Asia and exported to Latin America, Africa and other countries of Asia, as well as to the still-incipient trade in manufactured goods produced and traded within the region (see Table 4.3). Much of it, however, has to do with the new forms of organization of production since the crisis of Fordism. The post-Fordist structure of production links producers within a new international division of labour, while the relationship between ACCs and DCs has been transformed. The transfer of labour-intensive jobs to the DCs from the ACCs changed at some point between the 1970s and the 1990s, when the countries of Asia stopped being bastions of cheap labour. The great

TABLE 4.3 Growth in world trade: 1990 versus 1987–89 (%)

| Origin | Destination | | | | |
|---|---|---|---|---|---|
| | DCs | ACCs | Eastern Europe | Asian socialist countries | World |
| DCs | 19.2 | 11.5 | 11.4 | 7.3 | 11.4 |
| ACCs | 12.4 | 12.2 | 8.6 | -5.5 | 12.0 |
| Eastern Europe | -0.9 | 18.2 | -25.5 | -11.8 | -9.9 |
| Asian socialist countries | 17.3 | 12.5 | -17.7 | – | 11.9 |
| World | 11.9 | 12.2 | -11.7 | -1.8 | 10.4 |

*Source*: UNCTAD 1993: 16, table 16.

exception that proves the rule is China. However, the argument of Fröbel et al. is problematic in that it does not show the same displacement of investment in parts and components manufacturing to Latin America, where labour is cheaper in the 1990s than in Asia with the exception of China.

Most Latin American countries are primary exporters that concentrate on a few products, while Asian countries are highly diverse manufacturing exporters (Van Dijck 1990). Van Dijck argues, following Linder, that the availability of natural resources has a significant impact on the general development pattern of a country. However, 'the abundance of natural resources tends to delay the process of industrialization and reduce the need for industries oriented toward exports and substituting for exports' (Van Dijck 1990: 184). The result for resource-rich Latin America is that variations in international raw materials' prices have a significant effect on the balance of payments, given the lack of export-oriented industrialization, while this is not the case for East Asia. The deterioration in the terms of trade does not affect those countries in the same way it affects

TABLE 4.4 Participation in world trade of manufactured products from Latin America and Asia, 1980–90 (%)

|  | 1980 | 1990 | Annual growth rate 1987–90 |
|---|---|---|---|
| **Latin America** | | | |
| Argentina | 1.8 | 1.0 | 21.9 |
| Brazil | 7.1 | 4.2 | 7.4 |
| Chile | 0.4 | 0.2 | 23.6 |
| Colombia | 0.7 | 0.4 | 20.4 |
| Mexico | 1.2 | 3.1 | 14.6 |
| Peru | 0.5 | 0.2 | 19.1 |
| Costa Rica | 0.3 | 0.1 | 21.6 |
| Guatemala | 0.3 | 0.1 | 18.5 |
| **Asia** | | | |
| Indonesia | 0.5 | 2.4 | 32.4 |
| Malaysia | 2.3 | 4.2 | 31.2 |
| Philippines | 1.2 | 0.8 | 14.1 |
| Thailand | 1.5 | 3.8 | 34.2 |
| South Korea | 14.9 | 15.8 | 11.7 |
| Hong Kong | 17.1 | 19.8 | 19.5 |
| Singapore | 7.9 | 9.8 | 25.9 |
| Taiwan | 16.6 | 16.2 | 8.3 |

*Source*: UNCTAD 1993: 17, table 8.

Latin America, to the degree that they are exporters of manufactures and not raw materials (except for Indonesia), because they are countries without abundant natural resources.

An examination of a country's share of the total manufacturing exports of all developing countries highlights the contrast between the countries of Southeast Asia and Latin America. The Latin American countries with the greatest export-oriented industrialization have no significant role in the world market for developing-country manufactures. Singapore alone holds a market share in developing-country manufactures comparable to Brazil, Mexico and Argentina combined.

Amsden (1992–93) maintains that neither South Korea nor Taiwan developed on the basis of market-driven production costs. She argues that: 'in the sixties Japanese competition forced the Korean and Taiwanese governments to support basic industry, and from the eighties on public backing was necessary to enter high technology sectors.' The result was a process of permanent innovation and an *aggiornamento* of the industrial base. This in turn led to a modification in the manufacturing exports of Asian countries. Table 4.4 shows how Asia's industrial export growth became consolidated in the 1980s, with the four industrial countries (the former NIE) representing 61.6 per cent of all developing-country manufacturing exports. The four Dragons (now NIE), pursuing the same strategy,

TABLE 4.5 Asia: structure of manufacturing exports, 1973–90 (% of total exports)

|  | 1973 | 1980 | 1987 | 1990 |
| --- | --- | --- | --- | --- |
| All manufactures | 52.3 | 52.8 | 75.9 | 78.8 |
| Chemicals | 2.0 | 2.3 | 3.4 | 4.2 |
| Machinery and transportation equipment | 11.5 | 15.9 | 28.1 | 33.0 |
| Other manufactures | 38.8 | 34.6 | 44.4 | 41.7 |
| Textiles | 7.5 | 5.5 | 6.9 | 6.8 |
| Apparel | 11.9 | 9.4 | 11.9 | 10.0 |
| Iron and steel | 1.2 | 1.9 | 1.7 | 1.7 |
| Total raw materials | 46.7 | 44.9 | 22.3 | 20.1 |
| Total exports in US$ billions | – | – | 175.0 | 279.0 |

*Note*: Countries included in this category are Hong Kong, Singapore, Taiwan, South Korea (NIEs); Malaysia, Philippines, Indonesia and Thailand (ASEAN 4). China not included.

*Source*: UNCTAD 1993: 19, table 10.

advanced over the 1980s and by 1990 exported 11.2 per cent of all developing-country exports. Thus the countries of East Asia came to export 73.8 per cent of the total manufacturing exports from developing countries.

The countries of Latin America during that decade of economic depression lost ground in the world market for manufactures, with their share of developing-country exports falling from 15.1 to 10.8 per cent. It is notable that over the 1980s, a decade of economic restructuring, Chile ended up with a reduction in its share of developing-country manufacturing exports, from 0.4 to 0.2 per cent, a result experienced by all other countries of the region save Mexico. Latin America's loss of position can be explained by the accelerated export growth in the countries of Southeast Asia, more than by the destruction of companies or manufacturing exports, although that too was a factor in the reduction of the region's share of the world market in developing-country manufactures. Technological obsolescence and the lack of new investment, as will be seen in Chapter 5, kept the region from maintaining a competitive position, in addition to the economic depression itself.

Table 4.5 shows that Asian countries' manufacturing exports were more than 53 per cent of their total exports in 1973, growing to 78.8 per cent in 1990. However, the composition of manufacturing exports changed:

TABLE 4.6 Structure of markets of Asian countries, 1970–89 (% of total exports to each region or country)

| | North America | Western Europe | Japan | Latin America | Africa | Asian countries |
|---|---|---|---|---|---|---|
| **NIE** | | | | | | |
| 1970 | 39.5 | 20.7 | 11.9 | 1.7 | 3.0 | 23.2 |
| 1980 | 28.8 | 20.2 | 10.6 | 3.3 | 3.4 | 33.8 |
| 1989 | 36.2 | 17.9 | 13.7 | 1.3 | 1.0 | 29.9 |
| **ASEAN 4** | | | | | | |
| 1970 | 21.4 | 17.9 | 28.7 | 0.7 | 0.6 | 30.7 |
| 1980 | 19.2 | 14.6 | 34.6 | 2.4 | 0.8 | 28.3 |
| 1989 | 20.8 | 16.8 | 26.0 | 0.4 | 0.8 | 35.1 |
| **China** | | | | | | |
| 1970 | 0.8 | 21.3 | 14.5 | 4.1 | 6.1 | 53.3 |
| 1980 | 5.3 | 17.2 | 4.9 | 1.9 | 5.5 | 65.3 |
| 1989 | 6.9 | 11.7 | 5.1 | 1.2 | 3.3 | 71.8 |

Source: UNCTAD 1993. Author's chart.

machinery and transportation equipment went from 11.5 per cent of total manufacturing exports in 1973 to 33 per cent in 1990; the chemical industry went from 2 per cent in 1973 to 4.2 per cent of total exports. Other exports, including textiles, apparel and steel grew slightly from 38.8 per cent in 1973 to 41.7 per cent in 1990, but these three traditional industries have either maintained their position in the structure of total exports or declined slightly. In other words, new and dynamic electronics exports must have been included under the category 'other exports'.

The achievements of this change in Asia's exports, taken together with the processes of technological change under way affecting Latin America's exports, have led to a marked turnabout in global commerce. But the European Economic Community's trade integration strategy is also important for understanding why intra-regional trade in Europe grew from 32 per cent of its total exports to 61 per cent from 1955 to 1990. In addition, the emergence of new production linkages from decentralized plants through subcontracting, as a result of the crisis of Fordism, is the key for understanding why from 1970 to 1990 intra-regional trade increased moderately for the aggregate of the world's countries, even though, as can be appreciated in Table 4.6, the phenomenon is more notable when countries are disaggregated into the NIE (Tigers) and the ASEAN 4 (Dragons).

The markets for Asia's manufacturing exports have been transformed, and one can see that groups of exporting countries pursued different strategies. For the recently industrialized countries (NIEs or Tigers), North America was and continues to be the most important market, representing 36 per cent of their total exports in 1989, followed by Asian countries (30 per cent). For the ASEAN 4 countries (or Dragons), the market of Asian countries themselves is most important. Similarly for China, Asian countries absorb 72 per cent of its exports.

For recently industrialized Asian countries, including China, trade with Asian countries is most meaningful. Not only does Asia represent the largest market for the exports of the NIEs and the ASEAN 4, but for the important Asian countries the presence of Asian trading partners is enormously significant. This is even true for Japan, which holds the largest share of international trade in the region (see Tables 4.5, 4.6 and 4.7).

Table 4.8 compares exports from Latin America with those of Southeast Asia. The data only cover up to 1989, but they give an idea of the starting point for the foreign trade and reinsertion reforms that were undertaken more generally from the end of the 1980s in Latin America and Eastern Europe. While manufacturing represents 78 per cent of Southeast Asia's exports, it represents only 33 per cent for Latin America's. It is true that throughout the 1980s manufacturing's share of the region's total exports doubled from 15 to 33 per cent, but it remains a smaller slice and is concentrated in a few countries (Colombia, Brazil, Mexico and, to a very small degree, Chile). What is alarming is that while in 1980 Southeast Asia's exports were 30 per cent greater than Latin America's, in 1989 they were 182 per cent greater. In other words, as a bloc Southeast Asia is an international competitor that began the 1990s in a position of great advantage.

Regarding primary products, an American speciality since colonial times, Southeast Asia exported 13 per cent less than Latin America in 1980, and 8 per cent less than our region in 1989. Regarding manufactures, the gap grew from 355 to 575 per cent more than Latin America. It could be that the international crisis affected the prices of raw materials which, when added to technological changes that reduced the global demand for them, led to a depression in Latin America's traditional exports. Buitelaar points out that in the period 1980–90, the proportion of exports in goods and services compared to the value of national production increased from 14 to 20 per cent. But the evidence shows that the reforms still haven't paid off in the industrialization of exports. On the contrary, in that sector there is even less diversification than Van Dijck found.

Chile would be a good example: although Chile's exports were diversi-

TABLE 4.7 Participation of Asian countries in the market of each region or country, 1970–89, (% of total exports to each region or country)

| | North America | Western Europe | Japan | Latin America | Africa | Asian countries |
|---|---|---|---|---|---|---|
| **NIE** | | | | | | |
| 1970 | 4.2 | 0.7 | 4.3 | 0.5 | 1.5 | 2.2 |
| 1980 | 6.8 | 1.5 | 5.9 | 1.8 | 3.2 | 5.5 |
| 1989 | 12.7 | 2.5 | 14.5 | 2.2 | 3.0 | 9.2 |
| **ASEAN 4** | | | | | | |
| 1970 | 1.8 | 0.5 | 8.4 | 0.2 | 0.3 | 2.3 |
| 1980 | 3.1 | 0.7 | 13.3 | 0.9 | 0.6 | 3.1 |
| 1989 | 2.7 | 0.8 | 10.1 | 0.3 | 1.0 | 4.0 |
| **China** | | | | | | |
| 1970 | 0.0* | 0.3 | 2.2 | 0.5 | 1.3 | 2.1 |
| 1980 | 0.4 | 0.4 | 0.8 | 0.3 | 1.6 | 3.1 |
| 1989 | 0.7 | 0.5 | 1.5 | 0.6 | 2.8 | 6.1 |

*Note:** The value is 0.04%.

*Source*: UNCTAD 1993. Author's chart.

fied from copper, it was not primarily towards manufactures, rather towards simply processed natural products (fruit, salmon and seafood, and lumber) with a few new metal/mechanical products and intermediate goods. Buitelaar (1989) affirms that the region's manufacturing exports grew from $15 to $40 billion and that half of that is represented by Brazil and 25 per cent by Mexico, but compared to total exports this does not modify the argument made by Van Dijck. The return to primary products is characteristic of nearly all of the rest of Latin America. Although there may be diversification away from traditional products, primary products continue to be the principal exports. Given this reality, Agosin and Ffrench Davis (1994) claim that for trade reform to be successful the aggregate value of new companies must be greater than that of the ones that close their doors, compensating with new exports the effect of the elimination of import substitution.

What is worrisome in this scenario of change in the patterns of international trade is that the rate of growth of OECD imports of Latin American goods (both primary and industrial) between 1986/89 and 1989/92 fell from 12.7 to 3.8 per cent, while OECD exports to the region grew dynamically from 12.2 to 14.9 per cent over the same period. In contrast, imports from Eastern Europe rose from 8.9 to 11.4 per cent and imports from the Asian Dragons displaced the Tigers in rate of growth (15.5 per cent in 1989/92 for the Dragons compared to 2.5 per cent for the Tigers in the same period).[6] It is worth noting that the growth rate of both internal and external OECD trade fell between 1986/89 and 1989/92. According to Ugarteche:

> The following elements are affecting Latin America's trade: 1) the appearance of the Asian Dragons (Indonesia, Thailand, Malaysia and Philippines); 2) the consolidation of the Asian Tigers (Hong Kong, Singapore,

TABLE 4.8 Latin American and Southeast Asian trade by product category, 1980–89 (in billions of US$)

|                              | Southeast Asia | | Latin America | |
| ---------------------------- | ----- | ----- | ----- | ----- |
|                              | 1980  | 1989  | 1980  | 1989  |
| Total primary exports        | 66.4  | 76.6  | 90.7  | 82.5  |
| Total manufacturing exports  | 72.2  | 268.3 | 15.8  | 39.7  |
| Total exports                | 138.6 | 345.0 | 106.6 | 122.2 |
| Primary exports (%)          | 48    | 22    | 85    | 67    |
| Manufacturing exports (%)    | 52    | 78    | 15    | 33    |

*Source*: UNCTAD 1992a: appendices 2–13.

Taiwan and South Korea); 3) China as an international economic actor; 4) the introduction of the countries of Eastern Europe; 5) the consolidation of economic blocs; and 6) the irrelevance of multilateral trade agreements. (Ugarteche 1994a: 172–3)

## Specialization among recently industrialized Latin American countries compared to Asian ones

Generally speaking, technological change has lowered demand for raw materials, while trade in manufactures requires higher levels of factor productivity. A study undertaken by Gurrieri on Argentina, Brazil and Mexico (Gurrieri 1994) suggests, based on Cantwell (1989), that technological capacity is a combination of the organizational and institutional knowledge, capacities and structures required for generating and managing technological change. However, says Gurrieri, since technological change is cumulative and involves specific knowledge on the part of each company, such national technological competencies do not change quickly, rather they follow stable technological trajectories. Evidently, this is an argument against Gerschenkron's 'catch-up' hypothesis, which when taken together with what Amsden (1989) says, leads one to think that the potential for rapid technological change in Latin America as a whole is rather limited.

Structural transformation has a growing influence on the evolution of comparative advantage and it is a causal factor in growth. However, he says, it should not be considered an off-shoot, an automatic result, of outward strategies for growth and stable macroeconomic policies, as the neoliberal theory holds. On the contrary, the creation of comparative advantage is a complex process in which the accumulation of physical capital interacts with the development of capacities and technology. From this arises the notion that although a structure of rational incentives can be meaningful for industrial development, the ability to respond to such incentives will depend on existing knowledge and capacity in the countries in question (Gurrieri 1994: 172–3).

Gurrieri makes a comparison between the export market shares of Asia's NIEs (Hong Kong, Singapore, South Korea and Taiwan) and Latin America's NIEs (Argentina, Brazil and Mexico), which allows for a deeper analysis of changes in the structure of trade and the importance of manufactures. He separates products into the following categories: agricultural products, fuels, other raw materials, industrial food products, traditional products, intensive raw materials products, intensive products in scale, products from speciality suppliers, products based on sciences, and others (see Table 4.9).

Taking 1970 as a starting point, the presence of the Asian countries is more or less the same as that of the Latin American countries (2.07 per cent of world trade for the four Asian countries versus 1.19 per cent for the three from Latin America). The 1990 evidence shows that the four Asian countries have achieved an increase in their share of world trade to 7.52 per cent, while the three Latin Americans barely reached 2.13 per cent of world trade. Raw materials for these Asian countries do not have much relevance in any of the categories, while for Latin America they do.

However, a close look at the data from Latin America shows a fall in the world market share for agricultural products, a sharp rise in that for fuels, primarily from Mexico, and a diversification of that for raw materials, possibly due to Latin America having bountiful natural resources and agricultural lands. The 'other raw materials' category leaps from 4.5 per cent of world trade to 9.8 per cent, while for the Asian countries under consideration, which have few natural resources, their market share grew slightly but insignificantly between 1970 and 1990.

The category 'traditional products' includes textiles, apparel and accessories, leather products, shoes, wood products, furniture, paper and printed products, ceramics, glass products, manufactured metal products (silverware, tools, etc.), real and costume jewellery, musical instruments, sports equipment, toys and games, and other miscellaneous products. In

TABLE 4.9 Participation in world exports, by product category, of certain Asian and Latin American countries, 1970–90 (%)

| | Asian countries[1] | | | Latin American countries[2] | | |
|---|---|---|---|---|---|---|
| | 1970 | 1979 | 1990 | 1970 | 1979 | 1990 |
| Total trade | 2.07 | 3.72 | 7.52 | 1.99 | 2.10 | 2.13 |
| Agricultural products | 2.58 | 3.29 | 3.53 | 5.84 | 5.21 | 5.23 |
| Fuels | 0.03 | 0.02 | 0.05 | 0.04 | 1.70 | 3.94 |
| Other raw materials | 0.71 | 0.82 | 0.90 | 4.50 | 6.38 | 9.80 |
| Food industries | 1.78 | 2.31 | 3.88 | 6.63 | 7.14 | 5.62 |
| Traditional products | 6.13 | 10.64 | 15.31 | 1.02 | 1.53 | 1.18 |
| Intensive raw materials products | 1.51 | 2.99 | 5.68 | 0.61 | 0.75 | 2.58 |
| Intensive products in scale | 0.95 | 2.95 | 6.09 | 0.60 | 1.12 | 1.84 |
| Products from specialized suppliers | 0.80 | 1.64 | 4.35 | 0.32 | 0.83 | 0.92 |
| Science-based products | 1.00 | 4.64 | 10.69 | 0.43 | 0.65 | 0.97 |
| Others | 5.13 | 5.82 | 5.55 | 10.32 | 7.59 | 0.67 |

*Source*: Guerrieri 1994: tables 1 and 3.   1. Hong Kong, Singapore, South Korea and Taiwan.   2. Argentina, Brazil and Mexico.

this low-tech category, the four Asian countries in 1970 held 6.13 per cent of the world market and by 1990 had reached 15.31 per cent of the world market in these products. The three Latin American countries went from 1.02 to 1.18 per cent. In other words, the existing technological capacity in newly industrialized Latin American countries was not utilized to manufacture these goods, while industries in those countries without natural resources made use of this sort of low technology to manufacture these products.

The category 'intensive raw materials products', which corresponds to the forward vertical integration of existing raw materials in the Latin American countries in question, shows an improvement, moving from 0.61 per cent in 1970 to 2.58 per cent in 1990. In the Asian countries, which lack raw materials, they went from 1.51 to 5.68 per cent, achieving double the market share of the Latin Americans. This is a clear indication that Latin America faces a problem of industrialization and technological paths, as well as entrepreneurial capacity.

The category 'intensive products in scale' includes products of organic and inorganic chemistry, other chemical materials and products, medical and pharmaceutical products, manufactures from rubber, iron and steel, television, media for sound and image recording and reproduction, home appliances, ships and other boats, railroad cars and equipment, highway vehicles (automobiles, trucks, motorcycles, etc.). This category implies a scale of technology somewhat more complex than the previous category, as well as large-scale production. The four Asian countries managed to multiply their world market share in these goods by a factor of six, moving from 0.95 to 6.09 per cent from 1979 to 1990. The three Latin American countries, which were somewhat behind the four Asians in 1970 with 0.60 per cent of the world market, increased their share to 2.58 per cent by 1990, but fell farther behind the Asians, whose share was double that of the Latin Americans.

The category 'products from specialized suppliers' includes the manufacture of agricultural machinery, metalworking machine tools, metalworking machinery, other machine tools for specialized industries, mining and construction machinery, machinery for textiles and leather factories, machinery for the paper and cardboard industry, other machinery and industrial equipment, electronic equipment and components, instruments for measuring, reviewing and analysis, optical products and other miscellaneous products. This category requires a much more complex technological level than the previous ones and arises from competence in the previous technological stages. In this realm, the Asian countries had an advantage over the Latin American ones in 1970, 0.80 per cent versus 0.32 per cent of the world market in these goods, which has traditionally

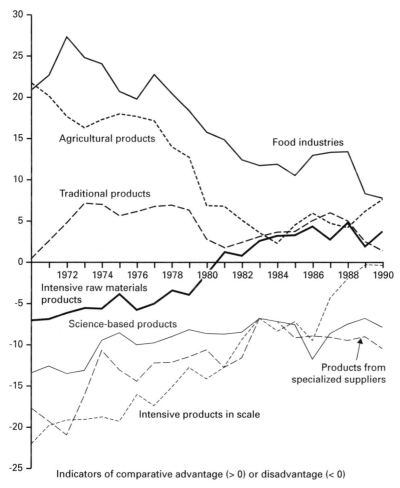

FIGURE 4.1 Pattern of trade specialization by product
(*Source*: Gurrieri 1994: 183)

been dominated by US and European industry with competition from the Japanese since the 1960s. By the year 1990, the evidence shows that the Asian countries managed to take over 4.35 per cent of the world market, while the Latin Americans increased their share to 0.92 per cent.

The category 'science- based products', the most advanced technologically, is where the Asian countries' greatest gains can be observed. This category includes organic synthetic dyes, radioactive and related materials, polymers and copolymers, antibiotics and other pharmaceutical products, nuclear reactors, machinery and other automatic data-processing equipment, telecommunications equipment, semiconductors, microelectronic circuits, electronic measuring instruments, electric machinery and other appliances, internal combustion engines, aeroplanes and related equipment, medical instruments, optical instruments and photographic equipment. The Asian countries moved from 1 per cent of the market in 1970 to 10.69 per cent of the world market in 1990, while the Latin Americans, who were behind the Asians with a 0.43 per cent market share, barely reached 0.97 per cent of the world market.

The four Asian countries examined developed industries with a higher technological content, while the Latin American countries got stuck in activities with a lower technological content. This indicates a lack of technological and industrial development policies and a lack of entrepreneurial capacity, compared to Asia. There has been some improvement in large-scale industries in Latin America, as well as in intensive raw materials industries, but although these have grown they did not keep pace with Asian development. This has less to do with liberalization policies and more to do with industrialization policies and the capacity to internalize acquired knowledge for manufacturing in the country itself.

Gurrieri lays out a process of product specialization begun in the three Latin American countries in the 1970s, and shows how it got stuck in the 1980s due to the so-called debt crisis (see Figure 4.1), when investment rates were depressed. He proposes that external adjustment for the three Latin American countries in question ought to be based on a complex and mixed strategy of reducing trade barriers (tariffs and 'grey zone') and selective interventionist policies to provide support for the required industrial reorientation and the necessary productive transformation, with the objective of maximizing technological linkages among companies and industries. Such policies could not be homogenous for all three countries, and much less so for the twenty-one countries of Latin America; rather, they should be attuned to the existing needs of each, depending on its degree of international competitiveness and product specialization.

The specific technological capacities and trade patterns of each country are the keys for selecting among available policy options. In this way the diversity of Latin America becomes relevant, and the region is not treated with the sort of generalization that includes everything and explains nothing (Gurrieri 1994: 200).

### In sum

Technological change has introduced new forms of international competition based on productivity differentials. This is what is referred to as international competitiveness within a new concept of production, defined by higher quality, just-in-time delivery and client-specific products, which maintains economies of scale and the environment required to achieve them. It is said that open-economy policies can help companies utilize these technologies to gain access to international markets, but this is not evident, particularly if competition is based on productivity.

Globalization is a word that includes a number of concepts: from widespread access to information to the integration of markets for goods, services, capital and labour. It is said that the globalization of the economy will allow for development. Under globalization, competition is based on productivity. The question is what will happen to those economies that have lower productivity relative to others. Theorists suggest that globalization will shelter only the richest and most productive economies, creating the impression that the gap between the North and the South is widening, and a gap is emerging between the North within the North and the South within the North, as well as between the North within the South and the South within the South. The economies that become integrated will be those of the Norths of countries, that is, the sectors of greatest productivity within national economies, able to compete with the same sectors of other economies. Excluded will be those of lower productivity, opening a complex social gap.

From the point of view of multilateralism, another interpretation of globalization is the growing tendency to form regional trading blocs that establish their own rules of the game rather than adopting the generalized rules of the Uruguay Round. The unilateral openings undertaken by Latin American countries have made the process of negotiation for integration into GATT a simple one, while among developed countries the negotiations are complex and slow and frequently contradictory. The question is whether regional blocs will turn out to be building blocks or stumbling blocks.

The evidence shows a growing tendency among advanced countries to use non-tariff trade barriers and to apply them to the light industries by which developing countries are attempting to achieve a new export take-off. The hypothesis would be that protectionism arises due to the number of competitors and the influence that has on reducing the market share for producers in developed countries, not due to the technological content of the goods produced.

Opening up and integrating are not synonyms in the globalized economy. There are regions, such as the European Union, that practise protectionism along with integration, and the countries of East Asia do the same. In Latin America, Colombia and Brazil would be two examples of protectionist integration. The process of globalization is leading to a dynamic process of trade in manufactures among developing countries, which possibly arises from the post-Fordist structure of production, but also from the need to find alternative markets in light of the existing barriers in the ACCs. A growing tendency towards intra-regional trade can be observed in Asia.

The development of Asia in this context has been achieved, given the lack of natural resources, by market integration and the efficient processing of natural resources brought from other regions of the world. On the contrary, Latin America, with its abundance of natural resources, has always been able to overcome problems in the balance of payments by increasing the volume of raw materials exports, as occurred during the 1980s. The obvious question is: What happens when the demand for raw materials falls because these are being replaced by new technologies?

Latin America's share of the world market in manufactures is embryonic. Brazil, Mexico and Argentina, taken together, hold a market share equivalent to that of Singapore, a city-state. It is said that free-market policies will move a country towards export-led development, which necessarily must be based on manufactures, since Latin America's raw materials are by and large being replaced by manufactured goods, but this is not evident. The tendency of the market is towards a renewed focus on raw materials in the region, as has been observed, along with the modernization of certain manufacturing industries in defence of company survival.

Manufacturing development in Southeast Asia was achieved with state intervention and without 'correct pricing'. It is not evident that Latin America can obtain the same results as Southeast Asia with 'correct pricing' and without state intervention. Although Latin America doubled its share of manufacturing exports from the beginning of the 1980s to the end of that decade, the absolute amount is barely 15 per cent greater and in real 1980 dollars it is worth less. In other words, the share has grown as an effect of the depression in raw materials prices. There is evidence of a notorious collapse in the comparative advantage of raw materials and of improvements in products based on sciences, scales and other specialized products.

## Notes

1. See also the response in *Foreign Affairs* by Clyde Prestowitz et al. (1994: 186–97) and Krugman's reply in the same issue (Krugman 1994c: 198–203).

2. Javier Iguíñiz (1995) undertakes an exercise using Ricardo's example of Portuguese wine and English cloth and following Krugman's reasoning.

3. Considering the outcome of Mexico's balance of payments crisis and 50

per cent currency devaluation in 1994, it would be interesting to know Drucker's new reading of this reality.

4. In the northern summer of 1995, two discussions between Japan and the United States on luxury cars and couriers just demonstrated this.

5. At the time of writing, MERCOSUR and the Andean Community are negotiating to form a single regional bloc in opposition to the United States due to the protectionism implicit in the set-up.

6. One detailed analysis of the patterns of recent OECD trade appears in Oscar Ugarteche (1994a: 164–79).

# 5. The Export-led Growth Model: The Theory, the Debate, the Evidence

Everything flows from an antecedent, everything is the antecedent of a future consequence ... or what's more likely, I know, it was Rosaura's fault.

(Marco Denevi, 'Rosaura a las Diez')

## The theory

In recent years import-substitution industrialization (ISI) policies have been modified in the light of the argument that the crisis was due to inefficiencies caused by protectionist barriers and excessive regulation. ISI policies rested on three pillars: protectionism, state intervention and an influx of foreign capital. Over the past decade, it has been argued that the governments of developing countries (DCs) are large and inefficient and that is what has made them poor. Protection made industry inefficient and, when capital flows reversed, the ISI model was left evidently inoperative. The DCs' ties to the world economy have been weak due to 'inward-focused' development policies premised on an erroneous belief in dependency (Dutt 1992). Excessive state regulation is an obstacle to the formation of new companies, acting as a tax on innovation and generating inefficiencies in distribution (De Soto 1986). The argument is that newly industrialized countries (NICs) that have abandoned 'inward-focused' development policies in favour of more market-oriented export policies have had success in achieving rapid growth – an example that could be followed by other countries to achieve the same results (Dutt 1992: 1159). Eliminating state intervention and protection has allowed those economies to rebound.

The empirical evidence shows that between 1965 and 1988, the OECD countries increased their GDP per capita at an average rate of 2.3 per cent, the NICs of Southeast Asia at 6.8 per cent, Sub-Saharan Africa at 0.2 per cent, South Asia at 1.8 per cent, and Latin America at 1.9 per cent. This argument and the evidence come in sharp contrast to the situation in the 1930s, when the same symptoms – a fall in export income, rising current accounts deficits due to a rise in international interest rates, problems with paying the debt and a lack of international credit – led countries to suspend debt payments as of 1931 and move from export-led growth to import substitution industrialization (Maddison 1985: part 1). In the 1980s, on the contrary, debt payments continued and economic policy changed towards greater openness and once again to export-led growth. The change was achieved through the application of structural reforms and it is argued that these have laid the basis for sustained economic growth.

'Adjustment programmes, which in general receive support from the International Monetary Fund (IMF) and the World Bank, seek to correct internal and external imbalances, and, to a greater or lesser degree, offer incentives and strengthen institutions' (World Bank 1990b: 133). If indeed the policies are uniform, the ways in which reforms have been implemented have varied and the policy mix is not the same across the region. The importance of deregulation is greater in some countries, of privatization in others, the change in the role of the state differs and the handling of labour policy is equally varied. However, generally speaking, the neoliberal paradigm has been embraced throughout Latin America (Hojman 1994). Hunt offers a succinct summary of the neoliberal paradigm:

1. It is desirable to maximize aggregate economic welfare.
2. Welfare maximization can only be achieved when the market value of goods and services produced at any given point in time is maximized.
3. Neo-classical theory is designed to show how these ends can be achieved through the operation of the free market.
4. In order to demonstrate this, it is necessary to make a number of explicit assumptions about the nature of the economic system. These assumptions include:
   (a) profit maximization by firms, which face cost structures characterized by the U-shaped cost curve;
   (b) utility maximization by consumers, who experience diminishing marginal utility in the consumption of various items;
   (c) an infinite range of production technologies (all of which experience diminishing returns to scale at some point);
   (d) perfectly competitive markets.

Given these suppositions, neo-classical theorists have generated the following propositions:

1. The price for goods and services which are generated by the unimpeded operation of the market (i.e. the forces of supply and demand) are

normally the correct prices[1] for the purposes of guiding resource allocation by producers and consumers.[2] This is because free-market equilibrium prices will simultaneously reflect marginal consumer preferences and marginal supply costs. However, where a particular form of resource use generates external costs or benefits, prices should be adjusted accordingly. Generation of external benefits should be rewarded and vice versa.

2. Factor prices should also be determined through the operation of the free market. In this way producers will be faced with correct information concerning the relative opportunity costs of different factors of production.

3. Given consumer preferences, firms' production costs, the total value of monetary demand and free markets are all given, there will be one set of equilibrium prices for all factors of production, intermediate products and final goods and services, in which all markets are cleared and the value of output will be maximized.

4. Given infinite technical choice and factor price flexibility, the maximum value of output, and hence, maximum social welfare, will always be achieved by the full employment of all factors of production. There will be no involuntary unemployment.

5. Relative factor prices determine factor income shares.

6. In the absence of government intervention, factor prices combined with the distribution of asset ownership determine interpersonal income distribution. This in turn determines, together with consumer tastes, the pattern of demand for final goods and services and hence, indirectly, the pattern of demand for factors of production.

7. The following propositions concerning growth can also be derived from the paradigm:

   (a) sustained growth of output with full employment is possible provided there is a positive propensity to save and to invest in excess of the amounts needed for capital maintenance;

   (b) output per worker will grow if the rate of savings and investment exceeds that which is required both for capital replacement and to equip any increase in the work-force;

   (c) investment will occur at a rate determined by the interaction of the social rate of time preference, which will determine the supply of savings for any given rate of interest, and the marginal productivity of capital, which will determine the amount of investment that producers are prepared to undertake at that rate of interest.

8. The main corollary of neo-classical theory is that, in any market, price distortion will lead to a distorted pattern of resource allocation with a consequent reduction in efficiency and welfare.

9. Hence, the key policy recommendation of the neo-classical paradigm is to remove all market distortions.[3] (Hunt 1989: 32–3)

Latin America has bet everything on one way forward: development led by exports/free market based on an internationally determined definition of correct pricing. The big question is, to paraphrase Pérez, whether these policies will help us cross the ocean, will be useful only for derailing the previous model, or will place the DCs on new rails but on the same side of the ocean and perhaps impede passing to the other side.

The reforms were not implemented as a result of government initiative; rather, they were conditionalities imposed by multilateral lending institutions to access assistance offered by the governments of the Paris Club and the private creditors of the London Club for restructuring existing debt. The reforms also came as conditions for financial assistance in the wake of the external crisis that appeared in the 1980s, whose causes, as we have seen, were endogenous and linked to the international recession and to the productivity crisis in the ACCs and the technological changes required to overcome it. In many cases, the conditionalities imposed by some institutions (the World Bank, for example) are subject to those imposed by the International Monetary Fund. To renegotiate an agreement with the Paris Club, a contingency agreement with the IMF is also required. What's more, bilateral aid packages have required structural adjustment agreements with the World Bank.

This is known as cross-conditionality (Griffiths-Jones 1988a) and it made debt negotiations rather complicated. To begin negotiating with the IMF, a country's negotiations with the World Bank had to have been concluded. And only after both of these negotiations were finished could a country begin to deal with the rest (Lizano and Charpentier 1986). Such negotiations not only touched on credit conditions, but also on the handling of development policy. In other words, the process of economic reform was forced upon Latin America at the beginning, but soon it began winning converts and political sympathy. The reforms proved themselves capable of bringing inflation under control, while openness and privatization gave new air to societies stifled by over a decade of economic crisis, shrinking national income, falling wages and the loss of hope in the future. The reforms were presented as the alternative to the economic depression that affected nearly all of Latin America. It ought to be kept in mind that the depression of the 1980s affected not only Latin America, but virtually every region of the world in various ways, including the ACCs.

Hojman (1994) described the change in accepted wisdom on economics in Latin America as moving from obligatory reforms to popular economic reforms. It had been argued (Killick 1984) that the unpopularity of the economic reforms would keep democratic governments from implementing them. However, it turned out that democratic governments were the ones that implemented them and won popular support for doing so, even though some were delegated democracies, such as those run by Fujimori, Menem or Durán Ballén. The reform process required follow-through, and that led to autocratic political styles, governments by decree, a direct call to 'the people', bypassing the political parties, and authoritarian presidential behaviour (Roxborough 1992: 425–6).[4]

The application of structural adjustment policies in Latin America, some analysts maintained, ought to resolve a double dilemma, addressing both the external and the internal causes of the crisis. External causes included high interest rates and the fall of raw materials prices, which adversely affect the balance of payments; chief among internal causes were inadequate exchange-rate policies that led to the overvaluation of currencies at the end of the 1970s and beginning of the 1980s, generating massive current accounts deficits and capital flight (Edwards 1991: 131–2). To avoid conceptual confusion, a distinction must be made between IMF stabilization programmes and World Bank structural adjustment programmes. The former are primarily oriented towards controlling inflation by seeking balance between internal and external flows in the short term, while the latter modify a country's domestic rules of the economic and political game (Meller 1991).

By the middle of the 1990s, the accepted wisdom was unequivocal: only neoliberal policies could get Latin America moving after a decade or more of crisis. The last country to begin reforms of this sort was Brazil, following the election of F. H. Cardoso in 1995. Paradoxically, the reforms in Brazil began following the Mexican crisis of December 1994, which cast doubt on the viability of the neoliberal model after the country rang up an unsustainable deficit in the current account financed by short-term resources, thus upsetting the balance of payments. Perhaps that explains why the Brazilian opening was toned down. In any case, ever since the birth of the republics, the economic history of Latin America has swung like a pendulum between the extremes of liberalism and protectionism, and today's policies are no exception. But in the past, more open economies meant more democracy, whereas today the relationship is the reverse: openness brings authoritarianism (Díaz Alejandro 1983).

This chapter sums up the reasoning for and against the free market promoted by the structural adjustment programmes of the World Bank, and examines what they have wrought in Latin America since implementation. The time frame is short for understanding whether we have begun to make the necessary voyage across the ocean noted in Chapter 2, or if we are still suffering the effects of the derailing of the previous model discussed in Chapter 3. But we hope to shed some light on the way the model really works, particularly regarding the external sector.

## The debate

**The arguments for export-led growth/free market: the World Bank doctrine** The argument in essence is that, by cutting back the state and implementing neoliberal policies, corruption can be avoided and resources can be allocated more efficiently in a changing world, leading to growth in exports and modernization of economic activity long suffocated by protectionist policies and a bloated state. The social consequences of such measures in the short term are the cost of a long-range structural adjustment. The opening rests on the fundamental supposition that the appropriate division of labour and the full use of a country's comparative advantages are best obtained by the free play of the market (World Bank 1987: 2–3).[5]

National economies have an inter-relation with the international economy which in some way affects their internal growth, but in the final analysis they grow by their own efforts. There continue to be external imbalances among industrialized countries and the problem of developing countries' debt will continue. Real interest rates remain high and the prices of raw materials continue to fall, causing greater problems for developing countries. New resources to support economic adjustment efforts are scarce. The long-term objectives of structural adjustment are to improve efficiency, achieve equity – understood as an improvement in income distribution – and increase the stock of physical and human capital (World Bank 1987: 4).

Three areas must be stressed to achieve long-term change:

1. *Trade Reform.* Countries ought to adopt externally oriented trade strategies. This implies removing anti-export biases, replacing quantitative restrictions by tariffs, and adopting more realistic exchange rates.
2. *Macroeconomic Policy.* Many governments need to reduce their fiscal deficits and offer incentives to enhance savings. The objective is to ensure positive real interest rates, competitive exchange rates and low inflation, not only to improve the internal supply of financial resources, but also to support trade reforms.
3. *Competitive National Environment.* Beyond trade reforms and macroeconomic policy, governments need to improve the response on the supply side of the economy, particularly by removing price controls, easing investment regulations and reforming labour laws. These policies will complement trade reforms and promote the adoption of technologies that minimize costs. But reforms alone will not re-establish growth. That requires increased capital flows as well (World Bank 1987: 4–5).

The old model for industrialization envisioned set stages. First light industries (textiles), then heavy industries (steel and industries based on steel and metals), then a leap to electronics and micro-electronics. But today countries do not have to follow that same path. Since new technologies are so portable, an engineering industry can be created without producing steel or metals, and the leap to micro-electronics can be taken without building giant industrial complexes. All countries protected their industries at one point or another, but those that achieved early industrialization (Europe and the United States) benefited from periods of free trade. In any case, their levels of protection were much lower than those that exist today in developing countries. States have taken on the function of assisting in decisions regarding technology selection and the provision of physical infrastructure (transport and communications). Another role for the state has been the provision of stable and flexible economic and social institutions, including everything from the rules of the game to non-inflationary macroeconomic policies (World Bank 1987: 7). The rules of the game define the use, ownership and conditions of physical, financial and intellectual assets.

In many developing countries the rules are not clear, they are interpreted in unforeseeable ways and are administered by a weighty bureaucracy. This raises the cost of doing business and acts as a disincentive to transactions that are essential for industrial specialization. Governments ought to continue playing a role in national education, a major bottleneck due to a lack of physical assets; providing transport, communications and energy infrastructure when the private sector is not prepared to do so (above all in communications and energy); providing a few regulations and standards, because more might be ineffective or counterproductive; support research and development in selected cases; and reform public enterprises, i.e. privatization (World Bank 1987: 7).

Based on these assumptions and debates regarding the efficiency of the state and the role of the market in solving Latin America's so-called debt crisis, a series of policies was recommended, known as the Washington Consensus (Meller 1992–93: 22; Williamson 1990). They emphasize the following:

1. Public sector reform including:

    a. Reduction of the fiscal deficit by between 1 and 2 per cent of GDP by cutting public spending. Also tax reform to broaden the tax base with low marginal rates.

    b. Privatization of public enterprises because the private sector is much more efficient than the public sector as a producer. Besides, cutting the number of public enterprises reduces transfers from the central government in the form of subsidies, which has a positive effect on public spending.

2. Liberalization and deregulation reforms to encourage competition in the domestic market. Among these are:

   a. Liberalization of the domestic capital market, which implies floating interest rates. Interest rates ought to be moderately positive.
   b. Trade liberalization, by replacing quantitative restrictions with low-level tariffs.
   c. Labour market flexibilization to encourage the required technological change by introducing mechanisms that allow companies to get out of one line of work and enter others.
   d. Positive treatment for foreign capital to promote the entrance of new capital, technology and know-how.

3. An elevated and stable real exchange rate to increase international competitiveness and promote exports.[6]

**Critiques of the export growth/free-market model** Theoretical critiques of the neoliberal model (Hunt 1989: 320–7) have been made by Arthur Lewis, Singer, Prebisch, Nurske, Myrdal and Emmanuel from various viewpoints ever since the 1950s. The central critique is that the model's suppositions do not reflect real world conditions. There are problems with income due to the elasticity of the demand for primary and manufactured goods in the ACCs (Singer, Nurske and Prebisch in Hunt 1989). The model fails to contemplate the implications of union strength in collective bargaining, or the capacity of advanced countries to set oligopolistic prices and thus retain improvements in productivity rather than transfer them to international commerce in the form of lower prices for manufactured goods (Prebisch and Emmanuel in Hunt 1989). And it ignores the incapacity of developing countries to retain the value of improvements in productivity in primary production, given the depressive effect on wages of the excess supply of labour (Lewis and Emmanuel in Hunt 1989). Hechsher-Ohlin's version of the theory of comparative advantage is critiqued for its presumption that all goods are technologically specific, which is not the case for raw materials or for simple manufactures. That undermines Hechsher-Ohlin's version because other technologies could render economies that lack their own raw materials more competitive, while the initial theory holds that having raw materials is a prerequisite for trade specialization (Hunt 1989: 320).

The strategy of 'outside-oriented' growth, which rests on the principle of comparative advantage, has been critiqued on an empirical basis for various reasons:

1. If all developing countries promoted the expansion of their manufactures, they would face a new wave of protectionism from the ACCs (Streeten 1982 in Hunt 1989: 321).

2. Countries outside Europe that have industrialized did *not* follow the path set by market-determined 'correct' factor pricing, the abandonment of public subsidies, and leaving interest, savings and investment rates to the whims of the market. In all countries that achieved industrialization, the state played a central role (Penrose 1992; Wade 1990; Amsden 1992–93).

3. There is no agreement regarding the contribution of liberalization policies to the success of East Asia, since it was the state that promoted exports while maintaining restrictions on imports (Sachs 1987 in Edwards and Larrain 1989).

4. Amsden suggests that Gerschenkron's belief that backwards countries should leap to the forefront of world technology in the most dynamic sectors is obsolete today since international competitiveness no longer depends only on product and process innovation and wages, but also on organizational structure (Amsden 1992–93).

5. The theory of comparative advantage presumes that productivity within a given industry varies from country to country, but that the exchange rate can be managed to offer low-wage countries advantages in labour-intensive goods (Krugman). This in reality is limited by the effect of the cost of imported goods on the costs of exported ones, and by the social impact of devaluations and resultant inflation (Amsden 1992–93).

6. Conventional price theory presumes that in all countries all companies in a given industry operate with the same production function, which is not true (Amsden 1992–93: 161–2). Besides, in dynamic industries at the forefront of world technology used by advanced countries, international competition has forced the adoption of globalization strategies based on 'organizational capacities', raising barriers to accessing families of technology (Amsden 1992–93: 162).

7. The potential for technological leaps, such as those suggested by Gerschenkron, poses some requirements regarding externalities that do not necessarily hold for developing countries. If indeed it is true that Germany and Russia at the end of the nineteenth century were able to incorporate new British technologies without going through the previous stages Great Britain had gone through, it is also true that there was a process of social development that allowed for it and educational levels that sustained it, a state that promoted it and a bourgeoisie that desired to achieve industrialization, none of which is the least evident elsewhere. Beyond the similarities and differences in strictly economic aspects, it is worth considering the critique made in Latin America regarding the crisis

of the 1980s which pointed to the lack of a proper business class and problems with externalities such as know-how, rules of the game and the usefulness of incorporating new technologies as far as employment is concerned, portable as these may be.

The phenomenon of Southeast Asia was linked to a process of permanent innovation, alongside restrictions on the balance of payments and on the external sector, maintaining an active role for the state and an outward orientation, distinct from the inward one adopted in Latin America. The outward focus consisted of opening to competition while retaining protection for domestic industries, so that such industries could link up to the international market without allowing international prices to become determinant domestically. The process of liberalization as proposed has the inverse effect: an inward focus, where international pricing becomes determinant in the formulation of domestic prices and linkages occur from the external sector towards the domestic sector.

8. Meller (1992–93: 185) synthesizes the critiques of Helleiner (1986) and Sachs (1986b) and indicates that reforms based on internal and external liberalization, deregulation and privatization in an imperfect 'next-to-optimum' world can show neither empirical evidence of achievement[7] nor a theoretical basis.

9. Other reservations point to the World Bank's openly hostile attitude towards governments and public enterprises in developing countries, based on the principle that everything related to public administration is inefficient and corrupt and that everything related to the private sector is efficient and honest. There is little evidence of this in Latin America, where the real situation is much more complex.

10. Structural adjustment programmes clearly interfere with a country's development strategy, with its management of economic policy and with its distributive and redistributive patterns. This interference was considered unacceptable up to the end of the 1980s (Meller 1991 and Feinberg 1986). The big change is that it became desirable in the 1990s.

11. 'Integration into the world economy is, apparently in all innocence, urged in the name of "liberalization", in spite of the fact that the international economy is not particularly "liberal"' (Penrose 1992: 238). This is so because, while the international economy is left to the free play of consumer and market demand, these are manipulated by very powerful private hierarchies. I refer here to the role played by transnational capital in globalization and to the fact that it controls the lion's share of trade in raw materials and in high-technology industrial goods in international markets. Penrose (1992) as well as Amsden (1992–93) maintain that none of the non-European countries that have managed to industrialize has done so on the basis of 'correct pricing' set by the free play of market

forces, without public subsidies, where rates of interest, savings and investment were determined by the free play of the market, and where economies were allowed to import freely or accept foreign investment with no state supports or restrictions. Penrose wonders, '[W]here did the government not play, in collaboration with local business and other elites, a very powerful role?' (Penrose 1992: 239).

The liberal nature of contemporary capitalism, says Penrose, is characterized by multinational companies which control a large share of the world market and which have specific nationalities and fly specific flags. Multinational companies have their hands in a growing majority of industrial and intermediate exports, in particular in industries such as high-technology, petrochemical and other chemicals, electronics, communications, pharmaceuticals, engineering, aviation and weapons, and so on. They control most service industries, such as banking, mass tourism, hotels and related products, just as they control the processing of agricultural goods. They are horizontally and vertically integrated, both functionally and geographically across national borders, and they base their operations on research and development backed by the immense real and financial resources at their disposal. These companies are the dynamic force of modern capitalism. In this world, trade is defined in large measure by pricing determined internally by the multinationals, and such prices are not, properly speaking, the result of the free play of the market. The entrance of new independent producers is complicated, given the economies of reach and of scale and the preferential access to finance that the multinationals enjoy. Japan, a new arrival to this modern industrial world, is not convinced by liberalism. It does not accept within its own borders the proposals put forward to other less-developed economies.

12. At the same time, while there is a lot of talk about liberalization and the free movement of the factors of production, no one mentions the movement of labour from south to north which results from the economic depression in the South and which the North seeks to block. If labour can not migrate to where there are jobs, perhaps investment could migrate to where there is cheap labour. In this way, some protection ought to be offered foreign investment so that jobs are created in developing economies. If direct foreign investment can not be attracted, then liberalization could well be counterproductive.[8] The cost is a loss of state autonomy.

13. Critiques from the viewpoint of dependency theory and self-centred development reaffirm that the development of Southeast Asia was not achieved by means of free-market policies, without a state and with export-led development. On the contrary, import substitution policies laid the basis for later achievements. The question is what would happen with markets and raw materials if all the countries of the world applied the

same external policy (Dutt 1992). Dutt presents a three-region model: North, NICs and South, to examine growth in the South as a result of the strategies employed in the NICs. The conclusion this model arrives at is that the NICs increased the gap between the ACCs and the DCs, excluding the NICs which were no longer developing countries. The more the gap widens, the more difficult the catch-up process will be. This does not mean that new NICs could not emerge in the South, but they will do so only if they can attract a portion of world spending away from the rest of the countries of the South, thus tending to make the gap between the rest of the South and the North even wider. A corollary, says Dutt, is that the longer it takes the countries of the South to develop, the more likely it is that NICs will become northern countries, producing investment goods and tending to produce an ever greater quantity of consumer goods to the detriment of the rest of the economies of the South. He concludes that attempts to raise investment rates, hold down wages or improve technology will be neutralized by deterioration in the terms of trade. Individual export success is possible, but it will come at the cost of other developing countries (the prisoner's paradox).

The conclusion is that for the countries of the South to advance by means of export-promotion policies, technological change and increasing the rate of savings – and thus to achieve a sustained and broad-based development – they will have to modify their relations with global trade and their dependent status therein. This model demonstrates the pattern of dependency: northern countries produce investment goods and growth in the North is determined by northern parameters, while growth in every other region depends on internal and external factors. Dutt calls the production of investment goods in the South a 'long-term change', and he suggests that it could best be achieved by protecting industries both in the NICs and in the North, and by promoting careful competition among producers in the South (Dutt 1992: 1168–9).

14. Other critiques of export-led growth and the free market from the viewpoint of dependency theory are made by Harry Magdoff (1992), who argues that 50 per cent of world trade is managed trade and that non-tariff (grey zone) barriers are still on the rise. In the second place, the broadening of direct investments, particularly by Japan and Germany, has transformed the structure of international property from being mostly controlled by US multinational interests, to being controlled by multi-nationals from other countries, above all in developed countries.[9] In addition, direct foreign investment (DFI) is increasingly being made within the ACCs (see Table 5.1).

The internationalization of finance capital is a feature of modern globalization. Between $2.5 and $3 trillion worth of goods and services are traded each year, while the market for Eurodollars exchanges $75 trillion annually, twenty-five times the total for world commerce, within an unstable world monetary system that points not towards a new integrated and ordered world, but rather towards chaos. At the same time, southern countries' share of manufacturing exports compared to the rest of the world, excluding the countries of Southeast Asia, fell by 30 per cent between 1966 and 1986. Meanwhile, trade competition between ACCs is tending towards the formation of blocs and away from multilateral trade.

Magdoff concludes that when the ACC economies lose dynamism they seek foreign markets to help themselves internally, but the inverse does not occur. This external search produces economic and political tensions among industrialized nations. Finally, he says, today's centrifugal tendencies are an echo of the past, of the period between the great crisis of the end of the nineteenth century and the beginning of the First World War, and the period between the Depression of the 1930s and the Second World War. While the lessons of the past may not hold today, the political and economic processes that gave rise to current trends did grow out of a similar situation (Magdoff 1992).

15. A different sort of critique can be made from the viewpoint of equity and the broadening of markets. From the neoclassical point of view, poverty is determined by the economic assets of people. In this way, factor remuneration will be the result of the allocation of assets in the economy. In economies where wealth is concentrated, this will result in a dynamic of greater income concentration, if income distribution policies are not in place. Income distribution, according to Fajnzylber (1986; 1990), is important because it allows for the broadening of the internal market and therefore a better competitive position for manufactures. The empirical evidence demonstrates that countries that have experienced rapid development, in both Southeast Asia and Southern and Central Europe, achieved it on the basis of more equitable income distribution, which

TABLE 5.1 Structure of accumulated foreign investment in developed and developing countries, 1967–89 (%)

|                      | 1967  | 1973  | 1980  | 1989  |
|----------------------|-------|-------|-------|-------|
| Developed countries  | 69.4  | 73.9  | 79.0  | 80.8  |
| Developing countries | 30.6  | 26.1  | 22.0  | 19.2  |
| Total                | 100.0 | 100.0 | 100.0 | 100.0 |

Source: Magdoff 1992: 6.

allowed for higher rates of savings, a better pattern of demand, greater innovation and therefore more growth, even though the causal relationship has not been definitively established. Adelman and Morris (1973) suggest, as well, that social equity should be considered fundamental for reasons related to justice and democracy, subjects that fall outside neoclassical theory. Adelman (1984) considers that, during international recessions, it is internal demand that will stimulate growth, and internal demand is related to the distribution of land and income. In other words, it is not only a question of justice, rather of economic dynamics in contrast to export-led growth during periods of international recession.

16. From a political standpoint, critiques of the neoliberal model include:

a. the model can be undermined by resistance from the political bureaucracy to the appropriation of power by the presidency;
b. the concentration of income and consumption can lead to explosions of social unrest (Chiapas in 1993, Córdoba in 1994 and Bolivia in 1995);
c. the appearance of radical populist or socialist political parties can pose radical alternatives;
d. the model can erode corporative mechanisms for solving problems; and
e. the model can worsen labour conflicts given the model's inherent tendency to concentrate income and consumption (Roxborough 1992: 427).

In other words, the successful functioning of the economic apparatus does not mean that the political apparatus or the systems for distributing economic benefits in society will experience similar success, and this might eventually undermine the functioning of the model itself. The model requires political regimes characterized by the concentration of political power in the presidency and Bonapartism, which in Latin America can be counterproductive. The model's direct beneficiaries are sectors who possess significant assets and the middle classes, while it works to the detriment of the rest of society.

17. The neoliberal model bets on the long term. The reforms must not be reversed if they are to result in a return on capital invested in real production. But that long term is politically questionable (Roxborough 1992) due to the economic restrictions implied for society as a whole, and in particular for those sectors of the popluation that do not possess significant assets and who are wage-earners.

## Latin America: The long-term evidence

It is worth reviewing the evidence of Latin America's crisis before going on to examine the effects of the application of the model and the current meaning of the reforms under way. First of all, however, it must be emphasized that the purpose of the reforms ought to be 'to cross the ocean': the incorporation of new technologies into the productive apparatus of developing countries and the modernization of their export sectors, replacing raw materials for which there is a shrinking demand with products for which demand is on the rise. It is certainly true that the policies and institutions which existed in Latin America up to the 1980s followed a technological model based on cheap energy. The policies of direct state intervention in production and price definition, and of import substitution, had a positive effect on GDP growth from the 1950s onwards. Average GDP growth in Latin America was 5.35 per cent and per capita GDP grew at a rate of 2 per cent; national income quadrupled and per capita income grew by 77 per cent between 1950 and 1980. In the decade from 1970 to 1980, exports rose at an average annual rate of 11.9 per cent in 1980 dollars, and per capita GDP at 3.1 per cent.

One result of this inward-oriented industrialization model was a deficit in the current accounts of the balance of payments that averaged annually at 26 per cent of the value of exported goods. This was financed by and large by long-term loans, raising the ratio of foreign debt to exports from 88 per cent between 1970 and 1975 to 218 per cent between 1975 and 1980. Edwards maintains that the problem was an exchange-rate policy

TABLE 5.2 Latin America: some aggregate macroeconomic indicators, 1970–94 (annual averages for the period)

|         | GDP variance per capita (%) | Inflation (%) | Exports (billions of 1980 US$) | GCF/GDP (%) | Current accounts deficit/exports of goods (%) |
|---------|------|------|------|------|------|
| 1970–75 | 3.5  | 30.1 | 41.8 | 20.8 | 24 |
| 1975–80 | 2.6  | 51.4 | 67.1 | 22.5 | 28 |
| 1980–85 | -0.6 | 131.4 | 76.7 | 19.5 | 23 |
| 1985–90 | -0.1 | 621.6 | 68.2 | 16.8 | 10 |
| 1990–94 | 0.9  | 632.7* | 76.9 | 16.8 | 23 |

*Note*: * See Table 5.4 for disaggregation by selected countries. Brazil distorts the figure.

*Source*: Author's chart from ECLAC data.

that caused national currencies to be overvalued, stunting exports and cheapening imports.[10] The ratio of internal savings to GNP was greater than 22 per cent and that of investment to GNP greater than 2 per cent between 1973 and 1980.[11]

As of 1981, when external problems worsened, export growth was halted by the fall in raw materials prices (see Table 5.2), as was the net transfer of resources by the rise in real international interest rates (see Table 5.3). This undercut the dynamism of the domestic economy by removing internal savings and transferring them overseas as debt payments. The proportions of these transfers varied, but there is evidence that they ranged from 3.4 per cent of GNP (Colombia) to 14.6 per cent of GNP (Mexico) for the period 1985–89, having grown from 2 per cent (Colombia) to 13 per cent (Bolivia) in the period 1982–84 (Meller 1992–93: 21). In both periods, the mean fell between 5 and 6 per cent of GNP. In other words, GNPs were really lower than usually considered, since these transfers ought to be subtracted from national savings to determine the real quantity of internal savings available for investment. In any case, these transfers overseas were a drag on investment, which fell from 22.5 per cent of GDP to 19.5 per cent between the final five years of the 1970s

TABLE 5.3 Foreign debt of Latin America: basic aggregate data, 1970–94 (annual averages by five-year period (%) and billions of 1980 US$)

|  | 1970–75 | 1975–80 | 1980–85 | 1985–90 | 1990–94 |
|---|---|---|---|---|---|
| Outstanding at end of period (1980 prices) | 98.7 | 205.3 | 292.5 | 277.1 | 294.2 |
| Net resource transfer (1980 prices) | 6.5 | 14.1 | -10.7 | -16.6 | 8.8 |
| Interests and utilities incurred (1980 prices) | 6.3 | 12.2 | 27.0 | 23.8 | 19.4 |
| Debt/exports of goods (%) | 88 | 218 | 354 | 429 | 368 |
| Annual increase in real debt (%) | 12.9 | 20.6 | 8.5 | -0.9 | 1.2 |
| Real prime interest rate (%) | 0.93 | 0.78 | 6.8 | 5.5 | 4.1 |
| Foreign payments (in % of GDP)* | 1.9* | 2.3* | 4.5 | 4.1 | 3.2* |
| Foreign payments/internal savings | 7.6* | 10.0* | 19.6 | 17.0 | 13.9 |

*Note*: * Figures correspond to the periods 1971–75, 1976–80 and 1990–92.
*Source*: Author's chart from ECLAC data.

and the first five years of the 1980s, and again to 16.8 per cent in the final
five years of that decade. In turn, this brought the dynamic of long-term
growth to a halt (Table 5.2). Per capita GDP fell at a rate of 0.6 per cent
in the first half of the 1980s and 0.1 per cent in the second half.

Due to problems arising from the price of raw materials and the rise
in international interest rates, imports had to be cut back and domestic
public spending curtailed to allow for debt servicing. The current accounts
deficit after debt servicing then improved, falling to 23 per cent and 10
per cent of average exports between the first and second halves of the
1980s. Per capita domestic product contracted, to the point that per capita
income in 1990 was the same as in 1978. Goods exports also shrank
between the first and the second half of the 1980s, from an average of
$76.6 billion constant dollars annually to $68.2 billion. These averages
hide the trend of real goods exports: unit prices fell 29 per cent while
volume rose 44 per cent between 1980 and 1987 (Ffrench-Davis and
Muñoz 1991: note 2). The final result was that income from total goods
exports fell 26 per cent in constant dollars, from $87.4 billion in 1980 to
$57.3 billion in 1986.

The reduction in consumption, which allowed for a corresponding
reduction in the current accounts deficit and thus for a level of savings
transferable overseas for debt servicing, was achieved through policies to
constrict demand implemented under IMF supervision. Thus, the region's
economic depression was an instrument for stabilizing the current accounts deficit. However, fiscal deficits grew for the same reason. Tax
income was depressed by the general downturn of the economy and the
fall in exports, and public spending rose due to the cost of debt servicing,
leading to record rates of inflation: from 51.4 per cent for the last five
years of the 1970s, to 131.4 per cent for the first five years of the 1980s,
and 621.6 per cent for the second five years of that decade (Table 5.2).
The effect of the economic depression was a drop in the ratio of internal
savings to GNP to below 18 per cent. The internal and external funding
gaps were financed fundamentally by holding back payments on the
foreign debt. As a result of this hold-back, and the capitalization of the
interest on it, as well as the fall in exports, the ratio of foreign debt to
goods exported rose from 354 per cent in the first half of the 1980s to
429 per cent in the second half.

In the 1980–90 period inflation rates rose substantially in the region as
a whole, and IMF stabilization policies were implemented to reduce them
and at the same time to allow for debt payments and international
negotiations. The introduction of stabilization policies was extremely
controversial. Structuralists proposed heterodox adjustments based on a
diagnosis that inflation was inertial, caused by companies raising their profit

margins to make up for falling economic activity. What they proposed was: reduce debt servicing, reactivate the internal economy, control exchange rates, maintain a differential interest rate for production and index all prices.[12] The IMF proposed an orthodox adjustment based on the diagnosis that the fiscal deficit was the only cause of inflation and difficulties in the

TABLE 5.4 Inflation and fiscal deficit for selected countries, 1982–94 (annual averages by period and years)

| Inflation | 1982–85 | 1986–90 | 1991 | 1992 | 1993 | 1994 |
|---|---|---|---|---|---|---|
| High inflation | | | | | | |
| Argentina | 492.2 | 1,382.3 | 84.0 | 17.6 | 7.7 | 3.6 |
| Bolivia | 2,743.0 | 26.4 | 14.5 | 10.5 | 9.4 | 8.9 |
| Brazil | 179.9 | 979.9 | 475.8 | 1,149.1 | 2,489.1 | 1,294.0 |
| Peru | 116.9 | 2,465.0 | 139.2 | 56.7 | 39.5 | 17.5 |
| Low inflation | | | | | | |
| Chile | 23.4 | 20.1 | 18.7 | 12.7 | 12.2 | 8.9 |
| Colombia | 20.3 | 26.3 | 26.8 | 25.2 | 22.6 | 23.0 |
| Mexico | 75.6 | 73.2 | 18.9 | 11.9 | 8.0 | 6.9 |
| Venezuela | 10.0 | 41.2 | 31.0 | 31.9 | 45.9 | 70.9 |
| Costa Rica | 30.2 | 18.9 | 25.3 | 17.0 | 9.0 | 17.4 |
| Guatemala | 11.6 | 24.6 | 10.2 | 14.2 | 11.6 | 12.5 |
| Fiscal deficit* (%) of GNP | | | | | | |
| High inflation | | | | | | |
| Argentina | | -4.6 | -1.6 | 0.4 | 1.1 | 0.1 |
| Bolivia | | -6.7 | -4.2 | -5.3 | -6.5 | -4.0 |
| Brazil | | -4.1 | 1.4 | -2.1 | 0.3 | – |
| Peru | | -3.7 | -1.5 | -1.6 | -1.4 | – |
| Low inflation | | | | | | |
| Chile | | 3.5 | 2.2 | 2.9 | 2.0 | 1.3 |
| Colombia | | -0.8 | 0.1 | -0.3 | 0.2 | – |
| Mexico | | -9.4 | -0.4 | 1.6 | 0.7 | 0.4 |
| Venezuela | | -3.3 | 0.6 | -5.8 | -3.5 | -7.0 |
| Costa Rica | | -3.3 | -3.2 | -1.9 | -1.9 | -4.6 |
| Guatemala | | -2.8 | -0.1 | -0.5 | -1.5 | -1.6 |

*Note*: * Fiscal deficit refers to the central government in all cases except: Argentina, in which case it refers to the national non-financial public sector; Brazil, Bolivia, Colombia, Chile and Venezuela, in which cases it refers to the non-financial public sector; and Mexico, in which case it refers to the consolidated public sector.

*Sources*: ECLAC 1994c: table A.5; and ECLAC 1991: table 12.

external sector were due to an overvaluation of the currency. For this they proposed: reducing public spending, raising taxes, raising interest rates and devaluation. In the end, the neoliberal thinking of the IMF held sway in stabilization efforts, but there were exceptions in Argentina (Plan Austral), Peru (Plan Inti) and Brazil (Plan Cruzado). These stabilization plans failed fairly quickly due to balance of payments limitations (Ocampo 1987; Fanelli and Frenkel 1987; Dancourt and Yong 1989; Pastor and Wise 1992).[13]

The limitations and 'success' of orthodox adjustment regarding inflation, however, had effects far beyond that goal. When public spending was cut to reduce the fiscal deficit, while at the same time an ever-greater percentage of the state budget was given over to debt servicing, and demand was restricted through policies to reduce real wages, the economy fell into a depression which spread and became a systemic crisis. Latin America's crisis was not endogenous, rather it was exogenous, caused and internalized by explicitly depressive policies implemented to control inflation.

While stabilization policies were being debated, negotiated and implemented, four rounds of negotiations were held with the banks and the Paris Club to make the problem of the debt and reducing public spending more manageable. Orthodox programmes achieved success at an immense social and political cost, yet once the economy was stabilized, the governments that had implemented them gained political support, while those governments that pursued heterodox adjustments lost popular support.

Between 1987 and 1994 both inflation and the fiscal deficit were reduced, but this did not occur homogeneously (see Table 5.4). Inflation reduction in Argentina, Bolivia and Peru (among high-inflation countries) and in Mexico (among low-inflation countries) was substantial. However, in Bolivia inflation was checked without reining in the fiscal deficit, while in the other countries the fiscal deficit was cut by 2 per cent of GNP approximately. The countries that did not undertake adjustment, such as Brazil, controlled the fiscal deficit but not inflation. The implementation of Brazil's Plan Real in July 1994 did manage to control inflation, the first successful heterodox programme. In Chile and Colombia inflation remained low and the fiscal balance either positive or nearly so, in a stable manner between 1987 and 1994.

Regarding the debt, there was a debate on the nature of the problem and possible solutions. In 1982 it was concluded that the debt problem had emerged as the result of the poor use of credit in areas that did not generate or save foreign exchange; in other words, credit for internal consumption, capital flight and activities by public enterprises that served only the internal market (Kuczynski 1988). There was a debate on whether this was a question of insolvency or bankruptcy, if the responsibility lay with the creditors (Devlin 1989; Darity and Horn 1988) or the debtors (Sachs 1989), or both (ECLAC 1988; Kisic 1987), or if the problem was the international context (Ugarteche 1986). There was discussion on the importance of the debt in society (George 1988), in the political system (Griffiths-Jones 1988a; Stallings and Kaufman 1989) and the way in which the crisis was managed (Williamson 1982; Sachs 1989; Svendsen 1987).

In the political arena there were reactions such as that of the governments of Peru, Nigeria and Cuba in 1985, who proclaimed unilateral limitations on debt payments (respectively 10, 30 and 0 per cent of exports). From the creditors' point of view, what occurred was a modification in the original terms of payment, through agreement on reducing the debt through discounted purchase (Baker Plan in 1985), a menu of options (Brady Plan in 1989) or partial cancellation and very lengthy terms for repayment (Toronto Terms for low-income countries, Houston Terms for those of medium income, for negotiations with the Paris Club). Between 1982 and 1990, there were four rounds of negotiations between the governments of Latin America and private international banks in search of a solution to the debt problem. By 1991 the Latin American crisis was considered to be over (BID 1992: Preface).

## The evidence from 1990 onwards

In the 1990s, low-level economic growth was re-established – 0.9 per cent average growth in per capita GDP – while inflation was held to the range of 3.6 per cent (Argentina) to 23 per cent (Colombia). Venezuela, with no orthodox adjustment and 70 per cent inflation, and Brazil, which undertook adjustment in July 1994 and had 1,294 per cent inflation, were the only atypical cases in the region until the Mexican crisis erupted in December 1994 (see Table 5.4). Fiscal deficits remained under 2 per cent of GNP, except for Bolivia (4 per cent), Costa Rica (4.6 per cent) and Venezuela (7 per cent), and that, along with the simultaneous change in the microeconomic rules of the game due to the implementation of Washington Consensus (WC) policies, gave rise to a new context for development. The first evaluation published in 1990 indicated few achievements for the implementation of adjustment policies during the 1980s (Williamson 1990). Successive evaluations showed more optimism, although the evidence regarding sustained growth is not overwhelming (IMF 1991–94).

Three variables are unchanged: the current accounts deficit of the balance of payments has returned to early-1980s levels (23 per cent of exports); the rate of investment has remained stagnant at 16.8 per cent of GDP, the same level as the average for the second half of the 1980s; and the ratio of debt to exports sits at the levels of the early 1980s (368 per cent, after having peaked at 429 per cent at the end of the 1980s). Overseas payments for debt servicing fell from 4.5 to 3.2 per cent of GDP between the beginning of the 1980s and the beginning of the 1990s, equivalent to an internal saving of 14 per cent.

Thus, the first evidence shows that although fiscal deficits were reduced (Table 5.4), there was inversely an increase in external deficits (Table 5.2). The balance between these two which the policies sought was not achieved. For the region as a whole, the ratio of the current accounts deficit to the export of goods and services rose from 2.7 per cent in 1990 to 32.3 per cent in 1994 (Table 5.6). The external deficit accumulated during the recovery in 1990–94, added up to $155.2 billion, which was financed through the influx of short- and long-term foreign capital (Table 5.5). However, the total resources obtained overseas added up to $270.7 billion.[14] The 45 per cent that corresponds to long-term capital can be divided into longer-term credit flows ($54.2 billion) and direct foreign investment for privatizations ($68.9 billion). The 55 per cent that corresponds to short-term assets adds up to $96.5 billion in bank credits and $51.1 billion in stock market investments.

Short-term financing of the current accounts deficit, through stock market investments and short-term credits, was obtained through capital flows attracted by interest rates and profit margins that were higher than in the ACCs. Real interest rates in Latin America are substantially higher than in the ACCs, making it more difficult and costly to re-establish the real rate of investment, while at the same time making it attractive to foreign capital. A rise in international interest rates can act as a detonator for capital to return to its source. It could then be said that half of the current accounts deficits has been financed by highly volatile assets. In other words, slight alterations in profitability in the ACCs could produce

TABLE 5.5 Foreign financial resources in Latin America, 1990–93 (billions of dollars)

|  | 1990 | 1991 | 1992 | 1993 | 1994 |
|---|---|---|---|---|---|
| Outstanding short-term debt | 78.1 | 88.4 | 93.1 | 96.8 | 96.5 |
| Net flow of long-term credits (including unsecured private sector credit lines) | 8.9 | 7.0 | 7.5 | 19.4 | 11.5 |
| Net foreign investment | 7.9 | 12.3 | 13.6 | 16.1 | 18.9 |
| Portfolio investment flows | 1.1 | 6.2 | 8.2 | 25.5 | 10.4 |

*Source*: World Bank 1994a: 204.

a massive outflow of money from the stock exchange, as well as cutbacks in short-term credits, affecting half of the financing of the current accounts deficit. At the same time, the direct foreign investment that resulted from privatizations was a one-time event, implying that perhaps current accounts deficits can not be sustained at the levels taken on during the economic recovery of the first half of the 1990s.

Privatizations have been an additional mechanism utilized for attempting to re-establish the internal rate of investment. Through the sale of public enterprises at prices that are profitable to the buyer, in the period 1991–93 foreign investment entered Latin America's economy at a rate equivalent to double that of the period 1987–89. It rose from $7.3 billion on an annual average in the earlier period to $12.479 billion in the later one (World Bank 1994a: 159). It was extraordinary that the privatization process, added to the process of liberalization, turned Latin America into the second greatest magnet for foreign capital in the world, after East Asia with its Tigers, Dragons and China. Argentina and Peru were the most important destinations for foreign capital in the region (World Bank 1994a: 161). Despite these massive flows, investment indicators remained stagnant, indicating that capital was flowing to privatizations, not real investment as yet. The potential for the real investment rate to rise as an effect of such investment is high, since it enjoys access to credits on the international market that are cheaper than in the local market and it

TABLE 5.6 Foreign debt in Latin America, 1980–94 (billions of US$ and %)

|  | 1980 | 1990 | 1991 | 1992 | 1993 | 1994 |
|---|---|---|---|---|---|---|
| Total debt contracted (in billions) | 257 | 476 | 490 | 500 | 526 | 547 |
| Outstanding with commercial banks* | 201.1 | 104.5 | 99.4 | 97.6 | 75.6 | – |
| Outstanding in bonds* | 16.7 | 77.41 | 80.4 | 83.1 | 114.7 | – |
| Exports of goods | 91.8 | 121.8 | 120.9 | 127.2 | 133.7 | 152.8 |
| Current accounts balance of the balance of payments | -28.7 | -3.6 | -18.8 | -37.1 | -46.0 | -49.7 |
| Ratio of current accounts deficit to exports (%) | -31.6 | -2.7 | -15.5 | -29.0 | -34.6 | -32.3 |
| Ratio of debt to goods and services exports | 199.6 | 264.2 | 269.1 | 258.4 | 261.3 | 247.3 |
| Ratio of interest due to exports | 19.1 | 12.7 | 13.3 | 12.0 | 11.9 | 12.0 |
| LIBOR | 13.6 | 8.3 | 6.1 | 3.9 | 3.8 | 6.0 |

*Note*: * Corresponds to 1987.

*Sources*: World Bank 1994a: 204; and ECLAC 1994c.

operates basically in the global market. This helps explain why the companies purchased were above all in the primary and telecommunications and transport sectors. It does not indicate a major change in the investment pattern in export manufacturing, at least in the two countries that received most of the foreign investment. Total foreign resources added up to $270.7 billion and the aggregate foreign deficit to $155 billion, leading to a notable increase in the supply of foreign exchange in Latin American economies. However, because of the oversupply of short-term foreign financing, the exchange rate became undervalued, producing an overvaluation of national currencies which

TABLE 5.7 Economic growth, exports and outstanding current accounts for nineteen Latin American countries, 1990–94

| Average per capita GNP (1943 US$) | Per capita GNP 1992 (US$) | Per capita GDP growth 1991–94 | Export growth 1991–94 | Out-standing current accounts 1990 | Out-standing current accounts 1994* | Real exchange rate** 1990–94 |
|---|---|---|---|---|---|---|
| **Above average** | | | | | | |
| Argentina | 6,050 | 6.05 | 5.5 | 1,093 | -10,500 | 76.3 |
| Brazil | 2,700 | 0.28 | 8.5 | -3,509 | -3,060 | 96.2 |
| Costa Rica | 7,960 | 2.48 | 12.3 | -561 | -515 | 101.9 |
| Chile | 2,730 | 4.58 | 9.1 | -744 | -645 | 65.0 |
| Mexico | 1,958 | 0.68 | 6.6 | -8,413 | -28,413 | 80.3 |
| Panama | 2,420 | 5.03 | 14.6 | 133 | -230 | 100.0 |
| Uruguay | 3,340 | 3.63 | 2.5 | 228 | -520 | 73.0 |
| Venezuela | 2,910 | 0.55 | -2.2 | 8,303 | -4,090 | 93.5 |
| Average | 3,017 | | | | | |
| **Below average** | | | | | | |
| Bolivia | 1,099 | 1.40 | 3.9 | -337 | -510 | 126.3 |
| Colombia | 1,330 | 2.10 | 6.5 | 714 | -302 | 76.3 |
| Ecuador | 1,070 | 1.33 | 7.8 | -273 | -440 | 77.3 |
| El Salvador | 1,170 | 2.48 | 9.6 | -381 | -315 | 82.8 |
| Guatemala | 980 | 1.03 | 7.8 | -235 | -510 | 84.6 |
| Honduras | 580 | 0.38 | 2.2 | -317 | -375 | 125.9 |
| Nicaragua | 340 | -3.25 | 1.8 | -507 | -855 | 103.2 |
| Paraguay | 1,380 | 0.10 | 1.1 | -44 | -740 | 94.5 |
| Peru | 950 | 2.45 | 7.5 | -1,914 | -2,895 | 84.0 |
| Average | 989 | | | | | |

*Notes*: * Estimated.    ** (1990=100)
*Source*: ECLAC 1994c.

Edwards pointed to as one of the problems of the previous model. This is a disincentive to exports and an incentive to imports, and explains why trade liberalization led to a surge in imports and why export income was slow to recover, as was reflected in growing current accounts deficits.[15]

Outstanding debt levels in constant dollars have returned to those of 1980–85; in current dollars, as can be seen in Table 5.6, these rose 15 per cent between 1990 and 1994. The ratio of debt to the export of goods and services fell due to the growth of the service economy, but the more common ratio of debt to goods exports remained at the level of the first part of the 1980s, 368 per cent (see Table 5.3).

The return of long-term credit in 1993 was due fundamentally to the operations of ADR companies[16] in New York, rather than to public debt (UNCTAD 1992b: 51). Bonds have been used to restructure the commercial bank debt. Brady bonds and others worth $114,622 million dollars were issued in 1993 (World Bank 1994a: 205) and debt to commercial banks was reduced from $201.1 billion in 1987 to $75 billion in 1994. The initiative to convert the debt into bonds and receive a reduction on the debt through the Brady Plan, according to UNCTAD (1991: 43–9) was successful in the case of Costa Rica, but not in the cases of Mexico or Venezuela. Success was determined by the capacity of the agreement to reduce debt. While in Costa Rica debt was bought at 16 per cent, in the cases of Mexico and Venezuela this occurred at higher rates. However, once credit was re-established, new forms of private financing were formalized in the bond market, even though to date only four countries in Latin America house such operations: Mexico, Venezuela, Brazil and Argentina (UNCTAD 1993: 49).

The impact of the inflow of short-term capital, plus stock market investments and privatizations, has been to reverse the net transfer of resources from the negative levels of the 1980s to positive ones in the 1990s, achieving what some called a positive external shock that has yet to alter the rate of real investment in the various economies. However, that positive shock seems to have resulted in undervalued exchange rates that are a disincentive to manufacturing exports and an incentive to the importation of finished goods.

### The evidence country by country

In analysing the data on economic growth by country (see Table 5.7), a first distinction can be made between countries with a per capita GNP above the 1992 average (US$1,943) and those with below-average per capita GNP. The median per capita income of those that are above average is $3,017, while for those below it is $989 dollars. This distinguishes the rich countries of Latin America from the poor ones. Among the rich countries are Argentina, Brazil, Mexico, Venezuela, Chile, Panama, Costa Rica and Uruguay, with Argentina the richest at $6,050 per capita GNP and Costa Rica the least rich with $1,961 per capita. Among the poor countries are those of Central America except Costa Rica, and the Andean countries except for Venezuela and Paraguay.

Then a distinction can be made regarding average annual GDP growth per capita between 1991 and 1994. Excluding the smaller island economies and Cuba, the data show a median per capita GDP growth of 1.8 per cent, with eight countries above that and nine below. What leaps out is the fact that, among the rich countries, Mexico, Brazil and Venezuela experienced little growth (0.68, 0.28 and 0.55 per cent respectively), far below the average for the period. Mexico, it should be noted, is the model of an open economy that managed to insert itself into the international economy on a new footing, that attracted the most important influx of capital in the region and whose goods exports represent more than half of all of Latin America's. Mexico's exports grew at a 6.6 per cent annual rate between 1991 and 1994, Brazil's at 8.5 per cent, while Venezuela's fell 2.2 per cent annually. The current accounts deficit in Mexico went from minus $8.4 billion in 1990 to an estimated minus $28.5 billion in 1994. In other words, liberalization in Mexico caused a massive external deficit, yet did not achieve faster economic growth.

The common denominator among the seventeen mainland Latin American countries is a weighty and growing current accounts deficit. This deficit was financed with volatile resources, causing exchange-rate undervaluations of greater than 15 per cent between 1990 and 1994 in

TABLE 5.8 Average wage index for selected countries of Latin America, 1980–94

|  | 1980 | 1990 | 1994 |
|---|---|---|---|
| Argentina | 100 | 79.4 | 85.7 |
| Brazil[a] | 100 | 130.8 | 162.7 |
| Colombia | 100 | 116.0 | 122.2 |
| Costa Rica | 100 | 86.5 | 94.7[b] |
| Chile | 100 | 104.8 | 124.6 |
| Mexico | 100 | 79.4 | 99.4 |
| Peru | 100 | 39.1 | 47.4 |
| Uruguay | 100 | 70.4 | 79.2 |

*Notes*: a. Corresponds to São Paulo.    b. Corresponds to 1993.
*Source*: ECLAC 1994c: table A6.

thirteen of the seventeen countries. Those with overvalued exchange rates were Costa Rica, Bolivia, Honduras and Nicaragua. Generally speaking, however, undervalued exchange rates are a common feature of the model, except in cases where there is no stock exchange, or where privatization processes moved slowly or have not begun; in other words, where the injection of foreign capital was not as important.

Average wages increased due to the recovery, or to the way the recovery was undertaken between 1990 and 1994, but they remain below 1980 levels except in Brazil and Colombia, countries that did not follow the policy recipe in the same manner as the rest of Latin America, and in Chile, which seems to have a more stable process of economic recovery as can be seen by its sustained growth over the 1980s (see Table 5.8). What this

TABLE 5.9  Ratio of exports to growth, 1991–94 (accumulated exports, average GDP growth)

| Median growth rate (1.8% ) of GDP per capita 1991–94 | Accumulated export growth | | | |
| --- | --- | --- | --- | --- |
| | Negative | Low 0–20% | Medium 20–40% | High over 40% |
| **(4% and 6%)** | | | | |
| Argentina | | | * | |
| Chile | | | | * |
| Panama | | | * | |
| **(1.8% and 4%)** | | | | |
| Uruguay | | * | | |
| Colombia | | | * | |
| El Salvador | | | * | |
| Peru | | * | | |
| Costa Rica | | | | * |
| **(0% and 1.8%)** | | | | |
| Brazil | | | * | |
| Mexico | | | * | |
| Venezuela | * | | | |
| Bolivia | | * | | |
| Ecuador | | | * | |
| Guatemala | | | * | |
| Honduras | | * | | |
| Paraguay | | * | | |
| **(-0%)** | | | | |
| Nicaragua | | * | | |

*Source*: ECLAC 1994c: author's table.

indicates is that wage recovery has little to do with the export dynamic, even though Brazil combined high export growth with low economic growth and a stable current accounts deficit during this period.

To get at the short-term results of the policy changes, we have undertaken an analysis of the evolution of economic growth and export development (see Table 5.9). The countries are divided into four categories: those with high per capita GDP growth (between 4 and 6 per cent annually), those with above average growth (1.8 to 4 per cent), those with below average growth (0 to 1.8 per cent) and those countries that experienced negative growth. The ranges of accumulated export growth between 1991 and 1994 are negative, low growth (0 to 20 per cent), medium growth (20 to 40 per cent) and high growth (over 40 per cent). Of the seventeen countries, eight experienced above average GDP growth, and nine below average:

1. Three countries (Argentina, Chile and Panama) experienced high per capita GDP growth (between 4 and 6 per cent annual average) and accumulated export growth between 1991 and 1994 greater than 20 per cent, one of which (Chile) achieved over 40 per cent in export growth.
2. Of the five countries that experienced medium per capita GDP growth (1.8 to 4 per cent), one (Costa Rica) had accumulated export growth of over 40 per cent during the period, two (Colombia and El Salvador) fell in the 20 to 40 per cent range, and two (Uruguay and Peru) were in the 0 to 20 per cent range.
3. Of the eight countries that are at or below the median regarding GDP growth, four (Brazil, Mexico, Ecuador and Guatemala) had accumulated export growth of between 20 and 40 per cent for the period, three (Bolivia, Honduras and Paraguay) fell into the 1 to 20 per cent range, and one (Venezuela) experienced a decline in exports.
4. One country (Nicaragua) experienced economic decline and export growth in the range of 0 to 20 per cent.

No common denominator between exports and economic growth seems to exist for the period examined. And there seems to be no common denominator between the implementation of neoliberal policies and export growth. However, there does seem to be one between growth and current accounts deficit. Apparently, the combination of an internal resource base, institutional consolidation and a diverse export base does lead to greater exports. That would be the common denominator between Brazil (which had export growth and low economic growth) and Costa Rica, Panama and El Salvador (which had export growth and economic growth). Factors that differentiate individual countries would include: peace in El Salvador leading to a return to economic normalcy, and normalization in Panama following the US invasion and the end of the US embargo that lasted from 1988 to 1990. It would be important to determine what Brazil and Costa Rica have in common, given their opposing policies and different insertions into the world market.

## In sum

Virtually every country in Latin America has applied structural adjustment policies based on the neoclassical theory of market perfection and of market distortion by the state. The way in which this change in the accepted wisdom about development occurred – from state-led to market-driven – can be directly attributed to pressure from international organizations. Initially, it was thought impossible to effect these changes in economic policy, due to the internal political situation of each country. However, when stabilization policies were implemented and inflation was brought under control, neoliberal policies to open the economy were widely embraced as the new accepted wisdom. Popular support for the governments that took this road was notable.

The evidence shows that open-economy policies have resulted in growing current accounts deficits that have been covered in part by short-term investments, stock purchases and short-term credits, and in part by long-term investments attracted mainly through privatizations. There is no evidence as yet that the real investment rate has recovered as a result of the sizeable flow of foreign capital. The long-term credits that have been extended are primarily for the private sector, as public-sector credit has not achieved a substantial recovery. Growth in exports between 1990 and 1994 has not yet achieved a recovery for the export sector, due to reasons related generally to the re-primarization of exports and their lack of industrialization, with Brazil, Mexico and Colombia being the exceptions.

Critiques of the neoclassical model implemented in the region have been varied, but in essence they address the question of the state. As long as the role of the state is not reconsidered and the direction of the economy is left to the market, it is likely that production levels will continue to be vulnerable. The reason for this lies in the perverse logic that holds sway. In economies with high financial concentration (as are all Latin American economies), the financial liberalization required by the model leads to high interest rates which attract short-term capital, yet depress the rate of real investment. This causes the exchange rate to become undervalued and the currency to become overvalued, which makes exports cheaper. At the same time liberalization causes a disincentive to exporting, leading to a growing current accounts deficit. In addition, once the market is entirely liberalized, imports of consumer goods tend to grow, since they are cheaper than the same goods produced domestically. The inability of the exchange rate to keep pace gives foreign products a preferential price, not so much as a consequence of the efficiency of foreign exporters as of the high cost of local production due to the undervalued exchange rate. In other words, these policies are having the same effect as very different ones applied in the 1970s, as some analysts have pointed out, only this time the imports are not capital goods, but consumer goods.

Liberalization is being promoted in a world economy that is not particularly liberal, but which is uniformly capitalist, with markets still dominated by transnational companies despite the technological changes that ought to allow for some modification in this regard. Latin America's capital stock became transnationalized once again in the 1990s, through privatizations and private sector loans, with the public sector paying its debts so that the private sector could become indebted. This transfer of resources from the public sector to the private sector would dynamize the economy and result in growth if only the private sector were honest and efficient as the theory argues. There was no evidence of this in Latin America in previous decades, which is the reason why the economic role of the state emerged in the first place.

The questions of whether these economic policies will help us cross the paradigmatic ocean, and whether the accompanying reforms to cut back the state will help us embrace the change in technological paradigm, are wide open. Similarly, the issue of equity remains on the table. No economy can develop without consolidating an internal market, and that results only from higher levels of equity, something the model does not even take into consideration. Development without an internal market leads to a dual economy, a defect which development theories tried to correct fifty years ago to achieve the economic and social integration of the population and the political stability that creates.

The country that is most completely integrated into the new world economy, Mexico, through its free trade deal with the United States, ended up with a low rate of economic growth, an unsustainable current accounts deficit – the financing of which is achieved through stock exchange operations and short-term credits – and a massive undervaluation of the exchange rate. What's more, internal political problems worsened, including an insurrectionary movement by part of the population that sees it has nothing to gain from the new economic policies, but quite a bit to lose. Before long, an external crisis hit, when international interest rates rose in December 1994.

While the debt crisis may be over as far as the international commercial banks are concerned, now that countries' debts to those creditors have been transformed into long-term bonds backed by the US Treasury, real levels of outstanding debt remain just as high as in the 1980s and the ratio of debt to exports remains unaltered. The reduction in real interest rates has brought some relief regarding debt servicing, but when these rise difficulties will return, primarily on the fiscal side, bringing even more pressure to bear on the current accounts balance.

APPENDIX 5.1 Foreign investment flows in developing countries, 1987–93 (millions of US$)

| Region | 1987–89 | 1990–93 |
|---|---|---|
| Sub-Saharan Africa | 1,685 | 1,585 |
| Asia | | |
| East Asia | 6,882 | 20,134 |
| South Asia | 408 | 615 |
| Pacific Islands | 190 | 472 |
| Central Europe and Central Asia | | |
| Eastern Europe and Central Asia | 111 | 3,655 |
| European Union | 1,822 | 3,123 |
| Rest of Europe | 415 | 792 |
| Middle East and North Africa | 1,670 | 1,527 |
| Latin America and Caribbean | 7,300 | 12,479 |

*Source*: World Bank: 1994a: 159.

## Notes

1. In a perfectly open economy, the law of the sole price must hold:
$$P = EP*$$
where:  P  = price of a unique good in national currency
        P*  = world price
        E   = nominal rate of exchange
If one assumes that international inflation is exogenous and negligible, then:
$$P = E$$
where * equals change over time. Thus internal inflation is derived from a persistent devaluation of the exchange rate. Once devaluations come to an end, internal prices ought to be equal to external ones.

2. A discussion on correct pricing in structural adjustment appears in Amsden (1992–93) and in Andrés Velasco (1991: 43–57).

3. The contribution of neoclassical theory to development theory is explained

by Hunt (1989 : 292–332). Her theoretical critique of the application of the neoclassical paradigm to development theory can be found on pp. 316–27.

4. Bonapartism is a situation where a political leader rejects being held to account by his base of social support, and instead tries to balance contradictory interests and develop independent measures. Examples in Latin America are Alan García, Alberto Fujimori, Collor de Melo, Menem, Durán Ballén, Carlos Andrés Pérez.

5. Wade (1990: 14–24) presents a synthesis of the neoclassical argument. He cites works by Balassa, Lal and Krueger. His reading is the opposite of that presented in the *World Development Report* of 1987, ch. 5, on the economic performance of forty-one countries broken down into those that are strongly externally oriented, moderately externally oriented, moderately internally oriented, and strongly internally oriented. He draws the conclusion that countries moderately internally oriented obtain better results than those moderately externally oriented, and that the countries judged strongly externally oriented are all in Southeast Asia, which possibly makes them atypical of the neoliberal model since all of them pursue managed trade and industrial policies rather than the application of the free-market model (pp. 17 and 18).

6. There is an acrid debate on this subject. See Lance Taylor (1987: 1407–35), for the structuralist point of view. John Williamson (1990) offers the neoclassical critique and José María Fanelli et al. (1990) provide a neostructural critique of Williamson.

7. *Ex ante*. It is worth remembering Lance Taylor's note that *ex-post* evidence tends to be more solid because the steps to reach goals tend to become broken in economic processes, as Penrose recalls (1992: note 5).

8. Penrose, paraphrasing Joan Robinson (and Oscar Wilde), says the misery of being exploited by capitalists is better than the misery of not being exploited at all.

9. On this point Ohmae is in agreement, and for this reason argues in favour of globalization among rich countries.

10. Of industrial and intermediate goods, given ISI.

11. The calculation of savings and investment levels in relation to GNP were made by a frequency analysis of a range of ten countries representing over 85 per cent of Latin America's GNP. These are: Argentina, Bolivia, Brazil, Chile, Colombia, Mexico, Peru, Venezuela, Costa Rica and Guatemala. The source is World Bank 1987: 177 (see appendix 2).

12. The literature on inertial inflation models came out of Mexico, Brazil and Argentina. In particular, see: Francisco Lopes 1986; Pérsio Arida and André Lara-Rezende 1995; and Jaime Ros 1987. Pérsio Arida (1987) contains articles which evaluate heterodox inflation control programmes and models of inertial inflation.

13. Those interested in a comprehensive analysis of the difficulties which the mentioned heterodox adjustment plans faced should read José Antonio Ocampo 1987: 7–51. José María Fanelli and Roberto Frenkel (1987: 55–117) evaluate their stabilization programme (the Plan Austral) in the same issue of *Trimestre Económico*. pp. 55–117. On Peru, see Oscar Dancourt and Ivory Yong 1989: 13–44; and Manuel Pastor and Carol Wise 1992: 83–117.

14. This figure was obtained by adding up the balance of short-term credits (under 360 days), plus the flow of long-term credits, foreign investment and external investment flows on account between 1990 and 1993, the most recent year for which there was World Bank data (1994).

15. Consumer goods due to trade liberalization and repressed demand from the 1980s.

16. American Depositary Receipts (ADRs) are registered financial documents issued in the United States, which certify that a specific number of foreign stocks have been deposited in the foreign branch of a US bank, which acts as guarantor in the country of origin. It is a way of offering credit by using the stock of companies in foreign countries as collateral. Mexican companies have made the most use of this mechanism to date (UNCTAD 1992b: 51).

# 6. Central America in the Global Economy

The previous chapters have sought to shed some light on debates and situations that affect Latin America as a whole. However, the region is so heterogeneous that to understand the impact of changes in the global economy we ought to reduce our focus to economies that are more or less homogeneous. Central America's dependence on trade with the United States and Europe is similar today to what it was when the countries became independent in the 1830s, and, generally speaking, the goods they export have not changed much (Woodward 1985: ch. 5). This chapter offers an overview of Central America in the context of the changes that took place between the 1970s and the 1990s, and suggests new ways in which those countries might seek insertion into the global economy. It also reviews the modifications in Central America's international economic relations and where those economies seem to be headed in the twenty-first century.

The hypothesis is that the processes of economic reform implemented in all the countries of the region since the end of the 1980s have had different results depending on previously existing conditions in each country: the degree of equity, the level of innovation in the export economy, institutionality, culture, wealth and belief in the future. In this way, the same policies had different results, according to cultural and political variables, as well as economic ones. Systemic factors pushed the region into crisis, but the way each country addressed them was different, depending less on the external elements that caused the crisis than on the internal elements around which a consensus could be built for a solution. Central America is a problematic region to analyse as a unit due to the state of war that existed in Nicaragua and El Salvador in the 1980s, to the political difficulties that have affected Guatemala since the 1950s, to the general backwardness of Honduras and to the degree of social homogeneity in Costa Rica since the 1948 revolution. This chapter seeks to draw an outline of where Central America sits in the framework of the new technological paradigm and examines what development options the region has in that context.

## The development path of Central American countries

Historically, the economies of Central America have specialized in a small group of similar agricultural exports. Coffee, bananas, sugar and cotton make up a large part of the foreign exchange earnings of these countries, complemented by meat and sea products in several of them. In the 1960s, an import-substitution process began with what turned out to be the most successful effort at integration in Latin America of that period. The countries of the region began to industrialize under the protection of a common external tariff and free trade within the Central American area. The industrialization process ought to have led to a parallel process of technological innovation to allow the countries to modify their export structure, but the evidence demonstrates that did not occur. The four variables proposed by Fajnzylber (see Chapter 2) for understanding a development pattern are:

1. The ratio of the income of the poorest 40 per cent of the population to that of the richest 10 per cent. The closer this ratio is to a value of one, the greater the equity. World Bank data on income distribution for the countries of the region are available only for 1980–82 in Costa Rica, Guatemala and Honduras.
2. Austerity, understood as a consumption model, is tracked by Fajnzylber through the proxy variable of the number of automobiles per 1,000 inhabitants, and the data are from 1992.
3. Competitiveness is expressed by the ratio of exports to imports of machinery and equipment. The higher the value, between 0 and 1, the greater the degree of innovation and competitiveness.
4. The fourth variable is the rate of per capita GDP growth. We have looked at 1970–90, the most recent twenty-year period; Fajnzylber looked at 1965–86.

Figure 6.1 shows these variables for the three countries for which all the data are available: Costa Rica, Guatemala and Honduras. For comparative purposes, Mexico and Taiwan have also been included, drawn from Fajnzylber. Evidently, Costa Rica's development pattern is closer to Mexico's, even though the four variables are much lower. In other words, Costa Rica is not following the Asian model, rather the US development model, but to a lesser degree than Mexico. The countries with greater income concentration are Honduras and Guatemala, which also experienced practically no average growth during the period. Their levels of consumption as defined above are low, which can be explained by the high degree of income concentration, rather than austerity policies or culture as in the Asian case. The small group of people who have high incomes have a high level of consumption, while the rest of society does not have that option, thus depressing aggregate consumption. Regarding innovation, Guatemala has a very low index, but Honduras has absolutely no innovation according to the terms defined. The four-variable kite in Honduras's case is actually a tiny triangle, because of the high degree of income concentration and the resulting low level of consumption in society as a whole. Average growth for the twenty years in question was virtually zero.

In Guatemala, income concentration is greater than in Latin America as a whole. In fact, it is double: a ratio of 0.16 between the poorest 40 per cent and the richest 10 per cent, compared to 0.30 for Latin America. In other words, the domestic market is quite restricted, giving rise to a relatively low consumption of automobiles but not to a high level of internal savings, as we shall see below. Competitiveness is less than one-quarter the Latin American average (0.08 and 0.30 respectively out of 1.00) and the rate of economic growth is much lower than in Latin America as a whole. In other words, Guatemala's development model has not incorporated the population into the process of capitalist modernization. This results from the lack of a land tenancy policy that would allow for better income distribution, and this is a major source of the political problems the country has suffered for the past forty years.

On Figure 6.1, Honduras is a triangle, not a kite, since it has no technological innovation or any exports of machinery and equipment. Just like Nicaragua, in 1992 its development pattern remained basically agricultural exports. Income concentration in Honduras is similar to Guatemala's (0.18), and thus there is a small internal market with the consequent problems of pressure on land common to the region. The level of consumption is low, due to high income concentration, and the resultant growth has been nearly zero.

In the World Bank data examined, there is no information on income distribution in El Salvador or Nicaragua, which makes it impossible to undertake the same sort of calculations. But the existing information on foreign trade, automobile consumption and growth indicates that income concentration in those countries is similar to that in Guatemala. In Nicaragua, income distribution is highly concentrated, consumption of automobiles is low due to the restricted internal market, it shows no technological innovation or international competitiveness and growth is negative. For the Nicaraguan case, however, other factors which affected its economic growth will be examined below. In the case of El Salvador,

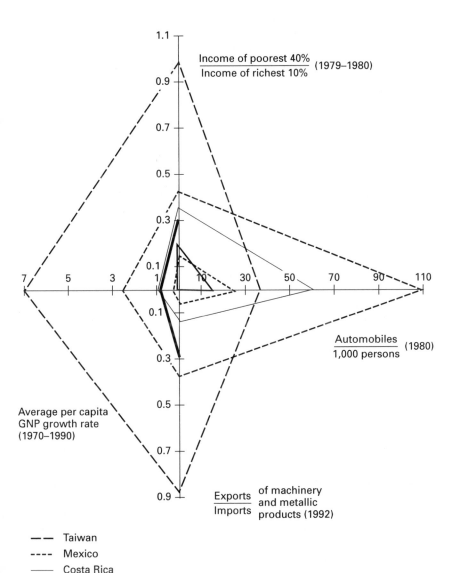

FIGURE 6.1 Profiles of Taiwan, Costa Rica, Guatemala, Honduras and Mexico (*Source*: Fajnzylber 1986: Appendix 3, Table 10)

the level of innovation and competitiveness is double Guatemala's, but still one-third of Costa Rica's, although its level of consumption is similar to that of Guatemala. It is another country affected by poor income distribution arising from unequal land tenancy, giving rise to serious political problems. The countries of Central America, with the exception of Costa Rica, have not followed the sort of rational land distribution policies undertaken in Southeast Asia, and that has impeded the growth of the domestic market. The lack of land reform, and not austerity policy or culture, explains the low consumption levels. In fact, the high-income sector follows a consumption pattern on the scale of the United States, a fact which aggravates the difficulties with accumulation.

The lack of competitiveness, understood as the ratio of metal-mechanic exports and transportation equipment to imports of the same goods, is due to the lack of development of these sectors in the early stages of import substitution. Import substitution was oriented towards light industry, and never achieved secondary substitution, except in the case of the chemical industry in Guatemala. While these elements are basic to the crisis of Central American countries, the fundamental problem is land tenancy. Other elements, ones that are truly systemic, are also factors in the region due to the high levels of foreign debt and the precarious export structure based on coffee, bananas, cotton and sugar.

## Elements of the Central American crisis: The Central American Common Market

Central America's economies were hit hard in the 1980s (see Table 6.1). Changes in the international economy had a significant effect on their primary export earnings, due to the fall in prices for bananas, coffee, sugar and cotton, products that make up the region's traditional export sector. But that was not the only factor, nor was it the most important. The external crisis faced as a common denominator by the five Central American nations was marginal compared to the domestic problems each society suffered (Dabene 1993). The political nature of the crises that arose in each country falls outside the scope of this chapter, which focuses on the development model followed, its results and the way in which the systemic crisis affected it. Undoubtedly, the economic development of El Salvador or Nicaragua cannot be explained without taking into account the effect of war in each country, nor can the difficulties Guatemala experienced with its investment rate be comprehended without an understanding of the factional conflict within its society.

An element that is common to the five countries of the region is their participation in the Central American Common Market (MCCA), created in 1960 to promote industrialization through an import-substitution strategy. The MCCA flowered with a high common external tariff and free trade within the Central American area. Thoumi (1989), based on studies evaluating the MCCA undertaken by the IADB and on the results of his own study, points out that the MCCA was the most successful of all the integration efforts of the 1970s. However, attempts to take the countries of the region towards a model of industrial development through the MCCA were limited by the resistance of the traditional oligarchies to improving income distribution to broaden the internal market. The ISI strategy never challenged either the traditional export structure or the policy of agricultural export growth; rather, it built upon them (Gallardo 1993: 142). In this way, the industrialization that occurred was a product of import substitution for the regional market, not for the domestic market of each country (Bulmer-Thomas 1983: 271).

The correct application of import-substitution policies would have meant a revolution for the agrarian sector, since the engine of the economy would have been displaced from the traditional oligarchy to new industrial sectors (Bulmer-Thomas 1989: 244). This gave rise to what Bulmer-Thomas (1989) calls a 'hybrid model' in which, after the MCCA was set up, public policies continued to favour export agriculture. The new tariff system stipulated low duties on imported intermediate and capital goods, but the real rate of tariff protection, though negative, did not place any binds on agricultural exports since they could not benefit from tariff protection for the internal market (Bulmer-Thomas 1989: 245).

Among the reasons for the crisis of the MCCA at the end of the 1960s was the lack of parity in industrial development, with some countries benefiting more than others, and a rise in extra-regional exports. In addition, the failure to develop agriculture for the internal market or to broaden the internal markets of each country added to the crisis. Finally, the decision of the Honduran government to carry out an agrarian reform in territories inhabited by migrants from El Salvador led to a brief war (known as the Soccer War) and the repatriation of 100,000 Salvadoreans; the two countries broke off relations and Honduras blocked intra-regional trade from crossing its borders.

Following the application of the model, dependence on the exterior grew instead of shrinking, due to the fact that industry had extra-regional, rather than intra-regional linkages. In addition, industry produced primarily consumer goods for a small market, thus pressuring the agricultural export sector for foreign exchange to keep the MCCA going. Policies to improve the productivity of traditional agriculture gave rise to increases in the volume of production in the 1970s, but the first world oil crisis hit the region hard. Agricultural export growth helped overcome the high cost of energy, but at the same time small farmers became further marginalized, leading to political conflict (Torres Rivas 1973).

At the beginning of the 1980s, the need for foreign exchange to pay the debt became the primary obstacle to intra-regional trade, and the postponement of payments arising from intra-regional trade compounded it, leading to a crisis in the integration plan. There is agreement that this integration model and the sort of insertion it offered the region were at a dead-end (Vacchino 1989). However, since neither the economic structure, nor the political one, has yet to be modified, questions regarding the long-term modernization of the region remain.

The notion of Central America as an economic unit is a complex one, given that it is made up of economies at different stages of development, with large differences in per capita GNP (Costa Rica's was six times that of Nicaragua in 1992). Per capita income in 1980 dollars was: Costa Rica, $1,156; El Salvador, $690; Guatemala, $578; Honduras, $342; and Nicaragua, $201. This tells us that the crisis affected each country in different ways, even though there were some common denominators (see Table 6.2).

The region as a whole has achieved, for example, a growing share of the foreign trade of Latin America, rising since the beginning of the 1970s. This can be explained by the dynamism of the Costa Rican export sector which at the beginning of the 1990s accounted for one-third of the region's exports, while at the same time Nicaragua's had shrunk to barely 5 per cent. This is an abrupt change from the beginning of the 1970s, when each Central American country accounted for 20 per cent of the region's exports. Converted to constant 1980 dollars, Costa Rica's exports suffered stagnation in the 1980s due to the fall in raw materials prices, with a slight recovery in the second half of that decade. The recovery took hold in the first half of the 1990s, reaching an annual average over 1990–94 of $1,012 million in 1980 dollars. Costa Rica is the model of success for the trade reform policies implemented in the region by the World Bank. All the other countries have seen their real exports shrink, despite the revitalization at the beginning of the 1990s in Honduras and El Salvador. It ought to be noted that the other countries also implemented trade reform policies early on, except for Nicaragua, which implemented them in 1990.

The crisis of the 1980s had many aspects in political, military and economic terms. The unifying element was the decline in export earnings due to the falling prices of the five raw materials exported by the region: cane sugar, cotton, coffee, bananas and meat. The foreign debt, an apparently unifying element, was not one, since Costa Rica and Nicaragua had high debt levels, while Guatemala's and El Salvador's were low. Honduras in this regard came in at the average for Latin America. Thus, the rise in interest rates affected the first two countries more than the rest. A brief country-by-country review will spell out the principal features of the crisis of the 1980s.[1]

**Nicaragua**  The country with the deepest crisis in the region had negative per capita GDP growth rates between 1975 and 1994. The movements that led the overthrow of the Somoza regime emerged in the middle of the 1970s and ended up dethroning the oligarchy that had managed both the nation's wealth and its development. In 1979 the Sandinista Front succeeded in overthrowing the government and taking power in the midst of internal convulsions, significant migratory movement and resistance to change on the part of some sectors of society. The external anti-Sandinista movement, the Contras, began in 1982 and took the country into low-intensity war in the coffee-producing zones of the north. Internal resistance to the government by the industrial elite, in addition to the US embargo, the war, production problems caused by the way the economy was managed and hyperinflation, led to the most dramatic drop in per capita GDP in the region and in all Latin America. Average annual inflation reached 8,544 per cent between 1985 and 1990 as a result of all of the above factors. Annual export earnings began to drop in the mid-1970s and fell 80 per cent between 1975–80 and 1990–94, in constant 1980 dollars.

Despite these difficulties, during the 1980s, efforts were made to maintain a high gross rate of capital formation, stabilizing it at an average of 18 per cent per year throughout the decade, a slight increase over the 1975–80 period. The high rate of capital formation combined with the fall in export earnings, stable import levels and an accumulation of debt taken on to cover growing current accounts deficits, generated ever greater deficits. This, plus the fall in agricultural production due to the reasons outlined above, explains the massive current accounts deficit, which reached 257 per cent of export earnings in the last five years of the 1980s.

After the change in regime in 1990, a policy of economic opening and stabilization led to an even more alarming current accounts deficit, 323 per cent of exports, but managed to reduce the fiscal deficit to one-half its former level, from 16.8 per cent of GDP at the end of the 1980s, to 7.4 per cent of average GDP between 1991 and 1994. Inflation fell from 8,544 per cent annual average during the second half of the 1980s to 12.2 per cent in 1994. The high current accounts deficit was due to the fact that exports had not as yet recovered and the liberalization of imports unleashed repressed demand from the 1980s. In addition, there was the growing debt due to the deficit itself. After 1990 the gross rate of capital formation dropped by 5 per cent of GDP due to cutbacks in public investment and high interest rates. Most of the growing current accounts deficit from 1990 to 1994, therefore, was due to additional consumption, plus debt servicing.

These are some explanations of how the systemic crisis interacted with the domestic crisis in Nicaragua. At the beginning of the 1970s, Nicaragua had a per capita income similar to that of Guatemala, greater than that of Honduras, and somewhat less than that of El Salvador and Costa Rica. By the beginning of the 1990s, per capita GDP was just one-sixth of Costa Rica's.

**Honduras** The Honduran crisis began at the beginning of the 1980s as part of the systemic crisis and internal political problems. Society was affected by a sizeable foreign debt and internal conflicts which weakened the country's political stability, creating uncertainty for investors. In this way, there was a fall in the gross rate of capital formation, from 22 per cent in the second half of the 1970s to 17 per cent in the second half of the 1980s when political stability returned. The fall in export prices occurred at nearly the same time as internal political problems, resulting in a decline in exports in constant dollars from $666 million in the mid-1970s to $595 million at the end of the 1980s. The ratio of the current accounts deficit to exports grew between the 1970s and the middle of the 1980s from 30.5 per cent to 41 per cent, and new debts were taken on to cover the gap. This spread was contained and reduced to 34 per cent by the beginning of the 1990s. The foreign debt, equivalent to 408 per cent of export earnings, weighed heavily in the second half of the 1980s, but was reduced to 217 per cent of goods exports by the first half of the 1990s. This was due to debt reduction and export-promotion policies which, though not very successful, managed to improve the country's export position.

Goods exports, meanwhile, went from an average of $595 million in constant 1980 dollars in 1985–90, to $688 million in 1990–94. The central government's budget deficit in the second half of the 1980s was 6.9 per cent of GDP, and it remained at an average of 6.1 per cent in the first part of the 1990s despite the implementation of an adjustment policy. In other words, the deficits in the current accounts and the central government budget remained relatively stable, equivalent to a very slight reduction of 0.6 per cent of GDP. The rate of inflation doubled with the application of economic reform and stabilization policies, from 10.8 to 21.1 per cent between 1985–90 and 1990–95.

**Guatemala** Another country affected by internal political upheavals, despite having a diversified export base, Guatemala suffered a fall in per capita income. The systemic crisis had a serious effect on exports, reducing them by 40 per cent between the second half of the 1970s and the first years of the 1990s. That decline was in part due to the fall in the prices of the raw materials Guatemala exports, and in part to the collapse of the Central American Common Market for which it produced. Its industries were oriented to regional exports, with intra-regional trade accounting for 28 per cent of total exports in 1970. Despite the crisis, manufactures continued at 29 per cent of total goods exports in 1992. In other words, the contraction of exports must have affected extra-regional primary exports and intra-regional manufacturing exports similarly, at least at the beginning.

In the 1980s, Guatemala was forced to change its development strategy. Intra-regional commerce fell from 25 to 10 per cent of total Central American trade between 1980 and 1989 (Gitli and Ryd 1991: 152), the combined result of internal political crises and the systemic crisis. Due to the latter crisis, the region's economies began to seek foreign exchange through extra-regional trade to cover payments on the foreign debt. They also suspended payment on debts generated by intra-regional trade, leading to the bankruptcy of the mechanism of commercial compensation (Central American Chamber for Compensation), which seriously affected the region's industrial exports, especially in the cases of Guatemala and El Salvador, and to a lesser degree Costa Rica.

The worsening of the internal war, added to the instability of the political regime and the hard line taken by the country's military in the 1980s, occurred in parallel with the collapse of the MCCA and led to a sharp reduction in the gross rate of capital formation to early 1970s levels. Between the middle of the 1970s and the end of the 1980s the gross rate of capital formation in the gross domestic product shrank from 19 to 12 per cent. Apparently, businessmen stopped investing and lived off the profits from their industries, while large landowners did the same, feeding the crisis and leading, along with the external factors noted, to a fall in per capita income.

**El Salvador**  Just like Nicaragua and Guatemala, El Salvador faced an internal war that lasted throughout the 1980s, but its political crisis began in 1972. During the period of military rule in the 1970s, the gross rate of capital formation remained high, but when the internal war became apparent in January 1980, it dropped off sharply. This can be explained in part by payments on the debt and the uncertainty caused by the state of war. Since the war took place in the countryside, as in Guatemala and Nicaragua, agricultural exports declined. However, what most affected this country and others in the region was the fall in the price of cotton and other agricultural products.

TABLE 6.1 Central America: basic indicators 1970–92 (annual averages for the period)

| | | Per capita GNP (US$) | Variation in per capita GDP (%) | Inflation (%) | Goods exports (millions of 1980 US$) | Tourism / goods export | GKF / GDP** | Current accounts deficit / exports (%) |
|---|---|---|---|---|---|---|---|---|
| **COSTA RICA** | 1970 | $1,139* | | | | | | |
| | 1980 | $998* | | | | | | |
| | 1992 | $1,156* | | | | | | |
| 1970–75 | | | 3.36 | 13.4 | 480 | – | 22 | -40.8 |
| 1975–80 | | | 2.05 | 11.6 | 923 | 8.3 | 23 | -45.4 |
| 1980–85 | | | -2.47 | 34.0 | 799 | 12.5 | 21 | -38.9 |
| 1985–90 | | | 0.92 | 17.6 | 808 | 15.2 | 20 | -34.6 |
| 1990–94 | | | 2.12 | 19.2 | 1,012 | 22.5 | 22 | -26.0 |
| **NICARAGUA** | 1970 | $1,112 | | | | | | |
| | 1980 | $585 | | | | | | |
| | 1992 | $201 | | | | | | |
| 1970–75 | | | 1.32 | – | 395 | – | 19 | -34.1 |
| 1975–80 | | | -5.65 | 19.6 | 650 | 4.4 | 17 | -33.4 |
| 1980–85 | | | -1.80 | 81.3 | 357 | 3.1 | 18 | -162.6 |
| 1985–90 | | | -6.05 | 8,544.3 | 202 | 1.9 | 18 | -256.6 |
| 1990–94 | | | -3.22 | 2,859.7 | 167 | 9.6 | 13 | -307.7 |

**EL SALVADOR**

| | | | | | | |
|---|---|---|---|---|---|---|
| 1970 | $709 | | | | | |
| 1980 | $623 | | | | | |
| 1992 | $690 | | | | | |
| 1970–75 | 2.06 | 8.3 | 510 | – | 16 | -11.7 |
| 1975–80 | -1.12 | 13.9 | 1,038 | 3.0 | 20 | -8.2 |
| 1980–85 | -4.58 | 16.7 | 681 | 3.3 | 13 | -29.3 |
| 1985–90 | 0.15 | 23.6 | 438 | 8.4 | 14 | -50.3 |
| 1990–94 | 2.14 | 14.1 | 387 | 12.1 | 15 | -56.5 |

**HONDURAS**

| | | | | | | |
|---|---|---|---|---|---|---|
| 1970 | $575 | | | | | |
| 1980 | $547 | | | | | |
| 1992 | $342 | | | | | |
| 1970–75 | -1.26 | 5.9 | 325 | – | 19 | -30.5 |
| 1975–80 | 2.50 | 10.1 | 667 | 2.8 | 22 | -33.4 |
| 1980–85 | -1.90 | 8.1 | 651 | 3.3 | 19 | -40.6 |
| 1985–90 | -0.05 | 10.8 | 595 | 3.2 | 17 | -34.5 |
| 1990–94 | -0.38 | 21.1 | 688 | 3.7 | 19 | -34.2 |

**GUATEMALA**

| | | | | | | |
|---|---|---|---|---|---|---|
| 1970 | $926 | | | | | |
| 1980 | $950 | | | | | |
| 1992 | $578 | | | | | |
| 1970–75 | 2.38 | 8.0 | 617 | – | 14 | -5.3 |
| 1975–80 | 2.22 | 9.8 | 1,250 | 6.2 | 19 | -12.7 |
| 1980–85 | -2.93 | 11.3 | 1,045 | 1.7 | 13 | -28.0 |
| 1985–90 | -0.58 | 25.7 | 753 | 5.7 | 12 | -31.1 |
| 1990–94 | 0.82 | 21.6 | 784 | 12.0 | 12 | -36.3 |

*Notes:* * 1980 dollars    ** The available data are for 1990–92.

*Sources:* ECLAC, *Balance de la economía de América Latina*, 1993; for per capita GNP, 1992: World Bank 1994b; per capita GNP, 1985: World Bank 1987; for per capita GNP, 1970: Woodward 1985: 364, table 4

## Systemic factors in the Central American crisis: Raw materials and foreign debt

To understand the systemic factors that affected the entire Central American region in the 1980s requires a review of trends in raw materials prices in the region and the existing demand for them over the long term. It further requires an examination of the countries' approach to indebtedness and the impact of the systemic crisis in that arena, in order to analyse the manner in which the crisis was internalized. And finally, it requires reviewing the changes under way regarding patterns of international insertion, in order to examine the solutions sought and to evaluate whether or not these fall within the parameters of the new international patterns of economic inter-relation.

**Export products and their prices** For all Central American countries the importance of agriculture in the economy was and continues to be greater than the average for Latin America. According to UNCTAD (1991: table 27), agricultural GDP was 15.7 per cent for all of Latin America in 1965 and fell to 9.2 per cent by 1988. For the countries of Central America, in 1992 the weight of agriculture in the GDP was still between 19 and 27 per cent of the total. In other words, the region's economies and their international insertion can not be understood without analysing the impact of international agricultural prices.

From the middle of the nineteenth century onwards, the region's export basket has centred on coffee and bananas, complemented from the beginning of the twentieth century by cotton and cane sugar (see Table 6.3) (Woodward 1985; Bulmer-Thomas 1989). Although the region's countries exported natural dyes (indigo and cochineal, primarily), the invention of anilines in the middle of the nineteenth century displaced these products from the world market and industrial coffee production began. Coffee trees were introduced to Costa Rica first by governor Tomás de Acosta before independence (1821) and from there were taken to Guatemala and the other countries. Honduras was the last to make coffee its primary product, taking it up only after the Second World War. Cane sugar was also promoted during the nineteenth century but it never had the importance of coffee in foreign trade. Bananas were important first for Honduras and Costa Rica, but much less so than coffee.

The historical markets for the countries of the region were Germany and England, but in the 1880s there was a turn towards the United States, following the World Centenary Industrial and Cotton Exposition in New Orleans in 1885 and the establishment of maritime routes between that city and Central America's ports, sponsored by the New Orleans Chamber of Commerce that same decade. That was also the period when mining began in Honduras and Nicaragua.

In general, ports were developed on the Pacific coast, linked by railways to the important cities, and trade was carried on through Panama. Only at the end of the nineteenth century were ports built on the Atlantic coast in all the countries for banana exports. While coffee farms were located on the Pacific coast and were relatively small, the great banana plantations were located on the Atlantic coast. Coffee cultivation, however, was not homogeneous. Depending on the country, there may be large coffee plantations, as in El Salvador and Guatemala, or small ones, as in the other three countries. Land tenancy is what lies at the root of the problem of income concentration, and pressures on land in the countries of the region is an element that has been present ever since the introduction of coffee.

TABLE 6.2 Central America: GDP structure by economic activity, 1970–92 (%)

|  | Agriculture | Manufacturing | Construction | Services |
|---|---|---|---|---|
| **Costa Rica** | | | | |
| 1970 | 25.0 | 15.1 | 4.7 | 55.2 |
| 1980 | 17.8 | 18.6 | 6.2 | 57.3 |
| 1992 | 19.4 | 19.0 | 3.5 | 57.1 |
| **Nicaragua** | | | | |
| 1970 | 26.3 | 17.5 | 3.2 | 52.4 |
| 1980 | 23.2 | 25.6 | 2.9 | 47.5 |
| 1992 | 24.5 | 21.6 | 2.8 | 50.5 |
| **El Salvador** | | | | |
| 1970 | 30.6 | 17.6 | 3.0 | 48.6 |
| 1980 | 27.8 | 15.0 | 3.4 | 53.6 |
| 1992 | 26.0 | 15.8 | 3.5 | 54.6 |
| **Honduras** | | | | |
| 1970 | 34.6 | 14.0 | 5.0 | 44.1 |
| 1980 | 21.4 | 16.9 | 5.3 | 54.5 |
| 1992 | 22.8 | 17.7 | 5.2 | 52.3 |
| **Guatemala** | | | | |
| 1970 | 30.1 | 14.6 | 2.2 | 53.0 |
| 1980 | 27.1 | 17.6 | 4.6 | 50.0 |
| 1992 | 27.7 | 15.5 | 3.3 | 52.9 |

*Source*: ECLAC, *Balance de la Economía de América Latina y el Caribe*, 1994, 1982, 1973.

The development of bananas in the region was carried out by a banana transnational, the United Fruit Company (UFCO). UFCO, owned by a North American (Minor Cooper Keith), became the owner of the region's railways (International Railways of Central America) and of the large fleet of steamships that linked Central America's coasts with the United States at the beginning of the twentieth century. Other banana companies, which linked the economies of that time to the world economy, were the Coyumel Fruit Co. and the Standard Fruit Co., previously known as Vaccaro Bros. In this way, British hegemony in the region gave way to US hegemony between the end of the nineteenth century and the end of the First World War. At the same time, the development of banana plantations gave rise to dual growth in the economy, with the Atlantic region becoming separate from the Pacific, a phenomenon that has also lasted to this day. The development of banana enclaves did not spark a process of economic development in the Atlantic region, beyond a rise in exports.

During the first half of the nineteenth century, transportation from the Atlantic coast to the Pacific coast was through Nicaragua, over the pass from the San Juan river to Lake Nicaragua. Feasibility studies for an interoceanic canal date from the first years of Central America's independence. Nicaragua, Costa Rica and Panama competed in the second half of the nineteenth century to be the site for a canal that would open a trade route for the countries of the region and link them to the United States. The routes proposed went through San Juan del Norte, Lake Nicaragua and San Juan del Sur in Nicaragua, which was used to transport passengers until a railway was built in Panama in 1855, along the route which eventually became the Panama Canal. In the 1880s telegraph lines linked Guatemala with the world, and telephone lines were installed in Honduras.

The combination of telecommunications, more efficient transportation systems and export dynamism, it was thought at the time, would lead to a process of industrialization. Instead, the region was turned into an exporter of raw materials and an importer of manufactured goods. Between 1870 and 1990 the volume exported by Guatemala grew by a factor of twenty, but the income from those exports were spent on importing manufactures (Woodward 1985: 163). A large part of those export earnings were invested outside the country and, despite the open immigration policies intended to attract European labour, the countries of the region did not become magnets for immigrants like the United States, Argentina or Brazil. From 1900 on, policies favouring foreign capital allowed the United Fruit Co. to develop, and later on Pan American Airways in air transportation. Generally speaking, from the end of the nineteenth century the governments of the region worked to favour foreign capital over their own; the exception was Costa Rica.

TABLE 6.3 Export structure of Central America, 1975–92 (% of total exports)[a]

| | Coffee | | | Cotton | | | Sugar | | | Bananas | | | Non-traditional | | |
|---|---|---|---|---|---|---|---|---|---|---|---|---|---|---|---|
| | 1975 | 1985 | 1992 | 1975 | 1985 | 1992 | 1975 | 1985 | 1992 | 1975 | 1985 | 1992 | 1975 | 1985 | 1992 |
| Costa Rica | 20 | 33 | 12 | –[b] | – | – | 10 | 1 | 2 | 29.0 | 22 | 28 | 33 | 38 | 56 |
| Nicaragua[c] | 18 | 42 | 21 | 19 | 31 | 12.0 | 6 | 4 | 9 | 0.2 | 5 | 5 | 37 | 9 | n/a |
| El Salvador | 34 | 62 | 26 | 15 | 4 | 0.3 | 16 | 3 | 8 | – | – | – | 33 | 28 | 64 |
| Honduras | 19 | 22 | 17 | n/a | 1 | n/a | – | – | – | 19.0 | 36 | 35 | – | 21 | 29 |
| Guatemala | 26 | 42 | 20 | 12 | 7 | 0.1 | 19 | 5 | 11 | 5.0 | 7 | 9 | 10 | 19 | 57 |
| Prices in 1980 US cents per lb[d] | 93.5 | 110.7 | 37.1 | 79.7 | 46.9 | 37.1 | 29.2 | 3.1 | 5.4 | 18.4 | 14.0 | 13.9 | | | |

*Notes*: a. 1975 data do not add up to 100% due to other traditional exports of lesser quantities.   b. – indicates that the county does not export that product.   c. Data for Nicaragua correspond to 1970, 1985 and 1992.   d. Prices calculated from ECLAC 1992a.

*Sources*: ECLAC, *Balance de la Economía de América Latina y el Caribe*, 1985; data for 1975 for Honduras: ECLAC, *Balance de la Economía de América Latina y el Caribe*, 1975.

In 1906, aboard the USS *Marblehead*, representatives of all the governments of the region, plus those representing the government of Porfirio Díaz O. in Mexico and that of Theodore Roosevelt in the United States, met to put an end to frequent border conflicts in the region and the difficulties that had arisen from the right to asylum in neighbouring countries. The presidents of Mexico and the United States acted as arbitrators to resolve the conflicts, setting a precedent for the relations between Central American countries and their two neighbours to the north, as far as promoting peace and cooperation was concerned. Since the governments of the region had difficulties achieving agreement among their policies, then as now, they sought the presence of their two larger neighbours from the north. They did not seek, then or now, the presence of countries from the south. Already in that period a northward view of their place in the world had taken hold in Central America. This did not change even during the search for economic integration in the MCCA or during the years of regional political conflict precipitated by Sandinismo in Nicaragua and the internal wars in El Salvador and Guatemala.

A hundred years later, the region seems unchanged, except for the industrializing impetus of the MCCA in the 1960s and 1970s which virtually collapsed in the 1980s for reasons explained above. Bulmer-Thomas suggests that the MCCA seems to have had an insignificant impact on the region's export specialization, as it was unable to compete effectively with the agricultural sector for the use of scarce resources (Bulmer-Thomas 1983: 286). In this way, the countries of Central America have remained dependent on agricultural exports whose prices have tended to fall over the 1980s and 1990s, and whose production is being substituted for by industrial goods. However, the increased use of land for these agricultural exports seems to have worsened social and political problems. In fact, one could say that the region's problems are the result of the success of export agriculture in the 1970s, not its failure. Today, the continued fall in agricultural income is occurring at the same time as processes of democratization take hold and the wars in each country wind down. The social impact of the change in global demand for the region's products occurs in a new political context.

The substitution of corn syrup for cane sugar as an industrial sweetener from the middle of the 1980s had the effect of lowering the price to a record 5 cents a pound in 1980 dollars. Cotton, whose productivity per hectare has grown due to cultivation techniques and the use of chemicals to control pests, was hit hard by competition from synthetic fibres, such that between 1960 and 1979 the use of cotton in finished goods fell from 68 to 48 per cent of total production in the world fibre market (ECLAC 1985). This tendency has been maintained, depressing prices due to oversupply, such that the real price fell from 80 cents to 37 cents a pound between 1975 and 1992, and throwing into question the long-term viability of this export. Coffee, due to the growing number of new exporters in Africa and Latin America, has tended to fall in price over the long term due to oversupply, leaving bananas as the only traditional product in the region that is neither being substituted for nor is experiencing dramatic improvements in productivity that might threaten a world glut. The fall in sugar and cotton prices explains the shrinking importance of those products in the region's export basket. The exception is Nicaragua, where, due to the overall contraction of production, cotton has a relatively high share (12 per cent in 1992) of total exports, but in constant dollars these are still half of El Salvador's and an eighth of Costa Rica's.

The fall in cotton and sugar prices, added to the fall in the price of coffee after the collapse of the International Coffee Organization, forced a modification of the export structure by making the traditional sectors, historically linked to coffee, sugar and cotton, less profitable, and weakening the landowning oligarchies. In this way, the countries that had some industrial base, small as it was, managed to convert it into a base for exports. ECLAC's classification of traditional and non-traditional products does not allow for an analysis of the industrial component of the non-traditional sector. For that reason we have chosen World Bank (1994b) data to delve deeper into the changes occurring in the region.

Proportionally, despite its depressed export levels, the country with the greatest industrial content to its exports is El Salvador, equivalent to 37 per cent of the total, nearly half of them (15 per cent) textiles and apparel (see Table 6.4). The machinery-equipment export sector which in 1970 accounted for 3 per cent of all exports has disappeared. In order of importance, Guatemala follows with industry accounting for 29 per cent of total exports, 1 per cent of it being machinery-equipment and 28 per cent other manufactures, including 5 per cent for textiles and apparel. Machinery-equipment exports also fell from 1970 to 1992 from 2 per cent to 1 per cent. Then comes Costa Rica with 27 per cent, made up of 4 per cent machinery-equipment and 23 per cent other manufactures. There is no account of apparel produced in export-processing zones. Honduras and Nicaragua follow with 13 per cent and 7 per cent respectively, although the trends are opposite in each country. While Honduras's exports are becoming more industrialized (from 8 to 13 per cent of total exports), Nicaragua's are de-industrializing (from 16 to 7 per cent of the total, from 1970 to 1992).

This indicates that there is no single way to resolve the national crisis in each country of the region since they do not spring from a single source, despite having the common denominator of a fall in raw materials prices. Bulmer-Thomas suggests that the roots of the current Central American

TABLE 6.4 Central America: export structure by product type, 1970–92 (%)

| | Fuels, minerals and metals | | Other primary products | | Machinery and transportation equipment | | Other manufactures | | Textiles and garments | |
|---|---|---|---|---|---|---|---|---|---|---|
| | 1970 | 1992 | 1970 | 1992 | 1970 | 1992 | 1970 | 1992 | 1970 | 1992 |
| Costa Rica | 1 | 1 | 80 | 72 | 3 | 4 | 17 | 23 | 4 | 0 |
| Nicaragua | 3 | 2 | 81 | 90 | 0 | 0 | 16 | 7 | 3 | 1 |
| El Salvador | 2 | 3 | 70 | 56 | 3 | 0 | 26 | 37 | 11 | 15 |
| Honduras | 9 | 3 | 82 | 84 | 0 | 0 | 8 | 13 | 2 | 3 |
| Guatemala | 0 | 2 | 72 | 68 | 2 | 1 | 26 | 28 | 8 | 5 |

*Source:* World Bank 1994b: World Statistical Annex, table 15.

crisis lie in the dislocations caused by change and are not due to a stagnation in production (Bulmer-Thomas 1983). The dramatic fall in Nicaragua's exports, explained in part by their prices and in part by the war, did not occur in El Salvador even though it shares a similar export structure, albeit with a greater proportion of manufactures. One hypothesis would have it that in the Nicaraguan case the regime did not manage to modernize society or replace the old order during the revolutionary period or even when that was over. It destroyed the old oligarchic state, but was not able to renew it with a modern state or to create a business class willing to work with the state on renewing the productive apparatus. In this sense, modifications in the structure of income distribution need to be identified in order to evaluate if the reforms introduced in the 1979–90 period led to a broadening of the internal market, or, in contrast, whether that structure remained concentrated with a restricted internal market and all the problems that poses for development. The export structure of Honduras appears, similarly, to be basically obsolete, with some attempts to renovate it with manufacturing exports, but without any solid industrial base (there is no machinery-equipment export industry, for example). In both countries, the lack of institutions charged with leading a renewal of management and technology is evident, in both the state and the private sector.

El Salvador and Guatemala, two countries that suffered internal wars in the 1980s, also have high rates of income concentration, but their industrial sectors occupy a greater share of exports than of the GDP, indicating that they are bases for industrial exports, perhaps due to the restrictions of the internal market. El Salvador had an industrial GDP of 15.6 per cent of the total GDP in 1990, while its manufacturing exports added up to 37 per cent of total exports in 1992. Guatemala also has an industrial sector oriented towards exports, taking up 15.5 per cent of total GDP, while its manufacturing exports are equivalent to 29 per cent of total exports. Both countries have high rates of income concentration and have managed to bring about change in their export structures during periods of internal conflict, despite the collapse of the MCCA. Finally, Costa Rica, a country that experienced social peace in the 1980s, with better income distribution and a broadened internal market, has a manufactures export sector that has been developing since the 1970s and which represents 27 per cent of all exports, while industry represents 19.6 per cent of its total GDP. Evidently, Costa Rica's strategy has been to substitute traditional agricultural products with others, such as flowers, herbs, etc., while simultaneously industrializing the derivatives of cane sugar (into alcohols and liquors) and reinforcing banana exports.

**Capital flows** Over the past twenty-five years, Central American countries have had an inter-relationship with international capital markets and international public lending institutions that has allowed them to run deficits in the current accounts and to achieve much higher levels of capital investment than the rest of Latin America. Just as in the rest of Latin America, external resources may not have been employed as well as they could have been in terms of saving foreign exchange or generating new foreign exchange to cover the loans. The differences between the countries are stark, and the impact of the crisis of the 1980s was differentiated. The blessing of having access to resources at a moment when other countries did not, in the end became the curse of taking on unsustainable and unviable debt levels. Debt ranged from 208 to 3,972 per cent of exports by 1990, with most of the countries falling below the Latin American average of 368 per cent. In Nicaragua, Honduras and El Salvador debt took up a greater share of total goods exports. It is worth pointing out that the increase in the debt burden is related to the fall in export earnings. However, an analysis of the outstanding debt in constant 1980 dollars shows that Guatemala, Honduras and Nicaragua doubled their total debt between 1980 and 1985, while El Salvador's went up by 50 per cent and Costa Rica's remained stable.

The explanation of such a high level of indebtedness is political, since the creditor countries aligned themselves with or against some of the region's regimes. Thus, although exports suffered from falling prices and falling total demand for goods, import levels remained relatively stable or grew, and the relation GCF/GDP remained relatively stable in the three countries whose debt grew, as growing current accounts deficit in the balance of payments were covered by foreign governmental lending at a time when credit flows to the rest of Latin America were ostensibly shut off. Added to this were the costs of the military campaigns each government waged in its internal conflict, save Costa Rica. The levels of substantive public deficit plus the costs of debt servicing itself required an ever greater volume of credit.

The most dramatic case was Nicaragua. In the 1970s it maintained a manageable debt load, but as soon as the insurrection began its exports and GDP fell, leading to difficulties in managing its outstanding debt. This was a major controversy when the Sandinistas came to power, because of the nature of the debt. The central point of the debate was that loans had been used to facilitate capital flight and there had been corruption in the process, therefore there was no point in acknowledging the debt, even though at that time the private international banking system was the primary source of credit for the country. Nevertheless, a political decision was taken to acknowledge the debt and to renegotiate it in order to avoid any obstacles to the restoration of private bank credit (Weinert 1981). Commercial bank lending, however, was not re-established despite the negotiations, and the country turned principally to Third World and European governments for new credit. Later on, loans began to flow from socialist countries in Eastern Europe and from Cuba, both for military purchases and for consumption, while exports continued the downward slide begun in the 1970s (Ugarteche 1987). The economic actors were not prepared to assume a dynamic export role. Neither was the state prepared to replace the private sector, nor was the private sector prepared to take risks. So exports continued to fall and external deficits to grow, covered by fresh loans, until the debt/goods exports ratio hit the record of 3,972 per cent at the beginning of the 1990s. Only a small portion of the lending was used to finance projects that saved or generated foreign exchange, such that the outstanding debt could not be covered by the national economy.

Not unlike the support Nicaragua received from foreign governments, Honduras and Guatemala received similar credits in the 1980–95 period. Honduras continued to benefit from such lending in 1985–90, when these had ceased for Latin America as a whole. The exceptions in the region were El Salvador and Costa Rica. Costa Rica suffered a crisis in the balance of payments at the same time as the rest of Latin America, and it might well have suffered a greater crisis during the rest of the decade if it had not made prudent use of the new resources made available. It managed to reduce its outstanding debt by using the credits in activities, mainly tourism, that generated foreign exchange. El Salvador, despite growing current accounts deficits in relation to exports, did not make good use of loans, and rather financed deficits with transfers of capital from overseas from Salvadoran migrants and from the oligarchy, and in this way financed the war. But El Salvador's debt levels continued to deteriorate with the decline in export earnings due to falling prices for its principal products and to problems in the MCCA. The outstanding debt in constant 1980 dollars fell from $1,505 million in 1985 to $1,402 million in 1990, reflecting both a policy of avoiding greater indebtedness and the difficulties the country experienced in obtaining governmental loans from the United States due to human rights violations.

The explanation of how Guatemala and El Salvador were able to reduce their debts in constant dollars, while the current accounts deficit grew worse in the second half of the 1980s, lies in the size of private transfers from overseas, which were essentially remittances from emigrants who sent dollars to their relatives. There are an estimated 800,000 Salvadoreans in the United States, each of whom sends home $300 dollars a year on average, adding up to $240 million annually, although other

TABLE 6.5 Foreign debt of Central America: basic statistics, 1970–92 (annual averages by five-year period, per cent and millions of 1980 dollars)

| | Outstanding debt at end of period | Annual increase in real debt (%) | Private transfers from overseas | Transfers/ outstanding current accounts | Debt/goods exports (%) |
|---|---|---|---|---|---|
| **Costa Rica** | | | | | |
| 1970–75 | 1,001 | * | * | * | – |
| 1975–80 | 3,183 | 26.6 | 14 | 4.4 | 213 |
| 1980–85 | 3,146 | 4.9 | 20 | 8.5 | 395 |
| 1985–90 | 2,476 | -3.6 | 28 | 11.5 | 370 |
| 1990–92 | 2,373 | -6.9 | 30 | 17.5 | 264 |
| **Nicaragua** | | | | | |
| 1970–75 | 921 | * | * | * | – |
| 1975–80 | 1,571 | 11.9 | 1 | 0.3 | 187 |
| 1980–85 | 3,751 | 20.7 | 2 | 0.7 | 864 |
| 1985–90 | 6,618 | 11.8 | 2 | 0.3 | 2,542 |
| 1990–92 | 6,376 | -0.1 | 1 | 0.3 | 3,972 |
| **El Salvador** | | | | | |
| 1970–75 | * | * | * | * | – |
| 1975–80 | 1,176 | * | 34 | 53.3 | 96 |
| 1980–85 | 1,505 | 6.8 | 50 | 31.7 | 226 |
| 1985–90 | 1,402 | -1.4 | 118 | 77.0 | 332 |
| 1990–92 | 1,379 | -1.2 | 208 | 126.1 | 386 |
| **Honduras** | | | | | |
| 1970–75 | 711** | * | * | * | – |
| 1975–80 | 1,261 | 15.5 | 4 | 2.8 | 136 |
| 1980–85 | 2,306 | 13.7 | 8 | 3.4 | 272 |
| 1985–90 | 2,235 | 3.5 | 10 | 5.8 | 408 |
| 1990–92 | 2,087 | -1.6 | 11 | 4.6 | 411 |
| **Guatemala** | | | | | |
| 1970–75 | 764** | * | * | * | – |
| 1975–80 | 1,057 | 85 | 129 | 134.5 | 71 |
| 1980–85 | 2,047 | 12.7 | 70 | 20.9 | 167 |
| 1985–90 | 1,639 | -2.9 | 60 | 50.8 | 248 |
| 1990–92 | 1,523 | -5.4 | 134 | 81.9 | 208 |

*Notes*: * Figures for total public and private debt for this period do not exist.
** Corresponds to 1976.

*Source*: Various editions of ECLAC, *Balance de la economía de América Latina*.

estimates put the total at $1.3 billion (Orellana 1992). Table 6.5 shows the importance of that category for financing the current accounts deficit. The available reliable information from 1976 on shows that remittances to El Salvador add up to some 53 per cent of the surplus in current accounts for the period 1976–80, and cover 32, 77 and 126 per cent of the deficit in the following five-year periods. This reduced the demand for foreign resources to cover the current accounts deficit and allowed the debt to be reduced between 1990 and 1992. In Guatemala the case is similar, although less dramatic, except in the period 1976–80 when its internal conflict had begun and the Salvadorean conflict had not yet reached post-1980 levels.

Apparently, those displaced by the war managed to migrate in important numbers and send remittances to their families back home, injecting a significant quantity of foreign exchange into the economy as a whole. This would explain the fact that import levels and debt payments were maintained even though exports fell off in those countries. For reasons that merit a sociological or anthropological analysis, this phenomenon did not occur in Nicaragua, where transfers from overseas were consistently insignificant in terms of the current accounts deficit. Although the proportion of remittances in relation to exports rose, that was due to the dramatic collapse of exports, and not to the size of the remittances, which totalled between $1 million and $2 million in 1980 dollars between 1976 and 1992. Honduras presents a case that is less extreme but similar: remittances were between 2.8 and 4.8 per cent of the current accounts deficit. In the case of Costa Rica, remittances were not important for two reasons: a high income level in the national economy, and social peace during the entire period, meaning no great displacement of people overseas. This would imply for both Guatemala and El Salvador that their linkages to the global economy are made in part by migrants and the relationships they establish with their country of origin, a phenomenon that does not exist for other countries in the region. The data for Nicaragua probably underestimate the effect on the balance of payments, since the emigrant population is significant, and, as Funkhouser (1990) points out, many families had at least one member living overseas during the 1980s. Funkhouser's argument is that when one family member migrates, he sends remittances to help maintain the family or to buy housing.

**Services in the new global economy**   One aspect that has changed in Central America is the share in foreign exchange earnings and linkages to the global economy related to tourism. The climatic advantages and the existence of attractive beaches in the region have given rise to a surge in tourism, which is growing ever more significant, particularly in Costa

TABLE 6.6 Some social indicators

| | Costa Rica 1986 | Costa Rica 1990 | Nicaragua 1986 | Nicaragua 1990 | El Salvador 1986 | El Salvador 1990 | Honduras 1986 | Honduras 1990 | Guatemala 1986 | Guatemala 1990 |
|---|---|---|---|---|---|---|---|---|---|---|
| Life expectancy[1] | 74 | 75 | 63 | 65 | 67 | 64 | 62 | 65 | 61 | 63 |
| % of students who finish primary school[2] | 75 | 76 | 85 | 35 | 68 | 31 | 27 | 43 | 38 | 36 |
| Daily calorie intake as % of minimum daily requirement | 118 | 124 | 105 | 105 | 91 | 105 | 95 | 96 | 99 | 107 |
| Low-weight births[3] | 9 | 6 | 15 | 15 | 13 | 15 | 9 | 20 | 18 | 14 |
| Malnourished children under 5 (slight + serious) | 46 | 6 | n/a | 12 | 58 | 15 | 31 | 25 | n/a | 42 |
| Urban poverty (% of population) | n/a | 8 | 21 | 21 | 20 | 20 | 14 | 31 | 66 | 17 |
| Rural poverty[4] (% of population) | n/a | 20 | 19 | 19 | 32 | 32 | 55 | 70 | 74 | 51 |
| Income of poorest 40% of population (% of GDP)[4] | 12.0 | 13.1 | – | – | 15.5 | – | – | 8.7 | – | 7.9 |

*Sources*: 1. UNICEF 1988 and 1992: Table 1.
2. UNICEF 1988 and 1992: Table 4.
3. UNICEF 1988 and 1992: Table 2.
4. PNUD 1995 and 1993: Charts 12 and 18; the 1986 figure is the average for 1985–89; the 1990 figure is the average for 1981–92.

Rica. The development of this aspect of the economy, taking into consideration improved transportation and new forms of communications, has led to growth in those countries that managed to set up basic infrastructure and the national conditions required to attract foreign tourists. This policy has had different results in Guatemala, Honduras and Costa Rica, with the latter experiencing dramatic growth in tourism earnings, from 8.3 per cent of goods exports earnings in the second half of the 1970s to 22.5 per cent in the first years of the 1990s. El Salvador, which has no explicit tourism promotion policy like its neighbours, has observed an increase from 3 per cent of exports to 112.1 per cent between the end of the 1970s and the beginning of the 1990s, a figure similar to that of Guatemala which does have an explicit policy. An explanation could be that as long as a country is not at peace, tourism promotion policies have no impact on tourists' perception of personal risk. However, in constant 1980 dollars, Costa Rica is followed by Guatemala in foreign exchange earnings from tourism, having doubled them between the end of the 1980s and the beginning of the 1990s. In other words, the approach of peace in Guatemala seems to have allowed for tourism promotion policies to take hold. Honduras and Nicaragua apparently have high percentages of income from tourism relative to exports, but that is mostly due to the depressed level of the export base, rather than to a surge in tourism. The establishment of air transportation services and communications systems for tourism are externalities that benefit goods exports and the economy as a whole, such that tourism in the region has become a modernizing and dynamizing sector that builds linkages with the international infrastructure required for that industry.

**Social effects of the systemic crisis**  A study undertaken by organizations grouped in the International Save the Children Federation, presented in Bogotá, Colombia, in April 1992, shows a marked deterioration in the living conditions of children. The contrast between the beginning of the 1980s and the end of that decade indicates a fall in living conditions for the population as a whole, parallel to a fall in GDP per capita, but with a sharper fall in conditions for boys, girls and women. The evidence seems to suggest that the weight of the economic depression fell more harshly on women and girls than on men and boys, although all were affected (ISCA 1992). The contradiction would seem to be that while medical conditions increased life expectancy from birth, living conditions deteriorated, although the averages do not seem to follow the same trend in all countries (see Table 6.6).

The data for Nicaragua do not seem to be trustworthy. It is hardly believable that, in an economic crisis of the magnitude that country suffered, the social indicators have remained stable, unless high indebtedness had been incurred to cover the basic needs of the population. In that case the data for the middle of the 1990s would show a reverse from the stable trend towards a natural deterioration derived from the fall in per capita income, given the crisis of international insertion in an open economy whose export goods are at depressed prices. The only social indicator that shows the impact of the systemic crisis, on top of the war and the situation of social instability prevalent in the 1980s, is the deterioration in education. Between the first years of the 1980s and the average for the decade, the percentage of school-age children that finished primary school fell from 85 to 35 per cent between 1980–86 and 1985–87. It is possible that when the most recent data are published the deterioration will be even sharper.

The data for El Salvador show that life expectancy shortened between 1986 and 1990, reflecting the deterioration of the economy. It is the only country in the region with that trend. The increase in life expectancy in the rest of the region could be explained by the implementation of public health campaigns which reduced infant mortality. In general, the proportion of boys/girls born underweight rose only in El Salvador and Honduras, having improved in the other three countries. The data for El Salvador seem to be a mirror of that for Nicaragua, and do not allow for an analysis of what really occurred in Salvadorean society during its economic crisis.

## Note

1. For a detailed critical analysis from a theoretical viewpoint see John Weeks 1993: ch. 1.

APPENDIX 6.1 Export products of Central America

| Costa Rica | Nicaragua | El Salvador | Honduras | Guatemala |
|---|---|---|---|---|
| Traditional agricultural products and metals | | | | |
| Coffee | Coffee | Coffee | Coffee | Coffee |
| Bananas | Bananas | Cane sugar | Bananas | Bananas |
| Cane sugar | Cane sugar | Cotton | Cane sugar | Cane sugar |
| Cacao | Meat | | Meat | Meat |
| Meat | Tobacco | | Tobacco | Cotton |
| | Cotton | | Cotton | |
| | Gold | | Wood | |
| | Other | | Zinc | |
| | | | Silver | |
| | | | Lead. | |
| Sea products, new agricultural products and manufactures | | | | |
| Shrimp and fish | Lobsters, shrimp and fish | Shrimp | Lobsters and shrimp | Cardamom |
| Plants, flowers and herbs | Sesame | Manufactured products | Manufactured products | Vegetables and root crops |
| Pineapples | Chemical manufactures | Perfume, cosmetics and toiletries | Soap | Chemical manufactures |
| Manufactured products | Other | Insecticides, fungicides and disinfectants | Wooden manufactures | Oil |
| Wooden manufactures | | Cotton thread | Other | Other |
| Liquors | | Apparel | | Agroindustrial products |
| Other | | | | Canned vegetables and meat |

*Source:* ECLAC 1992.

# 7. The Crisis of the Millennium and Its Expansion

World capitalism is in a severe crisis. Economic growth in developing countries failed to be what was expected after the economic reforms. Vulnerability and volatility seem to characterize growth dynamics today due to the impact of real-time information and the perfect opening of capital markets around the world, with few exceptions (China, Cuba and North Korea). US Federal Reserve Board president Alan Greenspan has been warning the international community, and US investors in particular, to slow down their expectations as it is recognized that the New York stock market is in a bubble. The question posed is how to slow down the bubble in order for it not to burst. The answer has been to raise interest rates slowly but it is not reacting, leaving a great uncertainty about when and how the Dow Jones Index will become normal, i.e. will be related to real economic growth and not to expectations of profit from speculation.

The IMF has lost its soul and its former Extended Structural Adjustment Fund Facility was turned into the Poverty Reduction and Growth Facility when its executive director resigned soon after being re-elected in the autumn of 1999 and US pressure on the World Bank led to the resignation of its senior economist Dr Joseph Stiglitz later that same year. International institutions created in order to guarantee world stability seem not to have succeeded after the changes introduced in 1971 with the free flotation of currencies. Discussions are taking place on a new international financial architecture that will replace the existing one. The lack of success with growth, in fact the shrinking of many African economies, and the evidence of huge income concentration in the world as shown in UNDP's *Human Development Report 1999* have resulted in an extensive debate on the usefulness of current theoretical thinking.

Meanwhile, international pressure to cancel the debt of poor countries under the Jubilee 2000 initiative has mounted. It is a world movement that has shaken the roots of power in the ACCs and forced the treasuries of the G7 to act on the subject and write off debts. This is something which has never been done before except in Germany in 1953 and in 1929, when creditor countries wrote off the German debt for various reasons.

The dangerous part is that a US-led consumption bubble gives the impression that everything is fine while all the industrial indices of the G7 except for the USA and Canada have negative growth for several quarters after mid-1997. The warnings from Greenspan should be seen in this light. The roadrunner has run off the cliff but continues to wiggle its feet.

After twenty years of trying to reverse the fall in the productivity of capital and labour caused by the exhaustion of the oil-based productive paradigm and the rise in oil prices, the underlying problem has emerged. The new theoretical and productive paradigms have not managed to solve satisfactorily the problems posed twenty-five years ago. Today, as in 1929 and 1876, there are growing doubts as to whether such theories can predict the future; if they cannot, they must be revised or discarded. Omerod, in his book *The Death of Economics* (1994) suggested precisely that five years ago. If the productive paradigm has not managed to solve the problem of falling productivity, it ought to be abandoned in favour of a more stable one. It has been suggested that the pace of innovation has choked off the possibility of recouping investments, that as the cost of capital rises due to technological complexity, the pace of innovation is keeping capitalists from recovering their capital and earning a profit.

In Chapter 2 it was argued that the crisis under way is a systemic one, caused by capital's inability to recover its productivity in Japan and Western Europe. The data from Englander and Gurney published in the *OECD Economic Studies* no. 22 are irrefutable (1994b). The United States may have gone slightly past the zero line, but the other developed economies are still experiencing negative growth in productivity. The Japanese crisis is a vivid expression of this fact.

Thirdly, the institutions set up following the Second World War to resolve the problems that arose in 1929 seem no longer to suffice. Every year 360 times more money changes hands in financial transactions than in commercial ones. This calls for a system of international regulation unthinkable before now. Neither the IMF nor the World Bank was set up to deal with this sort of reality. Even less prepared is the Bank of International Settlements in Basel, whose mission is to oversee the operations of commercial banks within their own national arenas. The changes outlined in this book indicate that national arenas have all but disappeared for some purposes, among them finance.

In *El Estado deudor* (1986, first part), Ugarteche concurred with Versluysen (1982) that the lack of a regulatory framework for international banking has had an infinite multiplier effect on credit. The workings of this infinite multiplier effect is the reason why every year financial operations move 360 times as much money as commercial ones. This surely makes no sense. Finance is the flip-side of the production of goods and services in all economic theory from Hume onwards. This new phenomenon calls for an institutional framework quite different from the one that has existed to date. We may be facing a discussion similar to the one that took place between White and Keynes on the pros and cons of a world central bank versus an international monetary fund, or the usefulness of a two-metal standard versus that of a dollar/gold standard. Perhaps today that discussion would focus on the usefulness of having three standard reserve currencies (yen-yuan, US dollar, Euro) versus the US dollar alone. No doubt we are facing the most serious questioning since the 1930s, in theoretical, productive and institutional terms. Until the answers are found, the systemic crisis will not be fully overcome.

## The Asian crisis

The Asian crisis cannot be understood in isolation from the Japanese crisis, nor could the downward slide of Japan be analysed without examining the derivative effects of the crises of its Asian neighbours.[1] The Asian miracle has disappeared from the screen and the world crisis has taken its place. Despite incredibly high export growth rates in Malaysia, Indonesia and Thailand, as noted in Chapter 4, and despite the complexity of their exports, the proportion represented by raw materials was still quite high. The revaluation of the Japanese yen in 1985 – from 238 to the dollar to 168 to the dollar (a rise of 29 per cent) – may well have pushed production out of Japan and into its neighbours over the second half of the 1980s. At that same moment China devalued its currency by 44 per cent – from 2,396 yuan to the dollar to 3,452 – while other Asian currencies remained stable. The combination of revaluation in Japan and devaluation in China against the dollar, effectively devalued the yuan by 66.66 per cent against the yen. With that push, China's manufacturing exports took off, going from $12.2 billion dollars annually during the first half of the 1980s to $32.5 billion annually in the second half. The Japanese

TABLE 7.1 Exports from China (annual average in US$ billions)

|                    | 1980–85 | 1986–90 | 1991–95 | 1996–97 |
|--------------------|---------|---------|---------|---------|
| Primary products   | 10.8    | 14.0    | 18.0    | 22.9    |
| Manufactured goods | 12.2    | 32.5    | 84.5    | 143.9   |

market is not only important for the NICs or the ASEAN 4, it is also crucial for China.

Monetary changes gave rise to a change in the pattern of Japanese production and caused what is known as the dislocation of production in Asia. Japanese factory-owners cut back on their production in Japan, and began buying parts and components for their finished goods from their Asian neighbours. This dislocation strengthened intra-regional trade because parts and components for Japan's exports to the world are being made in the region. Table 4.8 (see Chapter 4) shows what category of product grew most in Asian trade during the 1980s and continued growing into the 1990s: intensive raw materials products, intensive products in scale, products from speciality suppliers and products based on sciences. My hypothesis is that these products were produced for the Japanese market and were primarily components for re-export. That would explain the stagnation of the Japanese economy during the 1990s while Japan's total exports continued to grow, as did the foreign trade of the region including China. The big question is: If Japan is the engine of Asia's dynamism and it went into crisis in 1991, why did trade continue to grow for such a long time?

In 1994, the yuan was devalued by 61 per cent against the yen and by 49 per cent against the dollar (see Table 7.2). China's objective was to export a greater volume of manufactured goods than Japan and its Asian

TABLE 7.2 Value of the Chinese yuan compared to its trading partners

| Years | US$ | Yen |
| --- | --- | --- |
| 1983 | 1.975 | 0.008 |
| 1984 | 2.327 | 0.009 |
| 1985 | 2.396 | 0.012 |
| 1986 | 3.452 | 0.020 |
| 1987 | 3.722 | 0.023 |
| 1988 | 3.722 | 0.029 |
| 1989 | 3.765 | 0.027 |
| 1990 | 4.783 | 0.033 |
| 1991 | 5.333 | 0.039 |
| 1992 | 5.514 | 0.043 |
| 1993 | 5.761 | 0.052 |
| 1994 | 8.618 | 0.084 |
| 1995 | 8.350 | 0.089 |
| 1996 | 8.314 | 0.076 |
| 1997 | 8.289 | 0.068 |
| 1998 | 8.280 | – |

competitors that had stable exchange rates (South Korea, Taiwan, Thailand, Malaysia, Indonesia, Singapore and Hong Kong). From 1994 onwards the devaluation overshot its mark and had to be adjusted back. The yuan was revalued slightly against the dollar by 3.9 per cent in 1998, while against the yen the revaluation was 19 per cent. Japan's weak yen policy is viewed by China as a way of competing with its exports and it effectively presses China to devalue the yuan yet again. The effect of China's exchange-rate policy on the export structure is evident: manufacturing exports have tripled since 1991. This introduced an unthinkable degree of competition among Southeast Asian countries and put an end to the expansion of their exports. Parallel to the growth of China's exports, expectations of export growth among the four economies of Southeast Asia were reined in (see Table 7.3).

Table 7.1 shows that China's raw materials exports followed a natural trend of vegetative growth, while an explosion in manufacturing led to a tripling of those exports from the first five-year period in the sample. No doubt the exchange rate is one variable, in addition to export processing zones, trade liberalization and foreign investment laws and, above all, China's policy of not allowing international institutions to interfere in any way with its trade policies.

In Chapter 4 we pointed out the virtues of industrialization policies, but we also noted the difficulty of achieving correct industrialization policies. There are two groups of countries in Asia in this regard.

1. Japan, South Korea and Taiwan had directed public lending policies as well as special historical, political and cultural circumstances that pulled them out of the pack of industrializing countries, and made their development style not replicable. The lack of armies, the communist enemy and Confucian culture are three elements worth underlining (World Bank 1993). Equally important is the fact that South Korea and Taiwan were Japanese colonies during the first half of the twentieth century, and in the process came to have an efficient public administration. These countries managed to make the transition from import substitution to export sub-

TABLE 7.3  Export growth projections (%)

|             | Projected 1996 | Actual 1996 | Projected 1997 | Actual 1997 |
|-------------|----------------|-------------|----------------|-------------|
| Indonesia   | 14.3           | 7.9         | 15.0           | 10.0        |
| Malaysia    | 18.0           | 7.3         | 15.0           | 7.4         |
| Philippines | 25.0           | 17.7        | 23.0           | 22.8        |
| Thailand    | 22.0           | -1.7        | 7.7            | -0.5        |

stitution policies with a simulated free market and distorted prices (Wade 1990; Amsden 1989). The distortions created by the state in the process of import substitution were compensated for by exports (Jomo et al. 1997). These are economies without natural resources and thus had to make transformation the basis of their development.

2. The other group of countries is made up of Indonesia, Thailand and Malaysia which, according to the World Bank's 'Asian Miracle' (1993), were to open the way for a new generation of export-led economies. Up to the most recent date examined in Chapter 4, these were solid economies that maintained high rates of economic growth. They did not have industrialization policies, and rather were led by the export market which in turn induced industrialization and structural change. Jomo (Jomo et al. 1997) suggests that industrialization in these countries was derived from the industrial policies of Japan, Taiwan, South Korea and Singapore, which encouraged their companies to move to neighbouring countries. He further suggests that these economies depended on foreign investment for capital, technology and market access. These countries did not have agrarian reforms to help improve income distribution, as in South Korea and Taiwan, and functioned more as food suppliers for Asia until they began industrializing. These were economies that had natural resources. Socially and culturally they are much more heterogeneous than the economies of Northeast Asia. They did not have the nationalist thrust of Taiwan, South Korea or Japan. Continuity has been provided by the permanence in power of a monarch in Thailand since 1946 and a president in Indonesia from 1965 to 1998. It was not a stable continuity, rather one centred on a monolithic political regime. In Malaysia, a multi-ethnic coalition has remained in power. In Thailand, the regime has a liberal outlook, although there is state support for private activities, which is not the case in either Malaysia or Indonesia.

Following the *endaka* (30 per cent revaluation of the yen against the dollar in 1985, from 238 to 168 yen to the dollar), the operating costs in dollars of Japanese companies rose substantially, giving rise to a decentralization of production to neighbouring Asian countries in the Southeast, primarily Malaysia, Indonesia and Thailand. Korean and Taiwanese companies also migrated to the countries of Southeast Asia. This is known as the 'flying geese' ('*akamatsu*') process: a 'following' country imports goods from a developed one. It then proceeds to manufacture them, and finally it exports them. As a 'following' country progresses through stages on the technological scale, learning to produce goods of greater complexity, value and sophistication, others focus on their own, protecting nascent industries and promoting exports. The theory of the flying geese emphasizes national location over company control.

## Interpretations of the crisis

There are four theoretical viewpoints on the Asian crisis which could be summarized as follows:

1. Exchange rate. This argument is made by the Bank of International Settlements in its annual report dated 8 June 1998. The report maintains that the problem emerged when the dollar began to grow stronger in 1995 due to sustained economic growth in the United States, while the mark and the yen remained weak as a result of the weakness of the German and Japanese economies. Institutional investors pulled out of those currencies and moved into Asian currencies that both offered higher interest rates and were pegged to the US dollar. In other words, with a dollar that was gaining in value against the deutschmark and the yen, loaning money in the Asian countries now in crisis seemed to be risk-free and highly profitable. The exchange rates of the NICs and the ASEAN 4 were tied to the dollar and they were also gaining in value. In the end, short-term loans were used to finance growing current accounts deficits, which generated pressure on the balance of payments and led to falling reserves. In turn, this exerted downward pressure on the exchange rate and led to the crisis no one could predict.

The BIS admits that banking supervision was inadequate in the 1990s, allowing such crises to occur in several parts of the world. The general recommendation to prevent these problems is to have financial systems supervised in the international arena, and to adjust the demand for credit to maintain balance in domestic banking, so that the international financial system does not get squeezed.

2. Capital flows and financial panic. In the speech he gave upon receiving an honorary doctorate at the Universidad Católica in Lima on 30 June 1998, Rudiger Dornsbusch summed up everything that had been said to date and wondered how it could happen from one day to the next that something that was not even suspected could become such a disaster. That question leads us to reflect on the difficulties faced by economic theory today. Up to 1996, growth rates in Thailand were high. During the 1980s that country grew at a rate of 7.9 per cent annually; in the 1990s at 8.6 per cent annually, except for 1996 when it dropped to 6.7 per cent. Annual inflation was in the range of 4.4 to 5.9 per cent, and savings were an enviable 35 per cent of GDP on average. The fiscal surplus was 1.5 per cent of GDP in recent years (in the 1980s it was 3.4 per cent). The current accounts deficit was around 7 per cent of GDP, rising in 1995 and 1996 to 7.5 per cent, while the volume of foreign debt grew from $48.1 billion (average for 1991–95) to $78.1 billion in 1996.

Dornbusch suggests that the problem does not lie in the numbers, rather in vulnerability: 'Vulnerability means that if something starts to go wrong, suddenly everything starts to go wrong' (Dornbusch 1989: 9). Vulnerability is transmitted by a fragile financial system, which is under-capitalized for the level of debt, and which features a set-up for short-term debt servicing that can make it all come tumbling down in a flash. When this happens, domestic interest rates can not be raised to close off the demand for credit, nor can they be lowered. In the end they rise automatically due to the problems faced by its users. In a context of relatively fixed exchange rates, this is problematic. In May 1997 when it was decided to lower interest rates, a catastrophe ensued.

Dornbusch argues that you never know just how deep a puddle is until you step into it. He also says that if you manage to diagnose the symptoms and catch a crisis in time, then it won't happen here, but it may well occur somewhere else where it could not be foreseen. Don't fight to hang on to an exchange rate, let it float. The more you struggle, the worse the crisis and the more reserves will erode. Better to let it float before the disaster to avoid the steep fall and the cost in lost reserves that would have to be paid if it is postponed. Economic actors should never trust political actors to do the right thing, because they never do.

Vulnerability grows out of the interaction of domestic banking develop-ment, the international financial system, the development of consumer banking and the local property market. Dornbusch suggests that the Asian crisis is no different from the crisis of 1982 in Latin America or that of 1995 in Mexico. In the final analysis, Asia's crisis had many links with Japan's. Now Japan will have to lower taxes by some 3 per cent of GDP to stimulate its feeble economy and take some steps towards opening up the economy if it is to stave off what appears to be the impending collapse, in one way or another, of its financial system, of trust in the country and of what Japan achieved over five decades of sustained growth. The Japanese state cannot go on as it has. All of this puts pressure on China. If China devalues, Asia will deteriorate further and the world will end up losing. If China does not devalue, it will have serious problems maintaining growth and keeping its budget in line. Dornbusch concludes that a country's risk must be followed by keeping minute track of the short-term debt owed by every company and bank, since if a number of them mature at once it could precipitate a serious situation in which the country is highly vulnerable.

3. The fundamental factors. Corsetti, Pesenti and Roubini pin the blame not on capital flows or the panic that occurred in Asia, but rather on fundamentals:

- a significant revaluation of their currencies and a distorted exchange rate

- large and growing current accounts deficits
- a vicious circle of 'competitive devaluations'
- the contagion resulting not from irrational panic, but from fundamental factors
- excessive investment in high-risk, low-profit projects
- excessive indebtedness and excessive lending in the financial sector because the potential risks were cancelled out by implicit or explicit bail-out guarantees from the government
- current accounts deficits financed by an accumulation of short-term and unhedged loans
- excessive lending in the 1990s and a sudden reversal of such flows in 1997

4. Too much state/corruption. Charles Wolf of the Rand Coporation, a philosopher of the perfect market, argues that Asia's problems stem from having followed the Japanese development model, with its high degree of public intervention. The accumulation of errors evident in Asia was among the perverse effects of a development model based on state participation in and regulation of the market. The state/market link gave rise to an immeasurable degree of corruption, as the subjectivity of choices for rewards ended up rewarding the choosers as well. Wolf, a perfect market radical, points out the following problems:

- Wasted resources when decisions not based on the market are taken, as in the case of Indonesia investing in a national car industry and in airplane manufacture. These failures, due to the lack of market reasoning, lay bare the fact that Asia's economic growth came about through increases in the capital and labour base, not through increases in productivity.
- Structural imbalances that resulted from giving preference to export markets over national markets. As a consequence, national production was shortchanged and consumption levels repressed to satisfy external demand.
- Excess installed capacity in the manufacturing export sector based on the state's decision to choose 'winners'. The incapacity to take into account the saturation of demand while production continued expanding, which contributed to devaluations, falling prices and sudden adverse changes.
- A sense of security among favoured industries, people and companies. When these actors faced the market and were unable to operate satisfactorily, they and their foreign creditors expected to be rescued with additional resources from the state, be that state national or foreign. Such were the cases of Yamaichi Securities in Japan, or the Jalla group

in Korea, or the car industry in Timor. The government will always put up the difference, it was thought, when the market does not respond properly.
• Under-the-table decision-making and favouritism, exclusivity and corruption in processes that were hardly transparent had a corrosive effect on society and on the region's political systems.

Despite these most publicized explanations of the Asian crisis, which would later be expanded to cover the Russian crisis, I continue to believe that the root of the problem lies in a systemic crisis due to deficiencies in productivity.

## Systemic crisis and the crisis in productivity: A different reading of the Asian crisis

This book offers a different approach from those summed up above. My hypothesis is that problems with the productivity of capital have interrupted the steady growth of capitalism as it exists today. Capitalism as such has been immersed in a systemic crisis for two decades. It tried to break free by means of a new productive paradigm based on knowledge. That effort was accompanied by a new theoretical paradigm: Friedman and the perfect market. In this theoretical paradigm, money is the only thing that matters; everything else will be adjusted by the perfect nature of markets. It marked the end of the welfare state and the disappearance of Keynes from the academic curriculum. After two decades of trying to achieve a rebound in productivity in developed countries and in almost all capitalist countries (which today includes every country except Cuba, North Korea and China), this approach appears to have reached its zenith and begun a precipitous decline.

In 1971, when the dollar was detached from gold and the dollar/gold standard was abandoned in favour of the dollar standard, a series of systemic changes unfolded, leading to: the rise in oil prices, the surge in international lending, the rapid rise of international interest rates based on the US prime rate and the British London Interbank Offered Rate (LIBOR), the Latin American crisis, the change in the productive paradigm from one based on oil to one based on knowledge, the change in the theoretical paradigm for the economy from Keynes to Friedman, from the welfare state to the notion of the sole perfect market, which became universal after the fall of the Berlin Wall and the disappearance of the Soviet Union, and with them the end of really existing socialism, arriving at Fukuyama's *The End of History*. The existing institutions for spreading these paradigms across the globe have either outlived their utility or have shown themselves to be useless. Both the IMF and the World Bank, the two stabilizers of the world economy, have been bypassed. Rather, they have demonstrated that their policies and their theoretical instruments can do no more than transfer resources from one place to another. The cost of pursuing the theory now in vogue, of having the productive paradigm in place and persevering with the existing institutionality, is a world depression characterized by deflation.

The 1990s was supposed to be the decade of global economic take-off, after two decades of sluggish growth and productivity problems in the G7 countries. The rules of the game agreed to in the Washington Consensus did become universal, the borderless world captured the global imagination, new advances in telecommunications ought to have provided all the necessary information to the economic actors so they could make decisions in a global market with a single price and a single set of rules. During the 1990s, there was no opposing force on the global economic plane. The Asian miracle fulfilled its function with a healthy dose of state interventionism that was acceptable because of the region's high rates of economic growth. Latin America was back on the road to growth, at a low-to-average rate but greater than the negative rate of the 1980s. Unrestricted openings gave rise to a surge in foreign trade and the unchallenged belief in the credo 'export or die'.

Meanwhile, in the first third of 1994, China's currency was devalued by 40 per cent better to compete with exports from its Asian neighbours, including Japan which had shown symptoms of cooling off since 1990 (see Table 7.2). Problems collecting on bad loans disrupted the Japanese financial system, whose stock market, which had been experiencing problems since 1990, took a beating in 1994. From a peak of 23,000 points in 1990, the Nikkei index fell to around 16,000, where it has remained since 1994.

Apparently, in 1994 Japanese banks began making more and more short-term loans to their Asian partners at an interest rate that was close to zero. As a result, a growing volume of Asia's loans came due at the same time, much as occurred in Latin America in 1982 due to the change in short-term lending strategy to the region in 1978. The European banks followed suit, sowing great uncertainty in Europe's economy.

The total volume of all forms of capital operating in the world added up to $1,131 trillion dollars daily in 1992, and it was estimated to be around $1,400 trillion in 1998. In a single week, the quantity of dollars and other currencies that changes hands is equivalent to the total production of the United States in a year. In other words, the international capital market in all its forms is hundreds of times larger than the world production that sustains it. This occurred while the systemic crisis was brewing and changes were introduced to modify both the model of accumulation and the theory behind that model.

The long-term downward trend in the terms of trade between raw materials and manufactured products was acknowledged by Prebisch over sixty years ago. No one imagined that trend was going to become accentuated as a result of required technological change. The prices of raw materials in constant 1980 dollars fell drastically in the 1980s and continued falling in the 1990s. In the first months of 1997 some prices fell significantly, creating difficulties first for the economies of Thailand and Indonesia. Those two exported significant volumes of manufactured goods, but 40 per cent of their total exports were still raw materials. This introduced problems in their balance of payments, in light of the coincidence of due dates on their short-term loans from international creditors and subsequent problems of devaluation and its effects on internationalized stock exchanges. At the same time, Thailand and Indonesia were incapable of paying their short-term debts to Japan and Korea, causing problems in those countries. Japan already suffered productivity problems as noted, and the existing troubles in its financial system worsened. These problems spread later on when creditor banks had to write off the losses incurred. This led to an infusion of cash into US banks, but also to the recognition internationally that Japan's banks were in a sorry state, which up to that point had been only a domestic problem. Japanese losses were on the order of $612 billion, all of which had to be covered by the Japanese government.

Elsewhere, Europe's banks, with portfolios concentrated in Asia and Eastern Europe (see Table 7.4), had to absorb losses, and the pressure on their currencies (and in favour of the dollar) forced devaluations as indicated in Table 7.5. To the degree that Asia's economies suffered negative growth following the débâcle of 1997, the market for US and European

TABLE 7.4 International banking exposure, excluding Japan (US$ billions)

| Destination | European banks | US Banks |
|---|---|---|
| Europe, United States, Latin America | 133.6 | 63.4 |
| Asia (except Japan) | 132.4 | 29.4 |
| Eastern Europe | 84.8 | 10.4 |
| Others | 74.9 | 13.8 |
| Total | 425.7 | 117.0 |

Source: *The Wall Street Journal Américas* in *Diario El Comercio* (Lima), 7 October 1998, p. E6.

exports contracted. This led to a reduction in the profits of companies that operate in those markets, and subsequent problems on the New York stock exchange.

The New York stock exchange became the safe refuge for capital fleeing instability in Eastern Europe and Asia, such that a fall on the Tokyo exchange was accompanied by a rise in New York. The Dow Jones Average of the New York exchange went from 4,000 points in 1994 to a record 9,300 in March 1998. In October 1997, when the Asian financial crisis caused huge drops in its stock markets, the New York exchange was dragged down for a few days. International stabilizers worked quickly through the IMF to keep the crisis from deepening across the planet, but global instability became inevitable. Markets lost some of their credibility and economic trends took a turn for the worse.

August 31, 1998 will be remembered as a day analogous to 28 October 1929. Stock markets around the world collapsed and the New York stock exchange lost 512 points, equivalent to $500 billion for investors and $2 trillion in stock value. These figures are comparable only to the crisis of 1929. On top of the nose-dive of between 30 and 50 per cent that raw materials prices suffered over the previous year came the dramatic fall on stock markets, which had been unstable since October 1997. The big question is whether the crisis of 1929 will be repeated, or if this time it will be different.

In history, great crises have been characterized by a fall in the price of raw materials, a rise in interest rates in New York and London, a drop in stock values, the closing off of credit and capital flows to developing countries and moratoria on foreign debt payments. In the crisis that began in 1997, a rise in interest rates has not yet occurred and, perhaps having learned something from history, there is still discussion as to whether they

TABLE 7.5 Devaluations compared to US dollar (%)

| Currency | Per cent devaluation 1997/1996 |
| --- | --- |
| French franc | 16.00 |
| Swiss franc | 9.10 |
| German mark | 16.87 |
| Japanese yen | 12.67 |
| Pound sterling | 3.70 |
| Italian lira | 16.62 |
| Canadian dollar | 4.34 |
| Spanish peseta | 17.40 |

Source: Diario Gestión (Lima), 1 September 1998, p. 31.

will rise or fall. The collapse of stock markets has, however, led to panic sown by instability in Japan over the possibility of a devaluation of China's currency, which would set off a new round of devaluations as occurred in 1997. It is worth recalling that the Japanese yen reached its greatest value of 88 yen to the US dollar in 1994 and has since fallen to the range of 140 yen to the dollar, a devaluation of 59 per cent. The principal currencies of the world all lost significant value against the dollar (over 2 per cent) between 1996 and 1997. In 1997 all of them devalued in order to export more, on average greater than 10 per cent (see Table 7.5). In 1998 there was a slight correction of 2 per cent, which left all currencies still strongly devalued against the US dollar. Something more dramatic occurred in Asia, and in general we can conclude that throughout the world the policies of competitive devaluation characteristic of the 1930s are being implemented.

Over six weeks beginning in the middle of July 1998, the New York stock exchange (NYSE) lost 1,800 points, equivalent to 19 per cent of its capital value. The ups and downs of the stock market are an indication of the weakened health of the world economy and of the fact that the productivity problems of capital were not resolved between 1994 and today (see Table 7.6).

The great fluctuations in price levels – fibrilation to use a medical term – are indicative of the degree of instability the stock market has suffered since June 1997 when Asia's economic problems became apparent (see Table 7.7). From June 1997, the NYSE, whose value peaked at $37.2 trillion dollars, seven times the GDP of the United States, suffered losses that had to be absorbed by investors' accounts. The total value at closing on 31 August 1998 was $31.1 trillion dollars. In other words, on the New York exchange alone losses added up to $6 trillion, greater than the GDP of the United States. In some cases these were compensated for by profits, but in

TABLE 7.6 Greatest crashes in New York stock exchange history

| Date | Per cent drop |
| --- | --- |
| 28 October 1929 | 12.82 |
| 29 October 1929 | 11.73 |
| 12 August 1932 | 8.40 |
| 21 July 1933 | 7.80 |
| 18 October 1937 | 7.75 |
| 19 October 1987 | 22.61 |
| 31 August 1998 | 6.36 |

*Source*: *Diario Gestión* (Lima), 1 September 1998, p. 35.

others they were not. Without a doubt, all transactions that were done by credit ended up in losses for the lender, since the stock ended up being worth less than the amount lent for its purchase. Generally speaking, in history this is the way in which crises spread from the stock market to the banking system, and from the banking system to the drying up of capital flows, and from there to moratoria on debt payments by the Third World.

Table 7.7 shows the severity of the fluctuations between June 1997 and August 1998. Generally, following periods of high fibrilation the market settles at a low level from which it begins once again to gain investors' confidence. Naturally, no one knows where the bottom of the market lies, and some anticipate that the bubble of the NYSE will burst and it will return to its normal level of between 4,000 and 5,000 points. Others argue that the problems are over and it will stabilize in the 7,000 range. Others even more optimistic think it will recover to the 9,000 range. Most likely, if it follows the pattern of previous financial crises (Kindleberger 1985) it will stabilize in the 4,000 to 5,000 range, while the losses of all actors around the world are written off and the dust settles in all the other markets, both for commodities and for stocks and bonds. The tendency for commodities to fall will continue until world growth stabilizes, which necessarily will first go through a phase of retrenchment while losses are absorbed. Losses in Latin America's export income will result from the fall in the price of commodities, its principal export products.

As an effect of the deterioration in the balance of payments, the region is beginning to show signs of external weakness. Devaluations in Mexico,

TABLE 7.7  Greatest losses in US$ on the NYSE

| Dates | Points lost (1 point = US$1 billion) |
| --- | --- |
| 23 October 1997 | 554.26 |
| 27 October 1997 | 512.61 |
| 31 August 1998 | 508 |
| 19 October 1987 | 357.36 |
| 27 August 1998 | 299.43 |
| 4 August 1998 | 247.37 |
| 15 August 1997 | 222.2 |
| 9 January 1998 | 207.01 |
| 15 June 1998 | 195.03 |
| 23 July 1998 | 192.25 |
| 23 June 1997 | 190.58 |
| 13 October 1989 | 186.88 |

*Source*: *Diario Gestión* (Lima), 1 September 1998, p. 35.

Venezuela and Colombia are evidence of this. No doubt this will lead to debt payment problems like the ones shown by Ecuador, Pakistan and Romania in early 1999, as well as bond flotations in order to pay back the old bonds. This was the case for Argentina, Uruguay and Peru at the end of 1999. Latin America's stock markets are falling sharply as a result of the pull-out of national and foreign investors in favour of the safe haven of the US dollar.

The global economic system is thus infected by the systemic crisis as a result of globalization and the free movement of capital. A solution will have to be sought both on the technological plane and on the theoretical one to achieve recovery in the long-term cycle of economic growth. Recovering productivity is the key and it will give rise to new technological changes as well as new theoretical ones. It appears that the theory based on the law of the single market and the sole world price may not survive the great crisis of the millennium.

The fall in the forecast estimate for growth is part of the growing awareness of several key factors:

1. The crisis in the level of financial speculation in Asia was triggered by real causes: the fall in the price of rubber in Thailand and the fall in the price of oil that affected Indonesia, due to a climatic phenomenon.
2. Financing of current accounts deficits today is essentially done through short-term financing of foreign trade, and that feeds the internal financing of economies in a substantive way through the national banking system of each country.
3. Losses by Asia's domestic financial systems due to devaluations are transferred to the international banking system and to investment banking. This ends up causing difficulties making payments on short-term inter-bank debt.
4. The degree of exposure of stock markets in emerging countries to investment by volatile capital which flees at the first sign of any difficulties.
5. The repetition of the phenomenon of shortening the term of short-term credits produces a negative net transfer of capital, generating a rapid fall in the international reserves of the receiving country.
6. The linking of all these phenomena, as Mynski points out. The problems caused by such things as hedge financing and Ponzi schemes are expected to be resolved over the long term, but they are not. Then, when anything goes wrong with exports, projections, the stock market, the rate of exchange, etc., a crisis is triggered and they end up causing both credit and financial problems.

The likely result is that, if the banking systems of countries are allowed to go bankrupt, the impact on international investment banks and on the  international banking system will be devastating, because they are the creditors who must accrue the loss. Examples include the bankruptcy of Peregrine in Hong Kong on 12 January 1998, the bankruptcy of Yamaichi Securities and seven other banks in Tokyo during 1997, the possible bankruptcy of fifty-six Korean banks and the warning sent to the international banking system with the Korean and Indonesian crises. The issue was taken up at Davos, the annual economic summit in 1998 where governments, businessmen and academics discuss the long-term prospects for the world. It was also on the agenda at the G7 meeting in Birmingham in May 1998. In July 1998 one of the largest banks in the world and certainly the most important in Asia today, the Hong Kong and Shanghai Bank, announced huge losses and sought merger options.

Twice in the space of a few weeks, Michel Camdessus and Stanley Fischer, director and vice-director of the IMF, had to make emergency trips to the Far East. First, in December 1997, to Korea where elections were won by the leftist candidate Kim. Then, in February 1998, to Indonesia where President Suharto was re-elected the following month. In both countries, the economies had suffered traumatic devaluations and problems were foreseen in their national financial systems. In Korea, twenty-six banks were declared to be in a difficult state and the South Korean government injected US$29 billion through bonds issued to the banks in exchange for debt and stock. The government acquired $50

TABLE 7.8  Variations on stock exchanges, 23 October 1997 to 24 October 1998

| Losses | | Gains | |
| --- | --- | --- | --- |
| Caracas | -66.39 | London | 4.5 |
| Bogotá | -48.0 | New York | 7.7 |
| Buenos Aires | -44.5 | Frankfurt | 12.7 |
| Santiago | -42.9 | Paris | 18.8 |
| Malaysia | -39.4 | Madrid | 26.3 |
| São Paulo | -38.9 | | |
| Indonesia | -36.1 | | |
| Thailand | -34.9 | | |
| Lima | -34.8 | | |
| Korea | -33.6 | | |
| Mexico | -21.06 | | |
| Tokyo | -17.5 | | |
| Hong Kong | -11.9 | | |
| Taiwan | -8.6 | | |

*Source*: Bloomberg in *Diario Gestión* (Lima), 27 October 1998, p. 33

billion in bad loans at 50 per cent of their nominal value. That did not fix the $133 billion in short-term commercial credits left unpaid to Japanese and international banks as a result of the failure of Korea's clients in Thailand and Indonesia to pay. The Japanese banks were the most affected, and they were the same ones that finance Korea's trade with Japan, Korea's largest trading partner.

Indonesia seems to be on a worse footing than Thailand or Korea since its foreign exchange depended mostly on oil exports, and these collapsed. The economy is teetering between unpaid debts and the inability to stabilize prices following the 300 per cent devaluation in 1997. The resignation of Suharto in May 1998, two months after his re-election, is one indication that the economic and political powers-that-be distanced themselves from the longest-running dictatorship in Asia (thirty-two years in power) to allow for an economic reform that would begin cutting back the state. It ought to be recalled that the role of the Indonesian state was built by Suharto, and up to 1997 the state played an integral role in the country's economic miracle.

The recovery of banking assets in the three countries forms a complex part of the solution to the Asian crisis, and is what links the crisis to the international financial system. The creditors of the national banks are international banks, mostly European besides the Japanese. The risky moratoria on payments are the total ones, by which not a cent is paid to any creditor until the accounts are put in order. This was a first success of the IMF in Asia. The corresponding failure, however, was that to achieve this it had to depress Asia's economies, and that caused an even greater contraction in world demand both for finished goods and raw materials, given the importance of Asia in the world demand for goods and services.

Between July and December 1997, devaluations ranged from 17 per cent in Taiwan to 303 per cent in Indonesia. It was 100 per cent in Indonesia between 30 December 1997 and 12 January 1998. In other words, if the Indonesian case is at all representative, the instability that began in July 1997 has not yet ended. This could mark the beginning of a new round of devaluations and stock market losses. Malaysia, which contained the balance-of-payments crisis with capital controls, suffered a 61.7 per cent devaluation between July and December and its stock market lost 41.3 per cent of its value, according to its index. The Lima stock market, by comparison, lost 750 points, falling from 2,350 in July 1997 to 1,600 in January 1998, nearly 25 per cent of its value. All of Latin America's stock markets have experienced losses since July 1997. Even the Chilean fell 20 per cent between July 1997 and February 1998. The Mexican market fared best, up until the crisis of 31 August 1998. At that point Russia was going through a terrible shock that caused a 90 per cent loss in the value of its stock market. The rush of currency traders to dump rubles for dollars (followed by the public, once political instability was added to economic instability) made its exchange rate drop 700 per cent.

It would seem that the tendency of international capital to pull out from stocks is not restricted to emerging markets, but also affects the various investment instruments of the world's major markets. There has been a surge in the market for US Treasury bonds, which has reduced yields to their lowest level since 1977. These are signs that the Asian crisis is a crisis of the international system as a whole. Besides threatening the stability of the international banking system, this will affect all open national economies. When stock markets filled with international capital suffer losses, national investors, as a consequence, are also dragged down. If investments in the stock market are collateral for real investments, as is frequently the case, the collateral will be worth less than the loans they cover, and that can cause greater problems for economies in the process of recovery, particularly in Latin America and Africa.

There is a very high correlation between the Nikkei index of the Tokyo exchange and spot prices for the most important raw materials. In a week-by-week survey, from June 1997 to April 1998, the raw materials prices listed in Table 7.9 showed an extremely strong correlation with the Nikkei, suggesting that the Asian crisis is a mirror of the Japanese crisis, which is a crisis of productivity. In this way, the Asian crisis would be one more expression of the systemic crisis that affected Latin America in the previous decade and which is now sweeping Asia, Russia, Mexico and Japan. Speculation now has it that the surge of 2,000 points on the New York stock exchange following its October 1997 fall is reaching its end. Various analysts tell us that the 'bubble' will soon burst. If that is the case, then we would be faced with the generalization of the systemic crisis. The

TABLE 7.9 Correlation between raw materials prices and the Tokyo stock exchange index, June 1997 to April 1998

| Copper | 0.9 |
| Gold | 0.46 (with a statistical T of 14.39) |
| Zinc | 0.98 (with a statistical T of 42) |
| Aluminium | 0.95 |
| Oil | 0.98 (with a statistical T of 53.74) |
| Coffee | 0.62 |
| Cotton | 0.61 |

*Source*: Calculations by students of International Finance 98–1 at the Pontífica Universidad Católica del Perú. Thank you to my students, who used monthly ten-year series.

international manoeuvring of the United States seeks to avoid precisely that. The 31 August crash is a sign of the bursting of that bubble. The Japanese recession has seriously affected raw materials prices, and the Asian crisis accelerated that process. Metals prices have been falling sharply, although there was some relief in November 1997 when it seemed that the first round of losses in Thailand, Indonesia and Hong Kong were over. Then came Korea in December and Indonesia yet again in January 1998 with the accompanying mood swings regarding world growth. As a sense of world recession takes hold, raw materials prices are likely to fall even farther, until they reach their real floor. For Latin America this is very bad news, since the region depends mostly on exporting raw materials and its largest market is Asia. The diagnosis of the producers is that this is a crisis of overproduction. Up to May 1998, copper markets had been cut back as much as 110,000 tonnes in refined production, and they are expected to drop as much as a further 250,000 tonnes due to the Asian crisis. Cutbacks in production are expected to last for three years at least. The same occurred with gold, which fell from $400 to $280 an ounce over the second half of 1997; with zinc, whose market closed entirely at one point because the price fell below the minimum of $1,200 a tonne; with aluminium, coffee, cotton; and oil, which fell from $23 per barrel during the Iraqi crisis in mid-1997 to $13.75 in March 1998 and is expected to reach $12 a barrel. The greatest losers may well be US and European commodities traders.

For developing economies that are wide open, this introduces instability in exchange rates as a result of the deterioration in the current accounts balance. More than 75 per cent of Latin America's exports face drops in price. The exception is silver which remained relatively stable after a short bubble. The El Niño phenomenon will also have negative impacts on agricultural and fishing exports and a positive one on food imports. This augurs poorly for Latin America's balance of payments for 1998 and 1999 in any case. It also offers elements for understanding why large investments in mining and energy have been suspended.

International interest rates will have to rise as a consequence of increases in the current accounts deficits of Latin America and Africa. In fact, Colombia and Argentina already issued Eurobonds in anticipation of the effects of their current accounts deficits on the balance of payments. Economies will also have to be slowed down or reoriented towards national markets, given the evidence that the international economy is cooling off. The United States intends to reduce interest rates in order to reactivate demand, since it considers the crisis to be one of underconsumption. In reality, everything we have seen shows the crisis to be one of overproduction. It is possible that Asian competition for G7 products will be fierce once the devaluations are over and it is clear which companies will survive the collapse. In addition, oversupply in Europe and the United States by companies that sell in Southeast Asia will lead to a fall in the prices of finished goods. That is why there is talk of deflation now. In other words, prices are falling not only for raw materials but also for finished goods, leading to bankruptcy for the large companies with tight margins that now dominate the world, except for those that merge or purchase Asian companies as a way to prevent a worse débâcle. All this could be bad news for developed economies, but less so for developing ones since it will cheapen imports.

Finally, national production in the manufacturing sector of our economies has been virtually liquidated, except for products sold on the Latin American market, which are essentially in primary and light industries. This could be a good moment for rethinking whether or not to have industry in Latin America. After all, the depths of a crisis is the best time to invest, because from that point everything goes up (Gerschenkron 1952). To do so would require strengthening integration schemes and the unification of industrial and agricultural promotion policies, thus dissolving the notion of the perfect market. In the contrary case, we are likely to see additional bankruptcies and the problems of financial vulnerability that they cause. In sum, the world economy is teetering on the verge of a depression characterized by deflation. And Latin America is part of the world economy.

### The systemic crisis viewed from Latin America[2]

The Mexican crisis of 1994 took some by surprise, particularly those who a few days previously, at the beginning of December 1994, had praised Mexico's growth and stability. The international press was filled with good omens for 1995 dreamed up by investment banks, multilateral organizations and international stockbrokers, all about the new, stable Mexico on course for integration with the United States and Canada after NAFTA came into effect. In October 1997 a phenomenon nearly identical to the Mexican crisis shook Asia's stock markets, dragging down Japan's banks and South Korea. Was it because of political reasons that adjustment did not work in Mexico, or is it that there is something in the concept of adjustment that does not work? What happened in Thailand such that no one saw it coming?

In any case, international organizations are all in a tizzy, worried that something indeed is wrong and that it may spread. Suddenly we hear a concern about balances that in theory ought to be maintained by the market. And there are new concerns about the functioning of international organizations. Perhaps it is time for a new Bretton Woods and a return to an economy based on the individual. General equilibrium appears not to have worked very well. The conceptual model claims that the external deficit is generated by public demand. Reducing public spending ought to reduce the external deficit. Both gaps, therefore, are exactly symmetrical. A hypothesis: given changes in the ways the economy works, the external deficit does not depend on public demand, rather it responds more to private demand.

Opening the economy, says the theory, ought to stabilize prices and set them at international levels, thus slowing national inflation to international levels. This is achieved by means of trade and financial liberalization, deregulation of prices and labour flexibility. A hypothesis: financial opening serves to cover up the new external deficit generated by private demand, and it covers it more than well. The effect of the financial opening has been to set national interest rates at levels that are approximately double international rates, as a result of the monopolistic structure of Latin America's banking systems and of the inefficiency of the banking system as a whole. The most recent effect has been an increase in international reserves due to short-term capital movements caused by high interest rates, leading to an undervaluation of Latin America's currencies.

The model of growth, says the theory, is led by export growth which ought to bring economic growth in its wake. A hypothesis: undervalued exchange rates can cause a substantial growth in imports, but only limited export growth. Widely publicized claims declared the debt crisis over in 1991. A hypothesis: it was not a debt crisis in the 1980s, rather an economic depression. The depression was being slowly overcome, although the debt problems remained, particularly regarding the fiscal angle. However, the systemic depression then swamped Latin America's recovery and returned it to its lowest point (1982).

Between 1987 and 1994 inflation and the fiscal deficit were both reduced, but this did not occur in a homogeneous fashion. Regarding inflation, there were substantial reductions in Argentina, Bolivia and Peru, among high-inflation countries, and in Mexico, among those with low inflation. However, in Bolivia inflation was reduced but not the fiscal deficit; in the rest of the countries the fiscal deficit was reduced by 2 per cent of GNP approximately. The countries that did not undertake adjustment, such as Brazil, controlled the fiscal deficit but not inflation. The application of the Plan Real in July 1994 was successful at controlling inflation, and would become the first successful heterodox adjustment plan. In Chile and Colombia inflation remained low and the fiscal balance was either positive or nearly so between 1987 and 1994.

Between 1994 and 1997 current accounts deficits grew substantially and so did capital flows. These were flows related to stock markets and the banking system via inter-bank lending. Primary exports continued to form the export base and intra-industrial exports became concentrated in Latin America. Although the logic of export-led growth remained, it was imports and the financing of them that played the largest role in the region's growth.

An observer of Latin America is left with the impression that there has been a return to a classical model of insertion into the world market, without major modifications, and that globalization works for imports but not for the national productive apparatus. It works even less so for transforming the content of exports, which theoretically, some say, ought to happen as in Southeast Asia as an automatic result of the application of the model. Some politicians in Latin America and other countries of the region claim we are the new Tigers. But we are immersed in a traditional Latin American development pattern, with all the historical fragilities and limitations that model brings, and the only tigers to be seen are made of paper or appear on the cartoons we see on cable television.

External balance in the short term calls for a reduction in the demand for imports. This is not possible politically, as was just seen in the discussion on selective consumption taxation in Japan. Long-term balance calls for export-promotion policies and state intervention in that area. This is theoretically unsustainable for Latin America's financial experts. Perhaps with the economy, as with life, it is reality that shows us the way forward: temporary tariffs, allowing the currency to float freely, non-tariff barriers used the way more developed countries use them. The alternative is an automatic adjustment.

## The development of the Asian crisis viewed from Latin America

During 1995, investors began pulling out of the Tokyo stock market and the Nikkei took a dive. Not only did they abandon the Japanese market, but they got out of the yen as well, moving their capital to New York. The New York stock market started growing at an unheard-of pace while the value of the yen against the dollar plummeted. In the end, the yen fell from its peak of 88 to the dollar to about 140 to the dollar: over 60 per cent. Along with the yen and the Nikkei, the price of raw materials fell. There has been a very high correlation between the Nikkei and basic raw materials prices since June 1997. The drop in the price of raw materials reached 30 to 50 per cent during the second half of 1997, and they continued to fall in 1998 causing current accounts deficits in economies that export them, such as Russia and Latin American and African countries. Russia relies on oil and gas exports as much as Mexico, Venezuela, Ecuador and Arab countries do.

The final result has been an increase in the demand for international lending, and requests for international capital flows are greater than ever. At the same time, the perception exists that changing dollars into any other currency or lending them to third countries is very risky. That led to the Brazilian crisis. The consequence has been the shrinking of capital flows and the weakening of the economies mentioned above. Chile, for example, which was solid until a few months ago, has seen its export earnings nose-dive along with the price of copper, and, like other countries, Chile has been forced to put the brakes on economic growth.

The first impact on raw materials exporting countries with open economies has been on the fiscal balance. The need to rein in the pace of economic growth led to lower tax revenue than anticipated. In addition, since the value of exports fell, so did the dollar taxes paid by export companies, which tend to be the largest taxpayers. That is how difficulties with macroeconomic growth become a fiscal problem, and it is a short step from there to a problem with the balance of payments, in a vicious cycle until prices begin to rise steadily again.

Meanwhile, the New York stock market took a beating. Between 17 July and 30 August 1998, the Dow Jones lost 1,800 points at a billion dollars in value per point, adding up to $1.8 trillion in losses. The way the troubles spread in chain reaction, and the panic that hit on 31 August were exactly like 1929 (Galbraith, 1961). To get from here to the next great cycle of growth for the world economy will require new ideas, new mechanisms and new technology, and we all hope for a quick recovery. In the meantime, the consequences of the crisis will be most evident in the world of banking.

### Notes

1. For this chapter, the author has consulted the articles in the NRoubini file on the Internet.

2. Several elements of this section were published between 1994 and 1998 in *Revista Moneda* of Peru's Central Reserve Bank.

# 8. Some Philosophical Problems Posed by the Systemic Crisis

The modern society in which we live is an outgrowth of industrial society, but modernity is no longer only that. The class contradictions which industrial society faced, and which were so severe, have been transformed. Today, the primary contradiction is between the right to a job and the impossibility of having one, at least a decent one. First of all, technology has radically modified the notion of employment, just as it did in the eighteenth century, by introducing new processes and new forms of social relations: 'The modern bourgeois society that has sprouted from the ruins of feudal society, has not done away with class antagonisms. It has but established new classes, new conditions of oppression, new forms of struggle in place of the old ones' (Marx and Engels 1932: 9).

Agnes Heller (1998) maintains that modernity is the combination of three logics: the logic of technology, the logic of the market and the logic of political institutions. These three are intimately related, though at any given moment one or another predominates. According to the logic of technology, modern man treats nature as an object and human beings as subjects. The world is conceived not as a living being, but as a place where problems are solved. Thus, it is an instrumentalist logic, by which science becomes absolute truth and truth as revelation (everything based on what was written in the Bible) disappears, leading Nietzsche to proclaim 'God is dead.' Truth in the sense of Christ's 'I am the truth' is replaced by science as discovered truth.

However, says Heller, besides technological imagination, beliefs are also founded on historical imagination. In pre-modern societies religion explained everything; in modern ones, science explains everything. Religious truth is immutable; scientific truth is continually changing. Scientific truth is cumulative; religious truth can not assimilate other truths, things are as they are. Science presupposes the dynamics of modernity, that the newest is the best because it contains more accumulated knowledge. In the modern world, science confronts religion and art as subversive because in essence they are not cumulative. The rationality of science gave rise to a counter-movement based on history known as Romanticism. The neoliberal approach, in this framework, takes the side of technological imagination and critiques Romanticism. In other words, it isolates itself from the individual and wraps itself in science and reason.

Heller suggests that by the logic of the market (what we now call modern society), function determines a person's place in society. When function determines a person's place, the markets for goods, services and labour are determinants. We all have needs and we have to satisfy them. In pre-modern societies, hierarchies determined people's function. People did not dress alike, did not receive equal education, did not have the same state of health nor the same rights. For one social stratum, reading and writing was elementary, for another knowing Latin was, for others it was not. Needs were differentiated by social strata. In pre-modern society no one envied those of other strata because it never occurred to anyone that he or she could have the same.

In modern society this all changes, because needs are satisfied quantitatively. The satisfying of needs is paid for with money. Romantics critique the quantification of needs and rationalists defend it as a sign of freedom. Money itself does not talk; everything depends on how much people are willing to pay for their needs, since service providers will offer their services to whoever will pay more. A lot of money will satisfy a lot of needs, and for rationalists it does not matter how that money is obtained. Modernity can not go back to a qualitative approach. It is quantitative in its essence. Modernity offers us the abstraction of needs in order to quantify them, which takes us back to Kant who said that man has three appetites: fame, money and power. If the three are indeterminate, it is because they are infinite. In this framework, progress is defined as the change in the locus of production for the market from luxury goods to basic goods. That is how everything is measured. The satisfying of needs, in reality, is an imaginary institution (Heller 1998).

Marx saw manufacturing as the modernity of his epoch that helped organize the world according to the logic of the market. 'Steam and machinery revolutionized industrial production' (Marx and Engels 1932: 10) in the same way that computers and information systems revolutionized it at the end of the twentieth century. 'Modern industry has established the world market ... [that] has given an immense development to commerce, to navigation, to communication by land' (p. 10). Just add air travel and we would have a good description of today. Every stage of evolution the bourgeoisie has gone through, says Marx, has been accompanied by a corresponding stage of political progress. It would be worth adding that political progress goes hand in hand with progress in economic theory and in the productive paradigm. In other words, not only the political regime advances, so do the economic and productive regimes, transforming social relations and international relations as well. In other words, the world changes in form, and what is considered truth is altered.

## Information, space and geography

Virtual society (Manrique 1997) was brought into this globalized world after the fall of the Berlin Wall. Virtuality lies in the immaterialness of its basis. The communications networks brought into being by the revolution of the new productive paradigm have given rise to a new world and have tossed out the old. There are elements that make up globalization and define the nature of the paradigm change in the sense of Kuhn (1972). One of the results of the introduction of the new knowledge-based paradigm in the middle of the 1970s was the acceleration and massification of information. More information is transmitted today than in the entire history of humanity, and that quantity is doubling at a dizzying pace that could be considered infinite. Humanity doubled its store of knowledge, measured by the number of books published, every thousand years up to the invention of Gutenberg's printing press, and every 120 years up to the invention of the typewriter towards the end of the nineteenth century. As I write this in May 1998, humanity's store of knowledge doubles every couple of months, and by the time this book is published that figure is likely to be out of date.

In fifteen years, between 1982 and 1997, microcomputers went from taking orders in BASIC, with 1K of RAM and no hard drive, to working with 3 gigabytes of hard drive memory and 32 megabytes of RAM. Today they use highly complex programmes that instead of requiring direct instructions use arrows and double clicks. The English term 'user friendly' is a good description of this system which allows anyone to communicate with computers without complicating their lives more than they wish. The rhythm of innovation in the computer industry has revolutionized the concept of knowledge and communication. For modern society this instrument is vital in universities, libraries, offices, studies, stores, factories – even in homes. In addition, the microprocessor revolution has affected everything modern life touches: money transfers by automatic teller, petrol stations, cash registers, speaking clocks, cars that announce in a loud voice that you are reversing, sound systems and compact discs, dashboard screens that indicate an open door or a seat-belt unbuckled. The microchip, the soul of everything digital, was invented in 1969 and put into widespread use in 1975. Twenty years later it is impossible to think of an aspect of modern life without machines that use microchips or microprocessors.

The means of production have changed, and so have ideas about the production of goods and services.

Globalization and the information revolution have gone hand in hand with a change in the technological paradigm. The world as we know it at the end of the twentieth century would be unthinkable without the scientific advances we enjoy today. The impact on the recovery of productivity in developed countries has been very positive, because such advances allow for savings in labour, raw materials and energy, besides accelerating the pace of innovation. They have also had a not-so-favourable impact. Savings in labour have led to irreversible structural unemployment, because the number of people required to produce a quantity of goods is smaller today than a decade ago. In this way the post-industrial epoch has begun; we are living in a post-industrial society. The labour force increasingly turns away from the manufacture of goods and towards services that have to do with the circulation of goods, or with their design, quality, delivery, maintenance, transport, marketing and so on.

In economies that were not industrial, like Latin America's, the leap to a post-industrial society is problematic. We never achieved the previous stage. Now the service economy in Latin America is the sum of quaternary services, the proper term for the services listed above, along with children selling candy in the street, to make a rather cruel metaphor. Right in front of a transnational bank with automatic tellers that process credit cards from across the world in real time (quaternary services), stand those who have no way to enter the labour force, no matter how hard they try. You can pay your phone bill, see your credit card balance in New York, withdraw money from your account in Geneva and hand a coin to whoever has been keeping an eye on your car. All of these – the banks, the credit cards, the cash machines and the children who watch cars and sell candy – are 'services' in the economy. The excess population (as far as the economic apparatus is concerned) with no jobs, who offer services that have little or no value added, has begun to appear all over the developed world, like the ghost of structural unemployment. Everything is services. Is it? Is a child selling candy in the street the same as a financial adviser? This is what scandalizes Forrester (1997).

The relation between countries producing raw materials and those that produce manufactures has deteriorated even further thanks to new technologies that allow for savings in raw materials by producing man-made substitutes and reducing the size of finished goods nearly to the point of needing no raw materials at all. To be seated like a beggar on top of a hill filled with minerals and dream about selling them to buy progress makes as much sense today as it did in the sixteenth century, except that now it doesn't even work in the long term. Extreme examples of what happens when countries bet on raw materials can be found in Santa María de Iquique, formerly the capital of saltpeter and today a ghost town, and Manaus, once the splendour of the rubber era and now forgotten. Iquitos, too, lost all relevance as far as production is concerned when synthetic rubber was invented. With a taste of nostalgia for mercury lamps, rubber and saltpeter, we can envision the future of the mineral wealth encased in the hills of the Andes. And that is our hope: an ancient past as a promise of the future.

With the acceleration of information and interactive communications in real time, distance or our sense of it has been lost. At any moment we can be in conversation via email with anyone in any part of the world. While we eat our supper, we can watch digital missiles being launched into a chimney in Iraq, and we are everywhere. There is no geography. That is, until we try to travel from South to North. Visas to the United States, Canada, Western Europe, Scandinavia and Japan have become the growing borders of history. The wall surrounding those countries excludes all who do not have the means, who cannot show the deed to their home, prove ownership of a car, produce an international credit card or proof of stable employment. They exclude those who do not come from rich countries, and thus national origin and geography become relevant once again. We are not in a world without borders. We are not even in the same world. A European Union passport avoids the hassle of obtaining visas and ensures better treatment in any port or airport of a developed country. The same thing happens with a Scandinavian, Japanese or US passport. The rest, except maybe for Mexico and Argentina, have problems. If the traveller is African or Asian, so much the worse. From the world without borders to global apartheid, even though there is a world without borders for those who have money.

Geography is the principle by which specialized goods are produced near the sources of the raw materials needed for those goods (Dollfus 1997). Chilean salmon garners a better price in Japan than Norwegian or Scottish salmon, while in the United States there is an additional 4.5 per cent tariff on it. Unskilled labour and its cost matter for such goods, but not in the case of sophisticated products for which only well-paid labour counts. In the global world, the European Union will not hire non-European nationals as consultants, the US government insists on using US goods and services, and the Japanese do not even consider the possibility of using employees or goods or services that are not Japanese for their consultancies. In other words, there is an economic apartheid in addition to the social one.

This would not really matter if the majority of the world's people – four-fifths of all humanity – did not live physically outside rich countries.

Besides, the geographic space outside rich countries makes up 80 per cent of the land surface of the earth. We are thus sitting outside a small walled space inhabited by 20 per cent of the world's population. We are perceived as the barbarian threat to Rome. Outside the walls there is life, there are people, there is space. This last item is what Europe and Japan lack. We are a space for breathing, rather than for producing. Dollfus (1997: 35) shows the world of globalization to be the world of concentration. Half of humanity lives on 3 per cent of the earth (in cities) and half of the world's wealth is produced on 1 per cent of the earth, 'notably on the great islands of the world metropolitan archipelago', which are: greater Tokyo, greater New York (stretching from Boston to Washington), greater Paris, and greater London. Dollfus suggests that there is a process of fragmentation under way even within those cities. Despite geography, for example, the jobless blacks of Harlem are not in the same place as the United Nations employees a few blocks away. They do not share the same horizons, ambitions or connections. Social distances tend to grow even within the world metropolitan archipelago. Outside it, the gaps are huge, because the few who have been incorporated into globalization in south-ern societies – people who get credit, who have well-paid jobs – make up about 10 per cent of the population. The 90 per cent who make up the rest watch from the outside, the way we watch the news on cable TV.

Geography also matters because distance today is a vital component of the concept of 'just-in-time' delivery. A month at sea is an obstacle for a commercial transaction that alternatively could be made with a supplier only five days away, or one day by train. Distance today is measured by the cost of transport and the lost profits caused by dormant capital during the time transport lasts. La Paz is twice as far from Lima as Puno, since it takes twice as much time by plane. Santiago is half as far as Buenos Aires from Lima, since it takes the same time in the air, but the fare is only half. The frequency of flights modifies the fare and $300 distant is certainly not the same as $100 distant. Besides, in terms of capital costs, a product at sea for a month freezes invested capital for a month, instead of obtaining that same product from a closer supplier.

Such considerations are turning globalization in Latin America into a regional process where the dynamism of world trade among the region's countries is basically manufacturing. Even those countries with a low manufacturing density, like Chile, have greater industrial dynamism within Latin America than outside it. Brazil, Colombia and Mexico are leading this process, without question.

## The French discussion on internationalization

A group of authors from the French school put forth their views in an issue of *La Pensée* at the beginning of 1997 (Sachs et al. 1997). In synthesis, they argue that globalization does not take place in the abstract but under certain conditions that have real restrictions. One is the lack of global governability and global rules of the game. Making the rules of the game universal does not make the global system universal; rather, only parts of it. Some argue that the structural changes under way cannot be reversed; others think these ought to regulated in some way. Margaret Thatcher's celebrated 1979 phrase 'There is no alternative ... ' (TINA) should not stop us from countering that globalization does not encompass everyone, that it creates degrees of concentration and clout that favour some and disadvantage others. Neither is Thatcher's dictum cause to leave things alone. We must think critically, because the lack of alternatives could become a catastrophe if we consider, for example, the plight of young professionals coming out of graduate school in Latin America who will not have the least opportunity to work in their chosen fields.

As is well known, the new globalization is essentially financial and in Latin America it benefits only the 10 per cent of the population that is credit-worthy. In this way, globalization will achieve neither economic development nor an improvement in income distribution, despite what some distorted income data may purport to show. The state has a role to play in the development process. The idea of eliminating the state as an actor is merely a swindle perpetrated by financial liberalization and is not a consequence of the end of the state's fundamental role in the promotion of investment and the stimulation of demand. One could add that this is especially the case in the most developed countries, where public spending represents one-third of GDP.

Ignacy Sachs affirms that these processes are as irreversible as global warming. In other words, we are not at a point of arrival, but rather at a point of departure from the accumulated achievements of capitalist development up to the end of the twentieth century. Globalization would be a higher phase of capitalism, to use Lenin's term, recalling imperialism. He says that the dual model of today is not meant to explain developing countries, but rather the developed ones, given the evident fragmentation under way there. Inequalities that violate the universal declaration of human rights, which includes the right to development, are increasing. He recalls Marx's words in the *Communist Manifesto* that the bourgeoisie gives production and consumption a cosmopolitan character in all countries. The difference between the end of the nineteenth century and the end of the twentieth is that in the former it was states that were the imperialists and in the latter it was transnational companies, along with the banks and other financial intermediaries, that control world investment, production and trade. The financial sphere is disassociated from the real one. It is, in the end, a return to the ideological nature of the pre-1929 debates, in which *economic* and *private* matters come first thanks to deregulation to allow for the free movement of capital, goods and services. He reminds us that the degree of openness in the world economy today is similar to that which existed before 1914, and that, therefore, the matter of developing internal markets remains on the table.

Ignacy Sachs reinforces the argument that there is a growing gap between North and South which creates fractures within the North and within the South, leaving the majorities excluded from globalization and impoverished. He recalls Hobsbawm's commentary on the fact that the economic miracles of the twentieth century have not been built on the free market, but rather by countering it. It would be worth adding that perhaps in economics there are no miracles, as Asia recently demonstrated.

Gibier maintains that by now globalization means continentalization and the formation of blocs that openly battle for the leadership of the world economy and to obtain greater benefits. In reality, he says in the spirit of Oman (1996), globalization is the sum of these regionalisms. The concept of the 'global village' was forged at the end of the nineteenth century with the telegraph revolution, steamships and the spread of the railway, and is not a new contribution. The communications revolution at the end of the nineteenth century was as important for that epoch as today's is for ours. He reminds us, as Oman (1996: 27–33) suggests, that this is not the first time the economy has been globalized. He says further that regarding the workings of world capitalism, a surplus in one country is at least equal to the deficits of all others or, more likely, equal to that of some of the others. But the others are not allowed to have deficits or surpluses, and we could say that they are 'encouraged' to find a balance. The adjustment of an economy is done in reference to 'other world-economies' and not to its own.

He almost goes so far as to remind us that there are countries that count and others that, after all, do not count for much; and there are some that are simply irrelevant. He suggests that the crisis and global adjustment correspond to a crisis in the model of accumulation: i.e. a crisis of the system. What is new in this phase is that international production is understood as the articulation of global 'production lines'. The axis is no longer production, rather the dispersion of production across the globe, a neo-Fordist approach noted by Aglietta where big production lines disappear and small ones in small factories dispersed across various regions of the world are linked to create big virtual production lines. He refers to this as nomadism. Small plants can open and close, and change location cheaply, depending on the production costs in a given place. This requires externalizing the services contracted in each case, such that the cost is reduced to the indispensable minimum while the flexibility to relocate production grows. This implies the incorporation of research and development – or conception/resolution – into production, since keeping products state of the art is more important than achieving optimum conditions for production. Profits are not derived from standardization, but rather from variety, which implies identifying the consumer and producing in a particular manner for that consumer. This is made possible due to new technologies. The great assets today are human assets and not physical ones; thus it is people and not machines that allow for technologies to be utilized.

Andreff reminds us that there are two notions on the table: the globalization of the economy and the globalization of capital. The latter is utilized to conceptualize the trend towards a world capitalism, whose theoretical matrix lies in the thought of the 1960s French school of the internationalization of capital. Chesnais affirms that the globalization of capital is distinct from the internationalization of capital that existed over the nineteenth century, particularly due to changes in the 1990s. The globalization of capital, he says, 'is a specific mode of functioning of world capitalism which must now be laid bare'. Its predominant features are:

1. Weak economic growth in economies once thought to be the 'engines' of the world economy.
2. Extremely high growth in the nominal value of financial assets in those economies.
3. The development of extremely high structural unemployment rates in OECD economies, and fragmentation in the levels of employee remuneration, which range so low that the beneficiaries fall into the categories of 'poor' or 'very poor'.
4. Parallel to the above phenomenon, the development of very high incomes based on finances, and the reconstitution of social groupings that could be defined as 'rentiers'.
5. A very unstable situation in the world, characterized by financial and monetary shocks that have the potential to become a serious international contagion, as was seen, for example, in the Mexican crisis.
6. The prolonged delay, year after year, of a significant relaunching of the international economy, the only sign of which to date has taken place in the United States.
7. Deflation that has become open and flagrant in industrialized countries,

above all in regard to the raw materials on which developing countries depend.

8. The marginalization of entire regions of the world from the world trading system, and an ever greater international concurrence at the centre of the system, generating serious trading conflicts among the great powers of the Triad.[1]

Chesnais calls the process a 'new regime of financial accumulation' to replace the previously existing 'regime of Fordist accumulation', though it was Boyer who along with Aglietta pointed out the end of Fordism. Sweezy could also be categorized in this line of a new model of financial accumulation. This new regime of accumulation revolves round three sectors: finance, the computer/telecommunications/other communications complex, and the marketing industry. Others call this the 'quaternary sector', since they are a new type of 'services'. 'Services' are the tertiary sector of the economy, manufactures the secondary and raw materials production the primary. Castoriadis claims that we are witnessing a step back for civilization, since the creations of capitalist society are now based on 'insignificance'.

Exclusion and marginalization are nothing more than different means of articulation within the new system, which is an integrated whole: globalization and exclusion are two sides of the same world-system coin. Besides, the change in inter-state relations is the basis for the new regime of accumulation, leading then to new relations of domination and political dependence among states which give rise to, or become, the new relations of globalized capital.

The global frame of reference comes from US business schools, where decision-making for companies on a world scale is taught, though the term also includes the world as a whole. In any case, it would be unthinkable to separate economics from politics or vice versa when analysing the changes under way. The analysis must be made jointly, Chesnais says, because the genesis of the globalized regime of financial accumulation lays politics and economics bare. The state is not outside the market, as neoliberals claim: 'The current triumph of the "market" would not have happened without the repeated political interventions of policy-makers from powerful capitalist states.'[2] Globalization, writes Chesnais paraphrasing the president of a transnational, exists to produce what a company wants, where it wants, how it wants, in the place where there is the least regulation of labour. Liberalization and financial deregulation were made possible by the abrogation of the Bretton Woods system in 1973, due to the particular role of currencies in the capitalist mode of accumulation, and due to the 'conservative revolution' that spread across the globe with Reagan and Thatcher and created a new sense of accepted wisdom. The new accepted wisdom is that the state is dysfunctional and blocks the development of markets.

## Power and the urge not to know

In *El horror económico*, Viviane Forrester (1997) reflects on the social costs of what we have discussed above. The central issues for her are lack of employment due to the intensive use of cybernetics, and 'laziness' and 'lack of interest' in paying attention to what is happening. Hers is a warning more than a review of the theory: 'For the first time [in Europe, I'd add] the human masses are no longer necessary from the material viewpoint – and even less so from the economic viewpoint – for that small minority that holds power, for whom the existence of human lives that evolve outside their intimate circle is only of utilitarian interest, as can be seen clearly every day' (Forrester 1997: 148).

Employment, for this author, is the glue of Western civilization; it is what allows people to feel useful and to enter into contact with one another. She notes that structural unemployment has increased in Europe, making a great number of people excluded, disposable. With technological change and changes in values, employment has become irrelevant.

> Today's world [is made up of] multinationals, transnationals, absolute liberalism, globalization, internationalization, deregulation, virtuality ... The world guided by cybernetics, automation and revolutionary technologies, now taking form and likely to rule from now on, seems to slip away, to take cover in hermetic, nearly esoteric, corners. It has stopped being synchronic with us. And naturally it has no link to the world of work, which is no longer of any use to it and which, when the system manages to perceive it, seems like an irritating bothersome parasite, embarrassingly disastrous, irrationally obstinate in its desire to exist ... The old decays and suffers, excluded from the new, which can't even imagine it. The new, reserved for a caste, imbues a brand-new order with 'reality', or perhaps it is 'unreality' ... It is a world that lives in the realm of cybernetics, state-of-the-art technologies, the vertigo of the immediate; a world in which speed gets confused with the here and now in a seamless space. There, ubiquity and simultaneousness reign ...
>
> And in that empire – you would think you were dreaming! – workers, poor devils, still believe they can have a 'labour market'. It's enough to make you laugh to keep from crying. In another epoch they had to learn to stay in their places. Now they must learn to have no place at all, and that is the message they are being given, rather discreetly for the moment. A majority of human beings are no longer necessary for the small group who, since they run the economy, hold power. (Forrester 1997: 29, 30, 31).

An individual with no role, with nothing to do in the world, has no reason to live, no apparent way to prolong his life. There are more and more people without any role in life, yet who somehow go on living for a rather long time. It is a sort of an extended living death, to put it bluntly. 'There are the excluded, rooted as no one else. They must be taken into account. Those pitiful bleets, those verses, leitmotifs and tunes that sound like tick-tocks calling unemployment "our greatest concern" and job creation 'our number one priority,' must be repeated incessantly to the four corners of the earth' (Forrester 1997: 38).

The author wants to call attention to the superficiality of political discourse in light of the reality that a person who does not work has no reason to live, because he has nothing that links him to society or to the economic system. Of course, speaking of Europe, Forrester refers to population groups that will not die of hunger if they have no work because they have a network of support, even if it is tenuous, and a minimum income ($560 dollars a month) that allows them to pay for some things. In reality, Forrester is intrigued by the fact that in a country as rich as France such a thing could occur. How is it possible that elegant Paris, chic and refined, can have people living in cardboard boxes? And how is it possible that there is so much indifference? More than a reflection on economics, which it is not, or a sociological text, which it is not either, Forrester's work is a wake-up call to the inhumanity of modern society. It is an essay on ethics. She does not explain what is happening, rather she underlines it. She is terrified by the prospect that 'the excluded' are a harbinger of future societies in which nearly all of us would be squeezed into that already-crowded category. Forrester is indignant at the indifference to all this. It is indifference, she maintains, that supports these regimes. She is referring to what in Lima we call '*alpinchismo*', in Spain is called '*pasotas*' and in Mexico '*valemadrismo*'. *Nothing matters, it's just normal.* That indifference, as Forrester notes, is the underpinning of the new social regime in which growing numbers of the excluded live alongside the temporarily included and the absolutely included. The danger does not lie in the situation itself, as much as in the blind acceptance of it, the widespread resignation towards what is presented to us as a package that is unavoidable. It is a new regime, and a regressive one: a return to nineteenth-century conceptions, except that the 'labour factor' has been eliminated.

Forrester's reflections on power at the beginning of the twenty-first century are not novel. They begin by reminding us that the ruling classes of the private economy may have at times lost control of the state, but they never lost power.

These classes (or castes) never stopped acting, supplanting, watching for their chance. Tempters, owners of all seduction, they were always offered incentives. Their privileges continue to make up the fantasies and desires of the majorities, even of those who claim to combat them. Money, control of strategic points, jobs to be distributed, links with other powerful people, domination of transactions, prestige, certain knowledge, the confidence of *savoir faire*, comfort, luxury are a few of the many means that have never been pried away from them ... Today their authority knows no limits: it has invaded everything, particularly the ways of thinking that keep crashing up against the logic of a power, firmly installed and organized, whose imprint is everywhere, ready to gobble up everything.

We have entered the era of liberalism, which has managed to impose its philosophy without formulating it, without even elucidating it as a doctrine, to the point where it has become materialized, active, without being discovered. Its domination imposes an imperious system, to use a totalitarian word, which for the moment is part of democracy. Truly, we are living the violence of tranquility. (Forrester 1997: 54)

That author takes us back to an important point of departure: today's liberalism has no philosophical underpinnings because it has no relation with humanity, and the real reason for the economy to exist is humanity. In other words, rather than a doctrine, it is the exercise of power. I would add that neither is it a theoretical paradigm. And power is the same as always: power that to serve its own ends decides the direction society as a whole should take, that dictates the economic steps, the currents of thought – and that makes money off every step. It may or may not control the state, but it certainly holds power. The powerful have the means. The powerful live in the jet set.

On the other side lies a scorned world on the road to extinction: the world of research, thought, extravagance, fervour. The world of the intellect, a term rejected with a contempt that is intentional, concerted, encouraged by society. That is because thought is dangerous. Because thought is subversive and can question this order of things that from a philosophical point of view is nowhere, even though from the point of view of power it seems perfect. When it was announced in March 1996 that employment was up in the United States, there was a crisis on the stock market. The meaning: things are the way they are and ought not to change. In the ubiquitous political discourse, we get salutes to the flag of 'jobs are what counts' and 'employment is our priority', just to make sure no one believes it. If the employment picture improves, the powerful become frightened, as if it were a ghost. Would it be senseless to expect respect, Forrester wonders?

She publicly denounces the ways in which the powerful have settled in and transformed society's values. The labour force was taken into account in a subordinated way by the powerful in the nineteenth and twentieth centuries, to produce and consume. At the beginning of the twenty-first century, the labour force is redundant. It is not wanted either to produce or to consume. It has no clout and no reason to exist; it is simply subordinated. Nowhere to go and nothing to do, labour gets no candles at its funeral.

Forrester's text does not help us grasp what is happening in terms of globalization; but it does let us know that in Europe things are not all rosy, even if reading about it from the perspective of Latin America is not exactly moving. What is new for them has always been the case for us. Indifference, indolence, unemployment, the precariousness of life. All this has been the case in Latin America for ever, though it never was of interest to Europe, much less the United States, as societies. However, it seems that we Latin Americans do care that such things are happening in Europe. Or perhaps the old saying that 'If they say it in Paris, it must be true' still holds, a surviving relic of the Enlightenment and the Encyclopaedists.

## Power, truth and crisis

Alain Touraine (1993: ch. 4) maintains that it is intellectuals who have always promoted rationalism, intellectuals who promoted scientific progress and the critique of past institutions and beliefs. From the Middle Ages on, they were the ones who struggled against truth as revelation. Touraine points out that when modernity became mass production and consumption in the twentieth century and the instruments of reason were or are utilized for the most mediocre and even irrational ends, the relationship of intellectuals to progress changed poles. The mass killings by the Nazis would be an extreme example of this. Intellectuals in the United States and France who are aware of this have sought to maintain their relationship with progress, defending wars of national liberation in countries that were colonies, for example, convinced that regimes born from an anti-colonial or anti-imperialist struggle were 'progressive'. In the 1970s, things shifted again, and anti-modernism became hegemonic. Just as the romantics of the nineteenth century were led by their dreams of the future, the intellectuals of the twentieth century were led by a sense of catastrophe. For the first time, social, economic and political transformations did not seem to have been thought out.

Foucault (Touraine 1993: 215–17) suggests that power has become ever less distinguishable from the categories of practice itself, such that in modern liberal society power is everywhere and is ever more diffuse. This ought to give life to culture and society and fill them with a dynamism of their own, separate from the power of the state and of big capital. Power is normalization and it is society as a whole that constantly sets that mechanism in motion, deepening the separation between what is normal and what is abnormal. Power is not a speech from a pulpit; it is an array of statements emerging autonomously from all institutions. This contradicts what Marx suggested for his day, that the government of the modern state was no more than a committee that administered the common affairs of the entire bourgeois class. That is, unless we differentiate between government and power and make the supposition that power outside the government is possible. In Latin America of the 1990s, more than ever before, there is a crossover between power and government. The government is still a business committee, but simultaneously it must face a range of many-faceted statements from what today is called civil society.

Truth has been transforming science (Marx) into market (Friedman, von Hayek and Walras previously), in an epochal change. The new truth is the market. It is the market that determines what is good and what is bad, who is useful and who is not, who deserves to eat and who does not. This is because he who does not work does not eat, since a subsidy to allow someone to eat interferes with the labour market – which employs fewer and fewer people and exploits them ever more – as well as with the market for goods. If that's the way things are, many questions about capital arise, especially when a world crisis erupts and raises doubts about how well the new truth grasps reality. If the market has to be worldwide in order to operate and provide greater access for the burgeoning industrial production of a small portion of world population in a small part of the globe, then that market settles in everywhere and creates linkages between every place, laying a foundation for the universalization of the crisis of capital we are currently experiencing. The national basis for industry has been gutted, but not the national nature of capital. Even if capital no longer carries a flag, power still does.

'In these [commercial] crises, a great part not only of the existing products, but also of the previously created productive forces, are periodically destroyed. In these crises, there breaks out an epidemic that in all earlier epochs would have seemed an absurdity – the epidemic of overproduction' (Marx and Engels 1932: 14–15). 'The conditions of bourgeois society are too narrow to comprise the wealth created by them' (p. 15). The big question is who will destroy overproduction and what role will the modern worker play.

One of the most overworked concepts of the 1990s is 'globalization'. The term has been used to refer to a number of phenomena and processes and has very different meanings. For the English school, the concept is related to the universalization of the neoliberal rules of the game. For

North Americans it has to do with the expansion of transnational companies in a borderless world, where only the interaction of transnationals – be they financial, service-related or productive – will allow for an increase in productivity and a new insertion for economies in the new global economy. For the French it has to do with the ways capital expands at the end of the twentieth century, and with the costs that capital expansion always brings for the economies of what used to be called the Third World.

It is impossible to think of globalization without some previous reference to a frequently and poorly used concept: competitiveness. Competitiveness alludes to the new forms of competition based on differences in productivity, incorporating quality, design and on-time delivery as fundamental elements. This new form of competition among various producers spread across the world leads to discussions about competitiveness and the capacity we have to be competitive in the global economy.

At the centre of the discussion, old debates about the three axes, liberalism vs mercantilism, globalization vs de-linking and state vs market, continually raise their heads. The debate on capitalism vs socialism disappeared with the fall of the Berlin Wall in 1989. Fukuyama wrote its death certificate in *The End of History* in 1990. Europe's really existing socialism collapsed that year and the word globalization was coined in a text by Keinichi Ohmae (Ohmae 1990). Was that a coincidence, or is there some relation between the resurgence of globalizing thought and the fall of existing socialism in Eastern Europe? Maybe Marx was referring to the end of history when he wrote that capitalism would collapse of its own weight and communism would emerge as a superior phase. Fukuyama suggests that capitalism as we understand it today is the end of history. However, this argument is being launched at a time when there is no opponent in sight and at a moment when internationalized capital, seeking new markets and ways of producing, looks very much like the capitalism described by Marx in the *Communist Manifesto*.

Clearly, now more than ever, we need new approaches from a socialist viewpoint to bring the meaning of the economy back to the individual. Globalization has been possible due to the spread of universal rules of the game contained within a theoretical framework of overall balance, which in light of events in Asia does not seem to work for anyone. It does not help us predict the future. And if it does not do that, then the theory will not work as a paradigm and ought to be replaced by one that does. In the name of science, the economic function of the individual has been forgotten, and that is senseless. After all, economics is the study of the transformation of nature by man. Or are we now to understand it as the study of financial (dis)equilibria?

The upshot is that the gap between rich and poor has widened enormously, causing migratory flows the rich do not want and a trend that runs counter to previous globalizations: rather than follow the expansion of capital from north to south, migration today flows in the opposite direction. Today it is not capital that generates desired or hoped-for employment, and the Philips curve has lost all value. So, for example, what is foreign investment for? Will export growth alone solve the problem of employment and development? As far as we can tell to date, it has solved neither the problem of capital nor that of its realization.

If one considers globalization to mean the migration of goods, services, capital and people across national borders, then it is a recurring phenomenon, one that the English school of Jenks, Hobson and other nineteenth-century writers baptized imperialism, from the title of Hobson's book. They alluded to British capital's need for expansion as a means of strengthening the Empire to face the great depression of the 1870s, and this drew it into wars and struggles to consolidate power overseas. It was the Marxist theorists of the early twentieth century who gave the concept a different content by including the direct involvement of the state as an exporter of goods, services, capital and people to the receiver state, to benefit the capitalists of the exporter state. The theories drawn up by Hilferding and reworked by Bukharin and Lenin somehow became extinguished during the 1970s, when studies of transnational companies (TNCs) demonstrated that these are really economic agents autonomous of the state and thus the denunciations by theorists at the beginning of the century of direct state involvement were imprecise or inexact. A new argument appeared that the logic of accumulation of TNCs was not to be found in the country receiving investment, rather TNCs simply went wherever it was most profitable. This led Latin American dependency theorists to point to the need for new development models that set foreign investment aside and placed public investment at the centre of a new approach to internal accumulation.

Several decades of policy efforts to break the hold of dependence ended up in an economic depression caused by over-indebtedness in an adverse international context and assets in technologies that were already obsolete. This led theorists to a new consensus, known as the Washington Consensus (Balassa et al. 1986), based on open economies and the truth of the market. Perhaps there is a problem with today's theory of general equilibria, since it was unable to predict the crisis now spreading across the globe. It is a systemic crisis that encompasses capital flows, pricing systems, and every country in the world. And it questions both the technology at the heart of production and the institutions created in the 1940s to avoid a crisis like the one we are facing today.

'And how does the bourgeoisie get over these crises? On the one hand, by the enforced destruction of a mass of productive forces; on the other, by the conquest of new markets, and by the more thorough exploitation of the old ones' (Marx and Engels 1932: 15). But all new markets were already conquered through the universalization of the law of the single price, implanted in modern ideology by the Bretton Woods institutions, and that was not sufficient. It only gave rise to 'more extensive and more destructive crises ... diminishing the means whereby crises are prevented' (p. 15). To paraphrase Marx, the forces that led to the destruction of modern industrial society based on Fordism are now turning on the bourgeoisie itself.

Workers' terror of unemployment and exclusion made them lose their consciousness of themselves as workers. 'The lower middle class, the small manufacturer, the shopkeeper, the artisan, the peasant, all of these fight against the bourgeoisie, to save from extinction their existence as fractions of the middle class' (Marx and Engels 1932: 19). This is a reactionary and self-defensive movement, and will not do for building a social alternative. 'The socialistic bourgeois want all the advantages of modern social conditions without the struggles and dangers necessarily resulting therefrom. They desire the existing state of society minus its revolutionary and disintegrating elements' (p. 38).

Modern society is made up of the included and the excluded. The lucky ones are included in the market and the unlucky ones are not even in the picture. To paraphrase Wilde, they have no right to be exploited. There will be no organized reaction at all to this situation as long as no one reopens the debate on socialism and communism and brings Marx's analysis from the *Manifesto* up to date. Not all wages are destined to fall. Nor are all workers destined to work in big industries. Technological changes have modified the relations of production and led to improvements in workers living standards in some places, while in others they have further gutted people's standard of living. Modern capital based on financial relations and on the so-called service economy has revolutionized the notion of the proletariat, the meaning of which must be updated. Does the proletariat include, as in the *Manifesto*, just those who have productive work in manufacturing? What about all the super-exploited labourers in services? What about all those who provide services to production? What about all those who can't even get a job? The notion of the lumpen proletariat was frozen in the England of the period in which the book was written. Who are today's lumpen proletarians? The excluded? Can we even speak of a working class? Do we need new, more precise analytical categories based on Marx's criteria? The epochal change calls for a theoretical revision and the formulation of new proposals based on Marx's concepts, if we are to retake the revolutionary dynamic that was lost among the political and economic crises of the past decade and the fall of really existing socialism, which, along with the failures in Latin America of Guyana, Chile, Nicaragua and Bolivia, battered efforts to make the concept of revolution viable.

To conclude, unity lies at the centre of Marx's thought. Unity did not exist in Latin America, plagued as it was by movements and parties divided by visions and persons who did not find and often did not search for ways to centre the struggle. At times, due to personality cults, we have suffered through a number of battles, often within the socialist movement itself, without ever getting to the larger struggle. Latin American socialism must be re-imagined, in light of the real experiences of socialism in the world, to allow for a resurgence of an alternative to a system that shunts the vast majority aside and oppresses it more and more. We are immersed in a great systemic crisis, like the one described in the *Manifesto* and this is the moment for thinking and proposing.

### Notes

1. By Triad he refers to the European Union, the United States and its NAFTA partners, and Japan.

2. It is they who in the end bring some order to the imbalances introduced by the market, as we have seen in Mexico, Thailand and Malaysia.

# Epilogue: Five Hypotheses on the Wrong Path Taken

In sum, these are the facts that form my frame of reference:

- Per capita growth in Latin America and Africa from the 1950s to the 1970s was between two and four times larger than growth in the 1990s.
- Between 1970 and 1980 Latin America's foreign debt doubled.
- Between 1980 and 1990, economic growth in Latin America stagnated and the region exported US$375 billion net for debt servicing, despite which the debt doubled again due to compounding interest.
- Beginning in the mid-1980s, structural adjustment policies were adopted throughout the world, and the World Bank moved from project-based lending to policy-based lending. It abandoned its role as a development bank to become a policy-making institution that intervenes in the internal affairs of countries.
- Per capita GDP of the world's ten richest countries doubled between 1985 and 1995, while per capita GDP of the ten poorest countries dropped 30 per cent; the gap between the richest country and the poorest, in per capita terms, grew from 70 times to 430 times.

Since June 1997 the world economic system has suffered volatility unseen since 1929. Stock prices on exchanges around the world have swung wildly in both directions. Raw materials prices have fallen some 40 to 50 per cent, while exchange rates in the most developed countries fell 20 per cent in relation to the dollar in 1997 and regained as much value in 1998. The Japanese yen declined 60 per cent and then recovered. The so-called Asian crisis found new expression in Russia, Mexico, Brazil and then the entire world outside of Europe, thus far. That crisis, an expression of overproduction, shows up the lack both of institutions capable of containing it geographically and of an economic theory that can explain it and therefore resolve it.

We are facing, in other words, a great theoretical, institutional and productive crisis, and its symptoms are financial. The stock exchanges in

New York, Frankfurt, Paris and Madrid are the only ones to have experienced any growth in the twelve months between October 1997 and October 1998, and even these suffered crashes and sudden reversals. In Asia and Latin America, and in Eastern Europe, stock exchanges collapsed. The improvements of 1999 had some relation to the war in Kosovo, which encouraged a rise in the prices of copper and oil and depressed the Euro. Perhaps more wars will be necessary to bring prices up, as was the case in the 1930s.

### First hypothesis: On liberalization and deregulation in Latin America – problems and results from the absence of choice

1. Liberalization and deregulation in Latin America have three objectives:

- to increase national savings to avoid the high foreign indebtedness of the 1970s
- to raise the value of the currency, which makes imports cheap and exports costly
- to balance the current accounts deficit of the balance of payments, which was very high as a result of low exchange rates and import-substitution policies

2. The concept known as structural adjustment, and the free-market policies that came with it, were introduced by means of the foreign debt. To be able to renegotiate the foreign debt, countries first had to reach an agreement with the International Monetary Fund which laid down conditions intended to fix problems with the exchange rate, national savings and the balance of payments. After signing an IMF accord, countries then had to sign a structural adjustment agreement with the World Bank containing policy prescriptions to:

- liberalize and deregulate foreign and domestic trade
- deregulate the labour market, known as labour flexibility
- liberalize and deregulate the financial system
- reduce the size of the state by eliminating subsidies, privatizing public enterprises and cutting back on both the role of the state and the number of public servants

After signing on to such a package, countries could enter into negotiations on the debt with the Paris Club and private creditors, and for accessing both the IDA facility at the World Bank for low-income countries and the Brady Plan for middle-income countries.

Agreements with the IMF, the World Bank, the Inter-American and

African Development Banks, and the Paris and London Clubs are all conditional on one another in such a way that if an agreement with one is not fulfilled, then they are all off the table. Usually, WTO accords, anti-drug agreements with the United States government, and international environmental accords, when these exist, are linked to them as well.

3. The argument used to convince governments of this drastic turn-about was: there is no alternative. The instrument: coercion. Governments were persuaded to implement these policies through debt negotiations. Such policies had to be implemented before public and private creditors would come to the table. In other words, follow the orders of the G7 governments laid down by the IMF and the WB, or there will be no dialogue. In 1979, Nicaragua was an exception; by 1990 there would be none.

4. The results by the 1990s were not what we had been led to expect. The effect of the opening of the economy on national savings was hardly what had been predicted. And it was the same story with growth, invest-ment and the external deficit. Investment rates did not return to the levels of the 1970s, while economic growth was half of what it had been previous to the crisis of the 1980s. Internal savings were depressed and replaced by external savings that are now private, when before they were public. Total national savings dropped slightly to 18 per cent of GDP in the 1990s, having been 20 per cent of GDP in the 1970s.

The explanation lies in the fact that capital flows are oriented towards increasing the consumption of imported goods and raising international reserves. This had a negative impact on exchange rates, raising the value of the currency and thus making imports cheap and exports costly. This began to come to an end with the Mexican crisis in 1994 and stopped definitively with the Brazilian crisis in 1999.

5. In a presentation at a conference on Globalization and Development

TABLE E.1 Latin America: selected macroeconomic indicators (% of GDP)

|  | Net capital inflow | Gross capital formation | GDP growth | Internal savings | External deficit |
|---|---|---|---|---|---|
| 1976–81 | 4.9 | 24.0 | 5.5 | 20.1 | 3.9 |
| 1983–90 | 1.2 | 16.7 | 1.6 | 15.7 | 1.0 |
| 1991–94 | 4.9 | 17.9 | 3.6 | 14.5 | 3.4 |
| 1995–96 | 4.9 | 18.0 | 1.9 | 15.0 | 3.0 |

*Source*: Ricardo Ffrench-Davis and Helmut Reisen 1998: 33, Table 2.2.

in Havana, held 18–22 January 1999, Andrés Solimano cited three effects of deregulation and liberalization:

- financial volatility
- rising income inequality
- loss of autonomy for economic policy-making

6. In the end, deregulation and liberalization engendered the following:

- a drop in internal savings
- a small rise in foreign savings
- a slight increase in real investment
- low economic growth
- great financial volatility
- greater income inequality
- loss of autonomy for defining economic policy

## Second hypothesis: On the crisis of the dollar, the end of the old international order and the creation of a new one in which developing countries have no defined role

1. The 1970s – with the dollar crisis of 1971, when the dollar went off the gold standard, and the oil crisis of 1973 – saw an end to the international order set up following the Second World War that was based on welfare economic policies, oil-based technology and the Bretton Woods institutions as stabilizers of a world system configured by the dollar/gold standard and stable exchange rates.

2. A new international economic order emerged, but it was not the one advocated by Third World countries in the NIEO pact of 1974. The new order was anchored in market policies, knowledge-based technology and Bretton Woods institutions as brokers and overseers of new economic policies and debt agreements.

3. The new order that emerged has the weakness of relying on knowledge-based technology whose defining principle is accelerated innovation. Investment in this new technology becomes less profitable as the rate of innovation increases, to the point that the world system becomes unstable.

In order to transform the technological basis of the economy, interest rates in the United States were raised at the end of the 1970s to attract capital circulating elsewhere in the world. In 1982, the so-called foreign debt crisis hit Latin America as a consequence. At that moment, in August 1982, a conference in Washington of bankers, academics and international bureaucrats gave rise to the so-called Washington Consensus in favour of market policies and their stable implementation across the board. Solidifying this consensus and putting it into action took the rest of the decade. In Latin America it was not until 1990 that all countries signed on to these policies. The population, worn down by the adjustment of the 1980s, acquiesced. The Washington Consensus became common sense.

## Third hypothesis: On ideological exhaustion, social disorganization and the crisis of the millennium

1. The 1990s provided a stage for governments of various stripes, backed by the IMF and the World Bank, to carry out the policies of economic opening. Worn down by adjustment, even the unions embraced them, and there was a brief moment of hope. With the fall of the Berlin Wall (1989), the disappearance of the USSR (1991), the defeat of the FSLN in Nicaragua (1990) and the books of Soto (*The Other Path*, 1986), Fukuyama (*The End of History*, 1990) and Ohmae (*The Borderless World*, 1990), the totalitarian approach that there is no alternative took root in society. If there was no alternative, there was no reason to speak out and no point in thinking. This paved the way for new right-wing political regimes in Latin America, leaving the role of opposition to the old right.

2. All governments except Cuba, took this path. And the disorganization of the left was such that the implementation of these policies faced no significant social opposition. On came the opening of the economy and the debt-reduction schemes of the Paris and London Clubs (multilateral lenders steered clear of debt reduction).

3. The promise was more than could be delivered, and a decade later we have sluggish economic growth, large current accounts deficits and overvalued exchange rates that catch up only through abrupt changes, as in the cases of Mexico in 1994, Brazil in 1999, and others to come. We also have economic polarization between the beneficiaries of the policies (about 20 per cent of the population) and those who are excluded, the 80 per cent who stand by and observe but perceive no benefit.

## Fourth hypothesis: On the systemic crisis that hit bottom in 1997 and its effects

1. In the middle of 1997 violent shock waves of the systemic crisis were felt, first in Asia, then in Russia, then in Brazil. Stock exchanges in the most developed countries became highly volatile and a door opened finally to address the crisis that had plagued the system really since the first half of the 1970s.

2. Suddenly there was a general recognition that exposure to short-term credit is too high all around the world, and that the level of internal

debt is equally high. And a warning went out about financial volatility and the contagion effect. Stock exchanges in every developing country crashed between 1997 and 1998, falling between 30 and 66 per cent, and the going was rocky in the world's major exchanges, although these ended up with a slight improvement. Alarm was raised that the world economy stood at the edge of the abyss. This is recent news and is not over yet.

- For Africa, Latin America and Asia, the foreign debt crunch of the 1970s is as yet unresolved, contrary to what had been thought.
- Neoliberal policies that were locked in and made irreversible are apparently going to change.
- Macro-indicators for the world's population as a whole show an improvement, but there is a small sector that has advanced quite a lot, and another larger one that has been left behind.
- Exchange rates in Latin America are undervalued and therefore GDP estimates are overvalued.
- External deficits in 1998 are larger than ever.
- National savings in 1998 are less than they have ever been in modern history.
- Latin America is much deeper in debt, thanks to short-term, primarily private-sector debt taken on since 1990.

### Fifth hypothesis: On definitive solutions and what will have to be considered if the South is to have a new, more sustainable order

1. The systemic crisis has caused raw materials prices to drop sharply and has weakened regional integration accords. The fall in export income for Latin American countries between 1997 and 1998 averaged around 20 per cent, with some exceptions. International interest rates for the moment are falling, but US and European rates are expected to rise sharply in the relatively short term. Falling export income and rising interest rates presage conflict over debt payments, which must be avoided because it would be an exact repetition of the crisis of 1982 – and identical to the problem faced in 1930, 1876 and 1825.

2. A definitive solution to the 1970s debt crisis could include:

- Total debt cancellation for the poorest countries.
- Reduction of debt taken on up to 1981 for middle-income countries.
- Limits on debt servicing, using the precedents of Peru in 1945 and Germany in 1953, setting an upper limit of 3 per cent of fiscal revenue or its equivalent in exports in a bisque clause.
- Conditionalities on budget use to avoid political corruption and waste;

resources ought to be oriented towards sustainable development and to the poorest sector of the population to promote their development; health, education and food ought to be priorities.
- Economic policies that place human beings first.
- An acknowledgement that there is a systemic crisis: that the economic theory is not working as it should; that international institutions are not providing a solution and have become part of the problem; and that the reigning technology must be modified.

3. A new international institutional framework is needed that will:

- Eliminate the IMF, since it is part of the problem, not the solution. IMF loans to Third World countries, such as Mexico, Korea, Russia and Brazil (to date), have brought on economic depression and increased debt levels, all in order to rescue the international banks.
- Create a World Central Bank with regional central banks to ensure that currencies have sufficient reserves. This would guarantee supervision and place a limit on the growth of credit. Today, the US dollar is a currency without reserves, and credit can be multiplied infinitely without any supervision at the source.
- Create a Debtors' Club to negotiate with both the multilateral banks and the London and Paris Clubs.
- Introduce bisque clauses in final agreements.
- Reorient the World Bank and the Inter-American, Asian and African Development Banks to focus on projects and leave policy to political institutions. Their purpose ought to be the welfare of the population, not the welfare of the transnational corporations or the international banks.
- Strengthen the United Nations system so that it is oriented towards peace, not war. Above all, so that it works towards the formulation of policies that contribute to the stability of the world economic system and lead towards a new, more just and balanced order. Otherwise, the system may break down due to the arrogance of one country that uses global institutions to assault, attack and manipulate the economies of developing countries, while hiding behind the blinds of multilateralism.

The systemic crisis combined with technological change caused a deterioration in the terms of trade that became even more accentuated during 1998. In other words, there has been a sudden worsening of a secular trend (see Table E.2 below). This deterioration in the terms of trade demonstrates that difficulties making debt payments are on the rise, just as occurred between 1929 and 1930, a working hypothesis noted above. Because of the inflexible nature of the Brady Plan and the accords with the Paris Club, maintaining the balance of payments has become so difficult that, for example, paying the foreign debt is causing internal problems.

The combination of region-wide recession, deterioration in the terms of trade and the drying up of short-term international inter-bank credit has led in the case of Ecuador to a complex result: to keep servicing the foreign debt the government had to suspend normal payroll expenditures for public servants during the first half of 1999. While this example may be extreme, it is indicative of a new trend which brings payment on the foreign debt into direct conflict with managing the national economy and with fulfilling domestic obligations in the public sector. The government must choose between allowing public servants, who live from their state salaries, to do their work and support themselves, or sticking to agreements with creditors. And public servants include doctors and nurses, teachers and university professors, bureaucrats and military personnel. From an ethical point of view there is no doubt where the government's responsibility lies.

Latin America is once again facing a situation of international conflict caused by overindebtedness that resulted from reckless borrowing and the way in which interest charges piled up during the 1980s. The many useless or unproductive loans were a good deal for those selling obsolete technology (which is what in the end was paid for), but a disaster for the governments that got stuck with the debts of public enterprises that either never functioned well or could have functioned better if they had not adopted useless technologies.

The return to a serious balance of payments crisis, as in 1982, ought

TABLE E.2 Changes in the terms of trade during 1998 (percentage losses or gains)

| Losses | | Gains | |
|---|---|---|---|
| Venezuela | -22.8 | Dominican Republic | 0.9 |
| Chile | -10.5 | El Salvador | 2.5 |
| Peru | -8.8 | Haiti | 2.8 |
| Ecuador | -8.4 | Costa Rica | 3.9 |
| Colombia | -6.3 | Uruguay | 4.8 |
| Paraguay | -4.8 | Guatemala | 5.3 |
| Bolivia | -4.5 | Nicaragua | 6.4 |
| Argentina | -4.5 | Honduras | 7.5 |
| Mexico | -2.6 | | |
| Panama | -1.8 | Unchanged | |
| Latin America | -4.1 | Brazil | 0.0 |

*Source*: BID 1999.

to lead to a reflection on the viability of the final debt agreements and the need to clear away outstanding loans that were tainted by corruption in the North and the South but which brought a net profit to the North. The issue of corruption in lending ought to be viewed from the angle of who came out on top in the end. The winners were nearly always the large companies selling inappropriate technology who got paid by their own governments, while the cost (in greater debt) was borne by Third World governments. Corruption in the South worked well for profitability in the North. After all, today it seems clear that such corruption began in the North where the big deals were cut.

In other words, once we begin to unravel the plot that led to the debt crisis, we can see that the rules of the game need to change in a way that will serve both parties, creditors and debtors, considering that in most cases, the debt has already been paid many times over due to the high interest rates charged.

The eight chapters in this book can be summed up as follows: the debt crisis in Latin America was in reality an economic depression, which

TABLE E.3  Latin American and Caribbean debt

| | Total debt/GNP (%) | Total debt (millions US$) | Long-term debt (%) | Long-term private debt (%) | Long-term private debt (millions US$) |
|---|---|---|---|---|---|
| Honduras | 111 | 4,453 | 89 | 11 | -10 |
| Nicaragua | 355 | 5,929 | 86 | 9 | -4 |
| Argentina | 32 | 93,841 | 80 | 74 | 92,682 |
| Bolivia | 32 | 5,174 | 87 | 7 | 44 |
| Brazil | 24 | 179,047 | 80 | 82 | 14,514 |
| Ecuador | 82 | 14,491 | 88 | 60 | 368 |
| Jamaica | 94 | 4,041 | 82 | 14 | 16 |
| Peru | 49 | 29,176 | 75 | 31 | 467 |
| Chile | 38 | 27,411 | 75 | 87 | 2,608 |
| Colombia | 35 | 28,859 | 80 | 72 | 4,127 |
| Mexico | 49 | 157,125 | 72 | 75 | 12,107 |
| Panama | 87 | 6,990 | 75 | 79 | 57 |
| Uruguay | 33 | 5,899 | 72 | 65 | 325 |
| Venezuela | 54 | 35,344 | 86 | 86 | 670 |
| Costa Rica | 38 | 3,454 | 89 | 89 | -24 |
| Dominican Rep. | 34 | 4,310 | 82 | 18 | -28 |
| El Salvador | 28 | 2,894 | 79 | 6 | 23 |
| Guatemala | 24 | 3,785 | 76 | 25 | -72 |
| Trinidad and Tobago | 45 | 2,242 | 87 | 55 | 23 |

*Source*: World Bank 1997: 7–11.

preceded the millennium crisis now affecting the capitalist system as a whole and was brought on by a drastic curtailment of foreign lending. Debt-management problems led Latin America to embrace new economic policies via conditionalities imposed progressively by the International Monetary Fund, the World Bank and the Inter-American Development Bank. As the crisis spread throughout the region, cross-conditionality among these three institutions forced the adoption of the free-market doctrine as a prerequisite for debt restructuring with the Paris and London Clubs. For the first time in contemporary economic history, cross-conditionality among international financial institutions placed restrictions on the administration of domestic economic policy and guaranteed the universal adoption of international rules of the game. As far as economics are concerned, one could say today there is a single central government, with some municipal differences, for all of Latin America except Brazil and Colombia. The same process was carried to Asia at the end of the 1990s.

The aggregate effects of these policies share several common features: slow recovery of per capita economic growth for the region as a whole, a sudden rise in imports, massive entrance of short-term capital, privatizations, overvalued exchange rates, extremely high interest rates in national banking systems and the failure of industrial exports to recover. Social effects include professionals being pushed into underemployment or into the unskilled service sector. Despite the avenues lined with fancy stores and restaurants in every Latin American capital, most of today's consumers are no better off than they were a decade ago; rather, a small group is more conspicuous in its consumption.

The rate of internal savings has remained consistently low, as has the rate of aggregate investment despite the wave of privatizations. Privatizations ought to have given rise to greater efficiency, but in many cases companies have simply been handed back to the same private hands whose monopolistic behaviour was the reason the state took them over in the first place. One effect of the unilateral opening of the economy has been to justify the presence of international actors in Latin America, and to encourage new countries, such as Spain, along with Chile, Mexico, Colombia and Venezuela, to become major investors.

In the productive realm, meanwhile, factor productivity growth in advanced capitalist countries continued the downward slide which had begun at the end of the 1960s and worsened in 1973 as a result of the rise in oil prices, encouraging the export of capital to developing countries. The spread of the productivity crisis throughout the system in the 1970s, compounded by the rise in oil prices, induced a turn away from the oil-based productive paradigm that had held sway since the 1930s. A new knowledge-based paradigm – based on human capital and innovation, and as much on processes and organization as on products – became the new way of thinking and doing economics, effectively modifying social relations as a whole. Such considerations as just-in-time delivery, quality and design are today determinants of international productivity. However, in Latin America the systemic productivity crisis is not viewed as a factor that affects the region, and is not taken into account in economic policy-making, despite the fact that it is evident among the economic actors. New as it is, the knowledge-based paradigm seems to be washed up already, and the capitalist system is facing a revolution in theory and in the means of production occurring at the same time as an institutional revolution. The same thing occurred in the 1930s and 1940s as a result of the crisis of 1929.

During the reign of the oil-based paradigm, particularly after the Second World War, a catch-up process among advanced capitalist countries eventually spread to the Asian Tigers, allowing them to move from import-substitution policies to secondary and then knowledge-based exports. Import substitution policies in Latin America, in contrast, except in Brazil, did not mature in this way, due to their very success in terms of growth and development and the inertia that wrought. Latin America's success came to an end in the early 1980s, leading many to conclude that the whole attempt at industrialization was a failure, rather than examining how the process was frustrated. Technological change disrupted Latin America's insertion into the global economy, a de-linking caused by the downward trend in raw materials prices, energy-saving measures that depressed oil prices, and the reorientation of credit towards the advanced countries for their own productive reconversion (thus cutting off credit while interest rates rose sharply). In other words, financing for the external deficit dried up at the same time that the deficit ballooned as a result of systemic changes.

Although new technologies reduce the need for raw materials, energy and labour in finished goods, thus raising factor productivity as a whole in absolute terms, paradoxically it is labour productivity that has risen while capital productivity has not yet done so. In Latin America these technologies are being incorporated slowly and no overall recovery in productivity has been observed to date. Generally speaking, it would seem that improvements in capital productivity are being suffocated by the ever-growing velocity of innovation, which blocks a rise in the rate of return on investment. The pace of innovation obliges companies to stay at the state of the art and maintain national know-how to achieve that, or be left behind.

If Latin America's crisis of the 1980s was part of a systemic crisis –

expressed at the beginning of the 1980s in a sharp contraction of credit combined with a rise in international interest rates and a sudden fall in raw materials prices – then we are facing the fourth crisis of this sort in history, following on those of 1826, 1876 and 1929, all of which shared these characteristics. However, in the 1980s there was no financial crisis in the developed world, which was the defining feature of the other three. The international financial crisis began only recently, in 1997. Now we are facing a crisis in the international model of capital accumulation, a result of low factor productivity, essentially capital productivity.

The end of the technological paradigm based on oil affected Eastern Europe, Latin America and Africa in the same fashion, but not Southeast Asia. At the same time, its impact on advanced capitalist economies was less than on developing economies. A tentative explanation could be that the countries of Southeast Asia were not as highly indebted, since the financial transmission belt did not exist in the same way as it did for Africans, Latin Americans and Eastern Europeans (particularly in the cases of Poland, Hungary, Czechoslovakia and the Soviet Union). That is, the cutting off of credit did not affect economic growth in South Korea, Taiwan, Singapore or Hong Kong, because their economies were producing surpluses. However, thanks to Japan's problems during the 1990s, Asia's economies underwent the same process that Latin America suffered in the 1980s. In the end, it is the entire world that is in crisis: the economic system, its theory and its knowledge-based productive paradigm, as well as its institutions, are all being questioned.

The positive results of import substitution policies in Latin America constituted obstacles to change or advancement in the processes of industrialization, as long as the external deficit generated by the model could be financed. In Asia, in contrast, the growth rate was not the only variable taken into account by policy-makers; external restrictions were also considered since the economies are poor in natural resources. In this sense, Latin America's bountiful store of resources has been its bane. The problem in Asia in the 1990s was over-reliance on a single market, Japan. The symptoms in both regions were identical: increases in short-term international indebtedness, low exchange rates and large current accounts deficits, and unwillingness to change the development model due to its previous economic success. Thus, a drop in raw materials prices dragged down the currency, and with it international reserves, economic stability and so on.

The opening up of Latin American and Eastern European economies wrought by the policies of international financial institutions occurred parallel to a new wave of internationalization of capital, this time called globalization. The only aspect that differentiates globalization from the same phenomenon at the end of the nineteenth century is that today information is transferred in real time, which accelerates the international movement of capital and merchandise. Asian countries benefited since this process allowed for the relocation of Japanese production to them. At the same time, the movement of people from South to North became more restricted, even though the borderless world is the salient feature of the developed economies. The combination of a borderless world for capital and growing borders for people seems to be what best describes the new internationalization of capital, as far as the relationship between high- and low-productivity countries is concerned.

The emergence of the doctrine of 'export or die' renewed Latin America's dependence on raw materials, and gave rise to an accelerated process of internationalization of banking. This follows a pattern observed at the end of the nineteenth century and again in the middle of the twentieth century when the same notion held sway. In Asia in the 1990s, 'export or die' turned out to mean 'just die'. In both regions the result has been growing external deficits financed by short-term capital and by the sale of public enterprises. In Asia this was taken to an extreme, as countries bet everything on a productive reconversion that did not occur.

In Latin America the role of the state has been reduced to collecting taxes, promoting education and building infrastructure, and that remains only because they believe physical infrastructure makes markets work better and education allows people a better chance of breaking into the market. In Southeast Asia, meanwhile, the state played and continues to play a preponderant role in assimilating new technology and overseeing changes in the model for export production. It is not yet clear which of these competing voices will win out once the crisis has passed: those that argue that the presence of the state distorts the perfect market, or the post-Keynesians who argue for greater state intervention in the economy.

In the United States, the European Union and Japan, a new mercantilism cloaks protection in free-market discourse, to paraphrase Joan Robinson, allowing it to flourish despite the creation of the World Trade Organization and its declared desire to reduce non-tariff barriers. Everywhere, it seems, Keynes is on the rebound, championing the notion that public spending or tax incentives are needed to raise depressed demand. From the comments of Schroeder's former finance minister Lafontaine in Germany to the speeches of Miyazawa in Japan, everything seems to indicate change; the rhetoric of World Bank chief economist Stiglitz points in the same direction.

Ohmae proposes globalization be defined as the integration of economies with over $10,000 per capita income in a borderless world. This implies a new process of linkage between the rich of developing countries and the developed economies, as well as the exclusion of the poor in developed economies and almost everyone in developing ones. The excluded add up to four-fifths of the world's population. The island of globalization is neither totally open nor totally competitive; it exists only for the rich. Globalization gives rise to South–North migratory pressures and to processes of social exclusion within national economies.

The new policies of unilateral opening pursued in Latin America presuppose the existence of economic agents who are agile risk-takers, well-informed operative institutions, stable rules of the game and a cultural level high enough to assimilate new technologies for increasing productivity. Given these prerequisites, the market is to take care of turning growth into development, of increasing the levels of value-added, of improving productivity and ensuring that international linkages benefit all countries. Central America's experience shows great disparities between countries in all these areas, and entirely different macroeconomic results from one country to the next despite the uniformity of the policies implemented. This tells us that the role of the state in the economy and the thinking that underlies economic policy today must be reconsidered. Central America, like much of Latin America, lives by the slogan 'export or die', but according to the data what the region has pursued is 'consume or die', financed by short-term international lending via the national banking systems. Central America's exports still rely on two basic products per country.

Conceptually, this evidence seems to indicate that international questions are a more important factor today than in the past, due to the quantity of information, the systems for international exchange of information and the velocity of innovation, factors from which Latin American economies cannot remain aloof. In addition, openings from outside to inside, export market to import market without state intervention, do not seem to bear the required fruit in terms of export growth or development. In Asia this was evidently the case. Policy-makers say that with time, in a decade or two, we will be better off, but they should recall what Keynes liked to say: in the long term, we'll all be dead. In Latin America, Asia and Africa, social demands and needs place pressure on growth in the short term. as do the structural bottlenecks in the external and fiscal sectors.

One alternative to self-centred development, in the sense of the delinking proposed by S. Amin (1990a), is open self-centred development, where the internal market becomes a base for export production, with an active role for the state in the promotion of technological linkage activities and the building of complementary relations among regional economies. This proposal would have the state act like a hinge that links private interests to larger national interests, and invests in innovation, adaptation and the spread of technology through universities and research centres in collaboration with the private sector. At the same time the state would protect embryonic industries and encourage mature ones to sell their products overseas, in the style of Southeast Asia. But the state must also have a redistributive role, not only through infrastructure spending but also in the area of pricing, to provide compensation to the poorest sector of the population. The focused anti-poverty programmes now coming into vogue are an acknowledgement of the need for public funding of this sort. However, focusing social programmes when a substantial part of the population lives below the poverty line is like covering the sun with your finger and believing you have blocked it from everyone's view.

The export-or-die dilemma ignores the basic requirements of development: improving living conditions for the population as a whole, building linkages within society and modernizing the social body without excluding anyone. The market will not accomplish this because the market cannot do so. It is the job of the state, not the market, to act as the transmission belt of modernization; the market works only where it is profitable. As a result of the way the market has been treated, a more appropriate slogan for Latin America than the stated goal of 'export or die' would be 'import and live' (with international credit and large external deficits).

Finally, without falling into cultural determinism, consideration must be given to the culture of the economic agents, who must learn to act rationally, instead of assuming the state will be the supreme protector of inefficiency. Inefficiency should not be protected and protection cannot be eternal, rather it should be provided for new ventures for a clearly defined period of time. The market acts on the basis of inefficiencies, and profits are made on the inefficiencies of others, not on absolute improvements in productivity or the conquest of new markets for new products. If the state is to help out in this process, it ought to prevent a resurgence of the *rentier* mentality that with a few notable exceptions has characterized the Latin American business class for the past forty years.

# Bibliography

Abreu, Alfonso et al. (1989) *Las zonas francas industriales en la República Dominicana: el éxito de una política económica.* Santo Domingo: Centro Internacional para el Desarrollo Económico.

Adelman, Irma (1984) 'Beyond Export-led Growth', *World Development,* vol. 12, no. 9 (September). London: Pergamon Press, 937–49.

Adelman, Irma and Cynthia T. Morris (1973) *Economic Growth and Social Equity in Developing Countries.* Stanford CA: Stanford University Press.

Agosin, Manuel R. (1992) 'Las experiencias de liberalización comercial en América Latina: lecciones y perspectives', *Pensamiento Iberoamericano. Revista de Economía Política,* no. 21. Madrid: Sociedad Estatal Quinto Centenario, 13–29.

Agosin, Manuel and Ricardo Ffrench-Davis (1994) 'Liberalización comercial y desarrollo en América Latina', *Nueva Sociedad,* no. 133 (September–October). Caracas, 54–71.

Amado V., José Daniel (1998) *Zonas francas industriales en el Proyocto de Ley General de Comercio Exterior.* Thesis. Lima: Pontificia Universidad Católica del Peru.

Amin, Ash (1994) 'Post Fordism: Models, Fantasies and Phantoms of Transition', in A. Amin (ed.), *Post Fordism: A Reader.* Oxford: Basil Blackwell.

Amin, Samir (1990a) *Delinking, Towards a Polycentric World.* London: Zed Books.

Amin, Samir (1990b) *Maldevelopment: Anatomy of a Global Failure.* London: Zed Books.

Amsden, Alice (1989) *Asia's Next Giant: South Korea and Late Industrialization.* New York and Oxford: Oxford University Press.

— (1992–93) '¿Puede competir Europa oriental "¿fijando correctamente los precios"?', *Pensamiento Iberoamericano. Revista de Economía Política,* vol. 11, nos 22/-23. Madrid: Sociedad Estatal Quinto Centenario, 159–87.

Antonelli, Cristiano (1990) 'La difusión internacional de innovaciones: pautas, determinantes y efectos', *Pensamiento Iberoamericano. Revista de Economía Política,* no. 16. Madrid: Sociedad Estatal Quinto Centenario, 45–55.

Arida, Pérsio (ed.) (1987) *Inflación cero.* Bogotá: Oveja Negra.

Arida, Pérsio and André Lara-Rezende (1985) 'Inertial Inflation and Monetary Reform in Brazil', in John Williamson (ed.), *Inflation and Indexation: Argentina, Brazil and Israel.* Cambridge MA: MIT.

Arrighi, Giovanni and Jessica Drangel (1986) 'The Stratification of the World-economy: An Exploration of the Semiperipheral Zone', *Review,* no. 10. 9–74.

Balassa, Bela (1981) *The Newly Industrializing Countries in the World Economy*. New York: Pergamon Press.

Balassa, Bela, Gerardo Bueno, Pedro Pablo Kuczynski and Mario Henrique Simonsen (1986) *Toward Renewed Economic Growth in Latin America*. Washington DC: Institute of International Economics.

Baumol, William J. (1989) 'Is There a U.S. Productivity Crisis?', *Science*, vol. 243, no. 3 (February), 611–15.

Baumol, William J., Sue Anne Batey Blackman and Edward N. Wolff (1991) *Productivity and American Leadership: The Long View*. Cambridge MA: MIT Press.

BID (Banco Interamericano de Desarrollo) (1971) *Cambio y transformación. La gran tarea de América Latina*, Washington DC: BID.

— (1990) *Progreso económico y social de América Latina*. Washington DC: BID.

— (1992) *Economic and Social Progress in Latin America*. Washington DC: Johns Hopkins University Press.

— (1999) *Integración y comercio en las Américas: implicancias de la crisis financiera internacional en la integración y el comercio de América latina*. Washington DC: BID.

Bloomfield, Arthur I. (1968) 'Patterns of Fluctuations in International Investment before 1914', *Princeton Studies in International Finance*, no. 21. Princeton NJ: Princeton University Press.

Bradford Jr, Colin (1992–93a) 'La experiencia del Este asiático en la reforma económica: opciones y retos para las antiguas economías socialistas', *Pensamiento Iberoamericano. Revista de Economía Política*, vol. 11, nos 22–23. Madrid: Sociedad Estatal Quinto Centenario, 259–62.

— (1992–93b) 'Las causes del dinamismo del Este asiático y el problema de la transferibilidad', *Pensamiento Iberoamericano. Revista de Economía Política*, vol. 11, nos 22–23. Madrid: Sociedad Estatal Quinto Centenario, 197–206.

Buchanan, James M. (1969) *Cost and Choice: An Inquiry in Economic Theory*. Chicago: Markhan Publishing.

Buchanan, James M. and Gordon Tullock (1962) *The Calculus of Consent: Logical Foundations of Constitutional Democracy*. Ann Arbor: University of Michigan Press.

Buitelaar, Rudolf (1989) 'El debate sobre el futuro de la industrialización en América Latina o cómo subir ia senda escarpada hacia crecimiento y equidad. Reseña tematica', *Pensamiento Iberoamericano. Revista de Economía Política*, no. 16. Madrid: Sociedad Estatal Quinto Centenario, 265–71.

Buitelaar, Rudolf M. and Leonard Mertens (1993) 'El desafío de la competitividad industrial', *Revista de la CEPAL*, no. 51 (December). Santiago de Chile: CEPAL, 51–69.

Bulmer-Thomas, Victor (1983) 'Economic Development over the Long Run: Central America since 1920', *Journal of Latin American Studies*, vol. 15, Part 2 (November). Cambridge MA: Cambridge University Press, 269–94.

— (1989) *La economía política de Centroamérica desde 1920*. Tegucigalpa: BCIE.

Cantwell, John (1989) *Technological Innovations and Multinational Corporations*. Oxford: Basil Blackwell.

— (1995) 'The Globalisation of Technology: What Remains of the Product Cycle Model?', *Cambridge Journal of Economics*, vol. 19, no. 1 (February). London: Academic Press, 155–74.

Caraçao, Joao M. G. (1990) 'Prospectiva, Complexidade e Mundança Europa de Hoje', *Pensamiento Iberoamericano. Revista de Economía Política*, no. 18. Madrid: Sociedad Estatal Quinto Centenario, 163–71.

Cardoso, Eliana and Albert Fishlow (1992) 'Latin America Economic Development: 1950–1980', in *Journal of Latin American Studies, Quincentenary Supplement*, vol. 24. Cambridge MA: Cambridge University Press, 197–218.

Cardoso, Fernando Henrique and Enzo Faletto (1979) *Dependency and Development in Latin America*. Berkeley CA: University of California Press.

Carroll, Cristopher, David Weil and Lawrence Summers (1993) *Savings and Growth: A Reinterpretation*. Paper presented at the Carnegie-Rochester Public Policy Conference, Bradley Policy Research Centre, 23–24 April.

Caves, Richard (1992) *Industrial Efficiency in Six Countries*. Cambridge MA: MIT Press.

Chu, Yun-han (1989) 'State Structure and Economic Adjustment', *International Organization*, vol. 43, no. 4 (autumn). Cambridge MA: MIT Press, 647–72.

Cohen, Benjamin J. (1990) 'The Political Economy of International Trade', *International Organization*, vol. 44, no. 2 (spring). Cambridge MA: MIT Press, 261–81.

Collier, David (ed.) (1979) *The New Authoritarianism in Latin America*. Princeton NJ: Princeton University Press.

Congdon, Tim (1988) *The Debt Threat*. New York: Basil Blackwell.

Corden, W. Max (1990) 'American Decline and the end of Hegemony', *SAIS Review*, vol. 10, no. 2 (summer–autumn). Washington DC: Johns Hopkins University Press, 13–26.

Crane, George T. and Abla Amawi (1991) *The Theoretical Evolution of International Political Economy*. New York: Oxford University Press.

Dabene, Olivier (1993) 'La invención y remanencia de una crisis: Centroamérica en los años 80', *Anuario de Estudios Centroamericanos*, vol. 19, no. 2. San José: University of Costa Rica, 25–50.

Dahlman, Carl (1994) 'New Elements of International Competitiveness. Implications for Developing Economies', in Colin Bradford Jr (ed.), *The New Paradigm of Systemic Competitiveness: Toward More Integrated Policies in Latin America*. Development Centre Documents. Paris: OECD, 69–95.

Dancourt, Oscar and Ivory Yong (1989) 'Sobre la hiperinflación peruana', *Economía*, vol. 12, no. 23. Lima: Pontificia Universidad Católica, 13–44.

Darity, William Jr and Bobbie L. Horn (1988) *The Loan Pushers: The Role of Commercial Banks in the International Debt Crisis*. Cambridge MA: Ballinger.

De Soto, Hernando (1986) *El otro Sendero, la revolución informal*. Lima: Ed. EL Barranco.

Devlin, Robert (1989) *The Supply Side of the Debt*. Princeton NJ: Princeton University Press.

Díaz Alejandro, Carlos (1983) 'Open Economy, Closed Polity?', in Diana Tussie (ed.), *Latin America in the World Economy: New Perspectives*. Aldershot: Gower, 21–53.

Dollfus, Olivier (1997) *La Mondialisation*. Paris: Presses des Sciences.

Doeringer, Peter and Paul Streeten (1990) 'How Economic Institutions Affect Economic Performance in Industrialized Countries: Lessons for Development', *World Development*, vol. 18, no. 9. London: Pergamon Press, 1249–53.

Dornbusch, Rudiger (1989) 'Los costes y beneficios de la integración económica regional. Una revisión', *Pensamiento Iberoamericano. Revista de Economía Política*, no. 15. Madrid: Sociedad Estatal Quinto Centenario, 25–54.

Dosi, Giovanni (1982) 'Technological Paradigms and Technical Trajectories: A Suggested Interpretation of the Determinants of Technical Change', *Research Policy*, vol. 11, no. 3 (June). North Holland: Elsevier.

Drucker, Peter (1993) *Post Capitalist Society*. Oxford: Butterworth-Heinemann.

Dutt, Amitava Krishna (1992) 'The NICs, Global Accumulation and Uneven Development: Implications of a Simple Three-Region Model', *World Development*, vol. 20, no. 8 (August). London: Pergamon Press, 1159–71.

ECLAC (Economic Commission for Latin America and the Caribbean) (1985) *América Latina y la economía mundial del algodón*, Estudios e Informes, no. 50. Santiago de Chile: ECLAC.

— (1988) *The Evolution of the External Debt Problem in Latin America and the Caribbean*, Estudios e Informes de la CEPAL, no. 72. Santiago de Chile: ECLAC.

— (1989) *Options to Reduce the Debt Burden*. Santiago de Chile: ECLAC.

— (1991) *Economic Survey of Latin America and the Caribbean 1989*. Santiago de Chile: ECLAC.

— (1992a) *Balance preliminar de América Latina y el Caribe 1992*. Santiago de Chile: ECLAC.

— (1992b) *Equidad y transformación productiva: un enfoque integrado*. Santiago de Chile: ECLAC.

— (1993) *Centroamérica: el camino de los noventa*. Mexico DF: ECLAC.

— (1994a) *Economic Survey of Latin America and the Caribbean 1992*, Vol. 1. Santiago de Chile: ECLAC.

— (1994b) *Export Processing in the Caribbean: Lessons from Four Case Studies*. Santo Domingo: Dominican Republic/Caribbean Development and Cooperation Commitee, LC/CAR/G:407, 21 April.

— (1994c) *Preliminary Overview of the Latin American and Caribbean Economy 1994*. Santiago de Chile: ECLAC.

— (1994d) *América Latina y el Caribe: políticas para mejorar la inserción en la economía mundial*. Santiago de Chile: ECLAC.

— (1994e) *Reestructuración y competitividad: bibliografía comentada*, Red de Reestructuración y competitividad, Serie Desarrollo Productivo no. 16 (November). Santiago de Chile: ECLAC.

Edwards, Sebastian (1991) 'Structural Adjustment Reforms and the Debt Crisis', in Patricio Meller (ed.), *The Latin American Development Debate. Neostructuralism, Neomonetarism and Adjustment Processes*. Boulder CO: Westview Press, 129–68.

Edwards, Sebastian and Felipe Larrain (1989) *Debt, Adjustment and Recovery*. Oxford: Basil Blackwell.

Edwards, Sebastian and Peter Montiel (1989) 'The Price of Postponed Adjustment', *Finance & Development*. Washington DC: IMF and International Bank for Reconstruction and Development, 34–7.

Eichengreen, Barry and Peter H. Lindert (eds) (1989) *The International Debt Crisis in Perspective*. Cambridge MA: MIT Press.

Englander, Steven and Andrew Gurney (1994a) 'Medium Term Determinants of OECD Productivity', *OECD Economic Studies*, no. 22 (spring). Paris. 49–110.

— (1994b) 'OECD Productivity Growth: Medium Term Trends', *OECD Economic Studies*, no. 22 (spring). Paris. 111–30.

Esser, Josef and Joachim Hirsch (1994) 'The Crisis of Fordism and the Dimensions of a "Post Fordist" Regional and Urban Structure', in Ash Amin (ed.), *Post Fordism: A Reader*. Oxford: Basil Blackwell, 71–98.

Evans, Peter (1979) *Dependent Development: The Alliance of Multinationals, State and Local Capital in Brazil*. Princeton NJ: Princeton University Press.

Fajnzylber, Fernando (1982) *Industrialización crecimiento y productividad*. Mexico: Editorial Nueva Imagen.

— (1983a) 'Intervención, autodeterminación e industrialización en la América Latina', *El Trimestre Economico*, vol. L(1), no. 197. Mexico: Fondo de Cultura Económica, 307–28.

— (1983b) *La industrialización trunca*. Mexico: Editorial Nueva Imagen.

— (1986) 'Reflexiones sobre las especificidades de América Latina y el Sudeste asiático y sus referentes en el mundo'. Mimeo.

— (1989) *Industrializacion en América Latina: de la 'caja negra' al 'casillero vacío'*, Cuadernos de la CEPAL, no. 60. Santiago de Chile: ECLAC.

— (1990) 'Sobre la impostergable transformación productiva de América Latina', *Pensamiento Iberoamericano. Revista de Economía Política*, vol. 16. Madrid: Sociedad Estatal Quinto Centenario, 85–129.

Fanelli, José María and Roberto Frenkel (1987) 'El Plan Austral: un año y medio después', *El Trimestre Económico*, vol. LIV, special issue (September). Mexico: Fondo de Cultura Económica, 55–117.

Fanelli, José María, Roberto Frenkel and Guillermo Rozenwurcel (1990) *Growth and Structural Reform in Latin America. Where we Stand.* 7 Documento CEDES, no. 57. Buenos Aires.

Feinberg, Richard E. (1986) *Más allá de la crisis de la deuda; bases para un nuevo enfoque*. Buenos Aires: Grupo Editorial Latinoamericano.

Ffrench-Davis, Ricardo and Oscar Muñoz (1991) 'Economic Development and the International Environment', in Patricio Meller (ed.), *The Latin American Development Debate. Neostructuralism, Neomonetarism and Adjustment Processes*. Boulder CO: Westview Press

Ffrench-Davis, Ricardo and Helmut Reisen (1998) *Mouvements de capitaux et performances des investissements*. Paris: OECD.

Fischer, Stanley (1993) 'Reforma económica en Rusia', *Pensamiento Iberoamericano. Revista de Economía Política*, vol. 1, nos 22–23. Madrid: Sociedad Estatal Quinto Centenario, 241–8.

Fishlow, Albert (1989) 'Latin American Failure against the Backdrop of Asian success', *The Annals of the American Academy of Political and Social Science*, vol. 505 (September). Newbury Park CA: Sage, 117–28.

— (1990) 'The Latin America State', *Journal of Economic Perspective*, vol. 4, no. 3 (summer). Stanford CA: Stanford University Press, 61–73.

Forrester, Viviane (1997) *El horror económico*. Fondo.

Forte F. and A. Peacock (eds) (1985) *Public Expenditure and Government Growth*. Oxford and New York: Blackwell.

Fröbel, Folker, Jürgen Heinrichs and Otto Kreye (1981) *The New International Division of Labour*. New York: Cambridge University Press.

Funkhouser, Edward (1990) *Mass Migration, Remittances, and Economic Adjustment: The Case of El Salvador in the 1980s*. Cambridge MA: Harvard University Press.

Galbraith, John Kenneth (1961) *The Great Crash, 1929*. Boston: Houghton Mifflin.

Gallardo, María Eugenia (1993) 'Central America in the 90s', in Wim Pelupessy and John Weeks (eds), *Economic Maladjustment in Central America*. London: Macmillan.

George, Susan (1988) *A Fate Worse than Debt: The World Financial Crisis and the Poor*. New York: Grove Press.

Gereffi, Gary (1990) 'Los nuevos desafíos de la industrialización: observaciones sobre el Sudeste Asiático y Latinoamérica', *Pensamiento Iberoamericano. Revistade Economía Política*, vol. 16. Madrid: Sociedad Estatal Quinto Centenario, 205–34.

Gerschenkron, Alexander (1952) 'Economic Backwardness in Historical Perspective', in Bert F. Hoselitz (ed.), *The Progress of Underdeveloped Areas*. Chicago: University of Chicago Press.

— (1962) *Economic Backwardness in Historical Perspective. A Book of Essays*. Cambridge MA: Belknap Press, Harvard University Press.

Gitli, Eduardo and Gunilla Ryd (1991) 'La integración latinoamericana frente a la Iniciativa de las Américas', *Pensamiento Iberoamericano. Revista de Economía Política*, no. 20. Madrid: Sociedad Estatal Quinto Centenario, 149–64.

Gold, Thomas (1981) *Dependent Development in Taiwan*. Doctoral thesis. Cambridge MA: Harvard University.

Grandi, Jorge (1991) 'Las dimensiones del Mercado Unico Europeo y América Latina: implicaciones y reflexiones sobre algunos interrogantes', *Pensamiento Iberoamericano. Revista de Economía Política*, no. 19. Madrid: Sociedad Estatal Quinto Centenario, 271–98.

Griffiths-Jones, Stephany (1988a) 'La condicionalidad cruzada o la expansión del ajuste obligatorio', *Pensamiento Iberoamericano. Revista de Economía Política*, no. 13. Madrid: Siglo XXI Espana Editores, 67–90.

— (1988b) *Managing World Debt*. New York: St Martin's Press.

Guitián, Manuel (1993) 'El proceso de ajuste y la reforma económica: diferencias aparentes y reales entre Este y Oeste', *Pensamiento Iberoamericano. Revista de Economía Política*, vol. 1, nos 22–23. Madrid: Sociedad Estatal Quinto Centenario, 113–38.

Gurrieri, Paolo (1994) 'International Competitiveness, Trade Integration and Technologic Interdependence', in Colin Bradford Jr (ed.), *The New Paradigm of Systemic Competitiveness: Towards More Integrated Policies in Latin America*. Paris: OECD, Development Centre Documents.

Gurrieri, Paolo and Carlo Milana (1995) 'Changes and Trends in the World Trade in High Technology products', *Cambridge Journal of Economics*, vol. 19, no. 1 (February). London: Academic Press, 225–242.

Hamilton, Alexander (1791) 'Report on Manufactures', in Samuel McKee Jr (ed.) (1934), *Papers on Public Credit, Commerce and Finance*. New York: Columbia University Press.

Hamilton, Clive (1989) 'The Irrelevance of Economic Liberalization in the Third World', *World Development*, vol. 17, no. 10. London: Pergamon Press, 1523–30.

Hansson, Par and Magnus Henrekson (1994) 'What Makes a Country Socially Capable of Catching up?', *Weltwirtschaft*, vol. 130, no. 4. Tubingen: Institut fur Weltwirtschaft an der Universitat Kiel, 760–84.

Harris, Nigel (1986) *The End of the Third World: Newly Industrializing Countries and the Decline of an Ideology.* London: I.B.Tauris.

Hart, Jeffrey (1995) 'Maquiladorization as a Global Process', in Steven Chan (ed.), *Foreign Direct Investment in a Changing Political Economy.* London: Macmillan.

Helleiner, Gerald K. (1987) 'Stabilization, Adjustment, and the Poor', *World Development*, vol. 15, no. 12. London: Pergamon Press, 1499–513.

— (ed.) (1986) *A World Divided The Less Developed Countries in the International Economy.* Cambridge MA: Cambridge University Press.

Heller, Agnes (1998) *Filosofía de la Modernidad.* Lima: Centro Antonio Ruiz de Montoya.

Herbert-Copley, Brent (1990) 'Technical Change in Latin American Manufacturing Firms: Review and Synthesis', *World Development*, vol. 18, no. 11 (November), Oxford: Pergamon Press, 1457–69.

Hirschman, Albert O. (1992) 'Industrialization and its Manifold Discontents: West, East and South', *World Development*, vol. 20, no. 9 (September). Oxford: Pergamon Press, 1225–32.

Hodne, Fritz (1975) *An Economic History of Norway 1815–1970.* Trondheim: Tapir.

Hojman, David E. (1994) 'The Political Economy of Recent Conversions to Market Economics in Latin America', *Journal of Latin American Studies*, vol. 26, Part 1. Oxford: Cambridge University Press, 191–19.

Hufbauer, Gary C. (1991) Las perspectives del comercio mundial en los noventa y sus implicaciones para los países en desarrollo', *Pensamiento Iberoamericano. Revista de Economía Política*, no. 20. Madrid: Sociedad Estatal Quinto Centenario, 43–51.

Hunt, Diana (1989) *Economic Theories of Development: An Analysis of Competing Paradigms.* New York and London: Harvester Wheatsheaf.

Iguíñiz, Javier (1995) *¿Compiten las naciones economicamente?.* Unpublished ms. Lima.

ILO–UNCTC (1988) *Economic and Social Effects of Mutinational Enterprises in Export Processing Zones. A Joint ILO–UNCTC Project.* Geneva: ILO–UNCTC.

IMF (International Monetary Fund) (1991–94) *Economic Outlook.* Washington DC: IMF.

ISCA (International Save the Children Federation) (1992) 'Impacto de la deuda externa y las políticas de ajuste sobre la niñez en América Latina'. Mimeo. Bogota: ISCA.

Jadresic, Alejandro (1990) 'Transformación productiva, crecimiento y competitividad internacional. Consideraciones sobre la experiencia chilena', *Pensamiento Iberoamericano. Revista de Economía Política*, no. 17. Madrid: Sociedad Estatal Quinto Centenario, 39–68.

Jenks, Leland H. (1963) *The Migration of British Capital to 1875* (3rd edn). London: Thomas Nelson.

Johnson, Chalmers (1987) 'Political Institutions and Economic Performance: The Government–Business Relationship in Japan, South Korea and Taiwan', in Frederic C. Deyo (ed.), *The Political Economy of the New Asian Industrialism.* Ithaca NY: Cornell University Press, 136–64.

Jomo, K.S. et al. (1997) *Southeast Asia's Misunderstood Miracle.* Boulder CO: Westview Press.

Kaplinsky, Raphael (1984) *Automation: The Technology and Society.* London: Longman.

Kaplinsky, Raphael and Kurt Hoffman (1988) *Driving Force: The Global Restructuring of Technology, Labour, and Investment in the Automobile and Components Industries*. Boulder CO: Westview Press.

Kennedy, Paul (1986) *Britain's Investment Overseas on the Eve of the First World War: The Use and Abuse of Numbers*. London: Macmillan.

— (1987) 'Review of David C.M. Platt', *Economic History Review*, 2nd Series, vol. XL, no. 2 (May). Oxford: Basil Blackwell, 307–9.

— (1993) *Preparing for the Twenty-First Century*. London: HarperCollins.

Kenwood, A. G. and Alam L. Lougheed (1992) *The Growth of the International Economy, 1820–1990* (3rd edn). London: Routledge.

Killick, Tony (ed.) (1984) *The Quest for Economic Stabilization: The IMF and the Third World*. New York and London: St Martin's Press and Heinemann Educational Books.

Kindleberger, Charles P. (1985) *A Financial History of Western Europe*. London: George Allen and Unwin

Kisic, Drago (1987) *De la corresponsabilidad a la moratoria: el caso de la deuda externa peruana 1970–1986*. Lima: Fundación Friedrich Ebert, CEPEI.

Krugman, Paul (1994a) *Peddling Prosperity. Economic Sense and Nonsense in the Age of Diminished Expectations*. New York and London: W.W. Norton.

— (1994b) 'Competitiveness: A Dangerous Obsession', *Foreign Affairs*, vol. 73, no. 2 (March–April). New York, 28–44.

— (1994c) 'Reply to Prestowitz et al.', *Foreign Affairs*, vol. 73, no. 4. New York, 198–203.

Kuczynski, Pedro Pablo (1988) *Latin American Debt*. Baltimore MD: Johns Hopkins University Press.

Kuhn, Thomas (1972) *The Structure of Scientific Revolutions*. Chicago/London: University of Chicago Press.

Kumar, Rajiv (1987) 'Performance of Foreign and Domestic Firms in Export Processing Zones', *World Development*, vol. 15, nos 10–11 (October/November). London: Pergamon Press, 1309–19.

Kuznetsov, Yevgeny (1993) 'Reestructuración industrial en Europa oriental: un caso especial de industrialización tardía?, Comentarios al artículo de Alice Amsden', *Pensamiento Iberoamericano. Revista de Economía Política*, vol. 11, nos 22–23,. Madrid: Sociedad Estatal Quinto Centenario, 189–92.

Lall, Sanjaya (1992) 'Technological Capabilities and Industrialization', *World Development*, vol. 20, no. 2. London: Pergamon Press, 165–86.

Leiva, Patricio (ed.) (1994) *La Ronda Uruguay y el desarrollo de América Latina*. Santiago de Chile: Centro Latinoamericano de Economía y Política Internacional-CLEPI.

Lim, Hyun-Chin (1985) *Dependent Development in Korea, 1963–1979*. Seoul: Seoul National University Press.

Lin, Ching-yuan (1988a) 'East Asia and Latin America as Contrasting Models', *Economic Development and Cultural Change*, vol. 36, no. 3 (April). Supplement. Chicago: University of Chicago Press, S153–S197.

— (1988b) *Latin America versus East Asia: A Comparative Development Perspective*. Gloucester NJ: Praeger.

Linder, Steffan (1961) *An Essay on Trade and Transformation*. New York: Wiley.

Lipietz, Alain (1985) *Mirages et miracles. Problèmes de l'industrialisation dans le Tiers Monde.* Paris: Editions La Découverte.

Lizano, Eduardo and Silvia Charpentier (1986) 'La condicionalidad cruzada y la deuda externa', *Comentarios sobre asuntos económicos*, no. 59. San José: Banco Central de Costa Rica.

Lopes, Francisco (1986) 'Inflaçao inercial, Hiperinflaçao e Desinflaçao: Notas e Conjectura', *Revista de ANPEC*, no. 9. Rio de Janeiro: Asociaçao Nacional de Pesquisas Economicas.

Ludlow, Peter M. (1989) 'The Future of the International Trading System', *Washington Quarterly. A Review of Strategic and International Issues*, vol. 12, no. 4. Cambridge MA, 157–69.

McKenzie, Richard (1989) 'The Decline of America: Myth or Fate?', *Society* (November–December). New Brunswick NJ, 41–8.

Maddison, Angus (1985) *Two Crises: Latin America and Asia, 1929–1938.* Paris: OECD, Development Centre Studies.

— (1990) 'El crecimiento postbélico y la crisis: una visión global', *Pensamiento Iberoamericano. Revista de Economía Política*, no. 18. Madrid: Sociedad Estatal Quinto Centenario, 13–42.

— (1991) *Dynamic Forces in Capitalist Development. A Long-Run Comparative Review.* New York and Oxford: Oxford University Press.

Magdoff, Harry (1992) 'Globalisation - To what end?', *Economic Review*, vol. 18, no. 5 (August). Colombo, Sri Lanka: The People's Bank, 2–11, 22–7, 33.

Mahaney, Mark S. (ed.) (1990) 'Symposium: American Foreign Policy in the 1990s', *SAIS Review*, vol. 10, no. 1 (winter–spring). Washington DC: Johns Hopkins University Press, 15–51.

Manrique, Nelson (1997) *La sociedad virtual y otros ensayos.* Lima: Pontificia Universidad Católica del Perú.

Marichal, Carlos (1989) *A Century of Debt Crisis in Latin America: From Independence to the Great Depression, 1820–1930.* Princeton NJ: Princeton University Press.

Marx, Karl and Friedrich Engels (1932) *Manifesto of the Communist Party.* New York: International Publishers.

Meller, Patricio (1991) 'IMF and World Bank Roles in the Latin American Foreign Debt Problem', in Patricio Meller (ed.), *The Latin American Development Debate. Neostructuralism, Neomonetarism and Adjustment Processes.* Boulder CO: Westview Press, 169–206.

— (1992–93) 'Ajuste y reformas económicas en America Latina: problemas y experiencias recientes', *Pensamiento Iberoamericano. Revista de Economía Política*, vol. 11, nos 22–23. Madrid: Sociedad Estatal Quinto Centenario, 15–58.

Mittelman, James (1995) 'Rethinking the International Division of Labour in the Context of Globalisation', *Third World Quarterly*, vol. 16, no. 2. Cambridge and London: Carfax Publishing Company, 273–95.

Morishima, Michio (1995) *Why has Japan 'Succeeded'. Western Technology and the Japanese Ethos.* Cambridge: Cambridge University Press.

Morss, Elliot R. (1991) 'The New Global Players: How They Compete and Collaborate', *World Development*, vol. 19, no. 1. London: Pergamon Press, 55–64.

Moya Espinal, (1986) 'Francisco Las zonas francas industriales y las empresas multinacionales: efectos económicos e impacto sobre el empleo en República

Dominicana'. Multinational Enterprises Programme Working Papers no. 46. OIT–CNUET.

Neal, Craig R. (1990) 'Macrofinancial indicators for 117 Developing and Industrial Countries'. Working Paper Series 58. Washington DC: World Bank, Office of the Vice President, Development Economics.

Niskanen, W.A. (1971) *Bureaucracy and Representative Government.* Chicago: Aldine Atherton.

Noland, Marcus (1992) 'Política comercial y desarrollo en la región del Asia-Pacífico', *Pensamiento Iberoamericano. Revista de Economía Política,* no. 21. Madrid: Sociedad Estatal Quinto Centenario, 217–33.

Nye, Joseph and Fredric Smoler (1991) 'Are We Really Going the Way of the British Empire?', *American Heritage* (May-June). 45–56.

Ocampo, José Antonio (1987) 'Una evaluación comparativa de cuatro planes antiinflacionarios recientes', *El Trimestre Económico,* vol. LIV, special issue (September). Mexico: Fondo de Cultura Económica, 7–51.

— (1991) 'Las nuevas teorías del comercio internacional y los países en vías de desarrollo', *Pensamiento Iberoamericano. Revista de Economía Política,* no. 20. Madrid: Sociedad Estatal Quinto Centenario, 193–214.

Ocampo, José Antonio and Leonardo Villar (1992) 'Trayectoria y vicisitudes de la apertura económica colombiana', *Pensamiento Iberoamericano. Revista de Economía Política,* no. 21. Madrid: Sociedad Estatal Quinto Centenario, 165–86.

O'Donnell, Guillermo (1973) *Modernization and Bureaucratic Authoritarianism: Studies in South American Politics.* Berkeley CA: University of California Press.

OECD (1991) *Economic Outlook,* no. 49 (July). Paris: OECD.

— (1992) *Historical Statistics 1960–1990.* Paris: OECD.

— (1993) *Economic Outlook,* no. 53 (June). Paris, OECD.

— (1994) *Economic Outlook,* no. 56 (December). Paris: OECD.

Offe, Claus (1990) 'Bienestar, nación y republica. Aspectos de la vía particular alemana del socialismo al capitalismo', *Pensamiento Iberoamericano. Revista de Economía Política,* no. 18. Madrid: Sociedad Estatal Quinto Centenario, 145–61.

Ohmae, Kenichi (1990) *The Borderless World. Power and Strategy in the Global Marketplace.* London: HarperCollins.

Oman, Charles (1994) *Globalisation and Regionalisation: The Challenge for Developing Countries.* Paris: OECD, Development Centre Studies.

— (1996) *Globalizacion y Regionalizacion: los desafíos políticos.* Lima: Fundacion Ebert.

Omerod, Paul (1994) *The Death of Economics.* London: Faber.

Ominami, Carlos (1988) 'Doce proposiciones acerca de América Latina en una era de profundo cambio tecnológico', *Pensamiento Iberoamericano. Revista de Economía Política,* vol. 21, no. 13, Madrid: Espana Editores, 49–66.

Ominami, Carlos (1991) 'Deindustrialization and Industrial Restructuring in Latin America: The examples of Argentina, Brazil and Chile', in Patricio Meller (ed.), *The Latin American Development Debate. Neostructuralism, Neomonetarism and Adjustment Processes,* Westview Press, Boulder CO, 79–101.

Orellana, Carlos (1992) 'Migración y remesas. Una evaluación de su impacto en la economía salvadorena', *Política Económica,* vol. I, no. 11 (February–March). San Salvador, 1–23.

Oshiro, Jorge (1995) 'Lo moderno en el Peru de los 90, Reseña', *Márgenes. Encuentro y debate*, vol. VIii, nos 13–14 (November). Lima, 237–48.

Pangestu, Mari (1995) 'Global Economic Developments: Implications for Developing Countries', *Indonesian Quarterly*, vol. 23, no. 1. Jakarta, 9–17.

Pastor, Manuel Jr and Carol Wise (1992) 'Peruvian Economic Policy in the 1980s: From Orthodoxy to Heterodoxy and Back', *Latin American Research Review*, vol. 27, no. 2. Albuquerque: University of New Mexico, 83–117.

Penrose, Edith (1992) 'Economic Liberalization: Openness and Integration – But what Kind?', *Development Policy Review*, vol. 10. London: Sage, 237–54.

Pérez, Carlota (1985) 'Microelectronics, Long Waves and World Structural Change: New Perspectives for Developing Countries', *World Development*, vol. 13, no. 3 (March). Oxford: Pergamon Press, 441–63.

— (1992) 'Cambio técnico, reestructuración competitiva y reforma institucional en los países en desarrollo', *El Trimestre Económico*, vol. LIX(1), no. 233 (January–March). Mexico: Fondo de Cultura Económica, 23–64.

Perkins, Dwight H. (1993) 'El enfoque "gradual" de las reformas de mercado en China', *Pensamiento Iberoamericano. Revista de Economía Política*, vol. 11, nos 22–23. Madrid: Sociedad Estatal Quinto Centenario, 121–54.

Pianta, Mario (1995) 'Technology and Growth in OECD Countries, 1970–1990', *Cambridge Journal of Economics*, vol. 19, no. 1 (February). London: Academic Press, 175–87.

PNUD (Programa de las Naciones Unidas pare el Desarrollo) (1993) *Informe sobre el desarrollo humano 1993*. Madrid: CIDEAL.

— (1995) *Informe sobre el desarrollo humano 1995*. Mexico: Harla SA.

Pollin, Robert and Alexander Cockburn (1991) 'The World, the Free Market and the Left', *The Nation* (25 February). 2–9.

Porter, Michael (1990) *The Competitive Advantage of Nations*. New York: Free Press.

Prestowitz, Clyde, Lester Thurow, Rudolf Scharping, Stephen Cohen and Benn Steil (1994) 'The Fight over Competitiveness. A Zero Sum Debate?', *Foreign Affairs*, vol. 73, no. 4. New York, 186–97.

Przeworski, Adam (1990) '¿Podriamos alimentar a todo el mundo? La irracionalidad del capitalismo y la inviabilidad del socialismo', *Pensamiento Iberoamericano. Revista de Economía Política*, no. 18. Madrid: Sociedad Estatal Quinto Centenario, 97–123.

Ramos, Joseph (1994) 'Sintesis del planteamiento de la CEPAL sobre la equidad y transformación productive', LC/G.1841 (December). Santiago de Chile: ECLAC, División de Desarrollo Productivo y Empresarial.

Rath, Amitav (1990) 'Science, Technology, and Policy in the Periphery: A Perspective from the Centre', *World Development*, vol. 18, no. 11 (November). Oxford: Pergamon Press, 1429–43.

Republica de Colombia (1990) 'Politicas pare las zones francas colombianas'. Mimeo. Bogotá: Ministerio de Desarrollo Económico.

Rojas, Mauricio (1991) 'Review of the Debate over the Origins of Latin American Industrialization and its Ideological Context', in Patricio Meller (ed.), *The Latin American Development Debate. Neostructuralism, Neomonetarism and Adjustment Processes*. Boulder CO: Westview Press.

Romer, Paul (1989) 'Capital Accumulation in the Theory of Long Run Growth', in Robere J. Barro (ed.), *Modern Business Cycle Theory*. Cambridge MA: Harvard University Press.

Ros, Jaime (1987) 'On models of Inertial Inflation'. Mimeo. Helsinki: World Institute for Development Economics Research (WIDER), July.

Rosenthal, Gert (1994) 'El desarrollo de América Latina y el Caribe y la Ronda Uruguay', in Patricio Leiva (ed.), *La Ronda Uruguay y el desarrollo de América Latina*. Santiago de Chile: Centro Latinoamericano de Economía y Política Internacional (CLEPI).

Roxborough, Ian (1992) 'Neoliberalism in Latin America: Limits and Alternatives', *Third World Quarterly*, vol. 13, no. 3. London: Carfax, 421–40.

Rubin, Steven (1998) *Tax Free Exporting Zones. A User's Manual*. London: Economist Publications.

Sachs, Ignacy, B. Gibier and F. Chesnais (1997) *La Pensée*, no. 309 (January-March). Paris.

Sachs, Jeffrey (1986a) 'Managing the LDC Debt Crisis', *Brooking Papers on Economic Activity*, no. 2. 397–432.

— (1986b) *The Bolivian Hyperinflation and Stabilization*, Discussion Paper no. 2073. Cambridge MA: NBER.

— (1987) *Trade and Exchange Rate Policies in Growth-oriented Adjustment Programs*. Paper presented to the symposium on Growth-oriented Adjustment Programs. Washington DC: IMF–World Bank.

— (1989) *Developing Country Debt and the World Economy*, Chicago: University of Chicago Press.

Scherer, F. M. (1992) International High-Technology Competition. Cambridge MA: Harvard University Press.

Schuldt, Jürgen (1995) *Repensando el desarrollo: hacia una concepción alternativa para los países andinos*. Quito: Centro Andino de Acción Popular-CAAP.

Schumpeter, Joseph A. (1943) *Capitalism, Socialism and Democracy*. London: Allen and Unwin.

Sheik, Anwar (1990) 'Crisis económicas y tasa decreciente de ganancia', in *Valor, acumulación y crisis*. Bogotá: Tercer Mundo Editores.

Soete, Luc (1985) 'International Diffusion of Technology, Industrial Development and Technological Leapfrogging', *World Development*, vol. 13, no. 3 (March). Oxford: Pergamon Press, 409–22.

Stallings, Barbara and Robert Kaufman (1989) *Debt and Democracy in Latin America*. Boulder CO: Westview Press.

Stiglitz (1993).

Streeten, Paul (1982) *Frontera de los estudios sobre el desarrollo*. Mexico: Fondo de Cultura Económica.

Subrahmanian K. K. and M. Pillai (1979) *Multinationals and Indian Exports*. Bombay: Allied Publishers.

SUFRAMA–Zona Franca de Manaos (1990) *Desarrollo del distrito industrial*. Manaos: SUFRAMA.

Svendsen, Knud Erik (1987) *The Failure of the International Debt Strategy*. Copenhagen: Centre for Development Research.

Szentes, Tamas (1990) 'La transición desde las "economías de planificación central-izada" a las "economías de mercado" en la Europa del Este y la URSS: la ruptura final con el estalinismo', *Pensamiento Iberoamericano. Revista de Economía Política*, no. 18. Madrid: Sociedad Estatal Quinto Centenario, 125–44.

Taylor, Lance (1987) 'Macro Policy in the Tropics: How Sensible People Stand?', *World Development*, vol. 15, no. 12 (December). London: Pergamon Press, 1407–35.

— (1993) 'La transición postsocialista desde el punto de vista de la economía del desarrollo', *Pensamiento Iberoamericano. Revista de Economía Política*, vol. 1, no. 22–23. Madrid: Sociedad Estatal Quinto Centenario, 141–79.

Thoumi, Francisco E. (1989) 'Bilateral Trade Flows and Economic Integration in Latin America and the Caribbean', *World Development*, vol. 17, no. 3 (March). Oxford: Pergamon Press, 421–9.

Thurow, Lester (1994) *Head to Head: The Coming Economic Battle among Japan, the United States and Europe*. London: Nicholas Brealey Publishing.

Torres-Rivas, Edelberto (1973) *Interpretación del desarrollo social centroamericano*. San José, Costa Rica: EDUCA.

Touraine, Alain (1993) *Crítica de la Modernidad*. Madrid: Ediciones Temas de Hoy.

Tussie, Diana (1991) 'La Ronda Uruguay, el sistema de comercio internacional y los países en desarrollo: consideraciones preliminares', *Pensamiento Iberoamericano. Revista de Economía Política*. no. 20. Madrid: Sociedad Estatal Quinto Centenario, 79–100.

Ugarteche, Oscar (1986) *El Estado deudor. Economía política de la deuda: Perú y Bolivia 1968–1984*. Lima: Instituto de Estudios Peruanos.

— (1987) 'Notas sobre la economía política de la deuda. El caso de Nicaragua'. Mimeo. Managua: Banco Central de Nicaragua.

— (1991) 'Europa del este: una aproximación. La crisis de la hegemonía y de los paradigmas', *Márgenes. Encuentro y debate*, vol. IV, no. 7 (January). Lima, 11–37.

— 'La recuperación económica en América Latina', *Nueva Sociedad*, no. 133, Caracas (September–October). 164–179.

— (1994b) '¿El fin de la male conciencia? Sobre lo moderno en el Peru de los 90', *Márgenes. Encuentro y debate*, vol. VII, no. 12 (November). Lima, 207–30.

UNCTAD (1991) *Trade and Development Report 1991*. New York: United Nations.

— (1992a) *Handbook of International Trade and Development Statistics 1991*. New York: United Nations.

— (1992b) *Trade and Development Report 1992*. New York: United Nations.

— (1993) *Trade and Development Report 1993*. New York: United Nations.

UNDP (1999) *Human Development Report 1999*, New York: Oxford University Press.

UNICEF (1988 and 1992) *Estado Mundial de la Infancia*. Barcelona: J&J Asociados.

UNIDO (1988) *Export Processing Zonesin Transition. The case of the Republic of Korea*, V.8825528 (10 June). Vienna: UNIDO.

United Nations (1986 and 1989) *National Accounts Statistics*. New York: United Nations.

Uthoff, Andras and Daniel Titelman (1994) 'Afluencia de capitales externos y políticas macroeconómicas', *Revista de la CEPAL*, no. 53 (August). Santiago de Chile: ECLAC, 13–29.

Vacchino, Juan Mario (1989) 'Esquemas latinoamericanos de integración: problemas y desarrollos', *Pensamiento Iberoamericano. Revista de Economía Política*, no. 15. Madrid: Sociedad Estatal Quinto Centenario, 57–84.

Van Dijck, Pitou (1990) 'Análisis comparativo entre América Latina y el Este asiático. Estructura, política y resultados económicos', *Pensamiento Iberoamericano. Revista de Economía Política*, no. 16. Madrid: Sociedad Estatal Quinto Centenario, 169–203.

Velasco, Andrés (1991) 'Monetarism vs. Structuralism: Some Macroeconomic Lessons', in Patricio Meller (ed.), *The Latin American Development Debate. Neostructuralism, Neomonetarism and Adjustment Processes*, Boulder CO: Westview Press, 43–57.

Vernon, Raymond (1989) 'The Japan–U.S. Bilateral Relationship: Its Role in the Global Economy', *The Washington Quarterly, A Review of Strategic and International Issues*, vol. 13, no. 3. Cambridge MA: 57–68.

Versluysen, Eugene (1982) *The Political Economy of International Finances*. London: St Martin's Press.

Viner, Jacob (1960) 'The Intellectual History of Laissez Faire', *Journal of Law and Economics*, vol. 3 (October). Chicago: University of Chicago Press, 45–69.

Wade, Robert (1990) *Governing the Market, Economic Theory and the Role of Government in East Asian Industrialization*. Princeton NJ: Princeton University Press.

Wallerstein, Immanuel (1974) 'Dependence in an Interdependent World: The Limited Possibilities of Transformation within the Capitalist World-economy', *African Studies Review*, no. 17. Atlanta GA, 1–26.

Warr, Peter (1989) 'Zonas francas industriales y política comercial', *Finanzas y Desarrollo*, vol. 26, no. 2 (June). Washington DC: Publicación trimestral del FMI y del Banco Mundial, 34–6.

Weeks, John (1993) 'Adjustment in Central America', in Wim Pelupessy and John Weeks (eds), *Economic Maladjustment in Central America*. London: Macmillan.

Weinert, Richard (1981) 'Nicaragua's Debt Renegotiation (Commentary)', *Cambridge Journal of Economics*, vol. 5, no. 2 (June). London and New York: Academic Press, 187–94.

Westphal, Larry (1991) 'La política industrial en una economía impulsada por las exportaciones: lecciones de la experiencia de Corea del Sur', *Pensamiento Iberoamericano. Revista de Economía Política*, no. 21. Madrid: Sociedad Estatal Quinto Centenario, 235–57.

Whee Rhee, Yung, Katharina Katterbach and Janette White (1990) *Free Trade Zones in Export Strategies*, PRE Industry Series Paper no. 36 (December). Washington DC: World Bank Industry and Energy Department.

Whitehead, Laurence (1989) 'Tigers in Latin America?', *The Annals of the American Academy of Political and Social Science*, vol. 505, (September). Newbury Park CA: Sage, 142–51.

Williamson, John (1982) *The Lending Policies of the International Monetary Fund, Policy Analysis in International Economics I*. Washington DC: Institute for International Economics.

— (ed.) (1990) *Latin American Adjustment: How Much Has Happened?* Washington DC: Institute of International Economics.

Willmore, Larry (1993a) 'Export Processing in Jamaica: Ownership, Linkages and Transfer of Technology'. ECLAC Working Paper no. 13.

— (1993b) 'Export Processing in Saint Lucia: Ownership, Linkages and Transfer of Technology'. ECLAC Working Paper no. 14.

— (1993c) 'Export Processing in Dominican Republic: Ownership, Linkages and Transfer of Technology'. ECLAC Working Paper no. 15.

Wolf, Charles Jr (1998) *Markets or Governments. Choosing between Imperfect Alternatives* (Rand Corporation Research Study). Cambridge MA: MIT Press.

Woodward, Ralph Lee (1985) *Central America. A Nation Divided*, 2nd edn. London and New York: Oxford University Press.

World Bank (1987) *World Development Report 1987*. New York and Oxford: Oxford University Press.

— (1990a) *Free Trade Zones in Export Strategies*. Industry Series Paper, no. 36. Washington DC: World Bank.

— (1990b) *Informe sobre el Desarrollo Mundial, 1990*. Washington DC: World Bank.

— (1992) *World Development Report 1992*. New York and Oxford: Oxford University Press.

— (1993) *The East Asian Miracle. Economic Growth and Public Policy*. New York and Oxford: Oxford University Press.

— (1994a) *World Debt Tables 1994–95: Vol. I. External Finance for Developing Countries*. Washington DC: World Bank.

— (1994b) *World Development Report 1994*. New York and Oxford: Oxford University Press.

— (1994c) *World Tables 1994*. Baltimore MD: Johns Hopkins University Press.

— (1997) *World Debt Tables, Vol. I*. Washington DC: Oxford University Press.

Zellner, Mike (1994) 'Mexico Bravo', *América Economía. La Revista de Negocios de América Latina*, no. 80 (February). New York: Nanbei Ltd, 26–7.

# Index